DUAL ALLEGIANCE

An Autobiography by

Ben Dunkelman

Macmillan of Canada   Toronto

Canadian Cataloguing in Publication Data

Dunkelman, Ben, 1913-
  Dual allegiance
Includes index.

ISBN 0-7705-1429-4

1. Dunkelman, Ben, 1913- 2. World War, 1939-1945—
Personal narratives, Canadian. 3. Israel-Arab War,
1948-1949—Personal narratives. I. Title.

D811.D865 940.54′81′71 C76-017146-7

Printed in Canada
for the Macmillan Company of Canada Limited
70 Bond Street, Toronto M5B 1X3

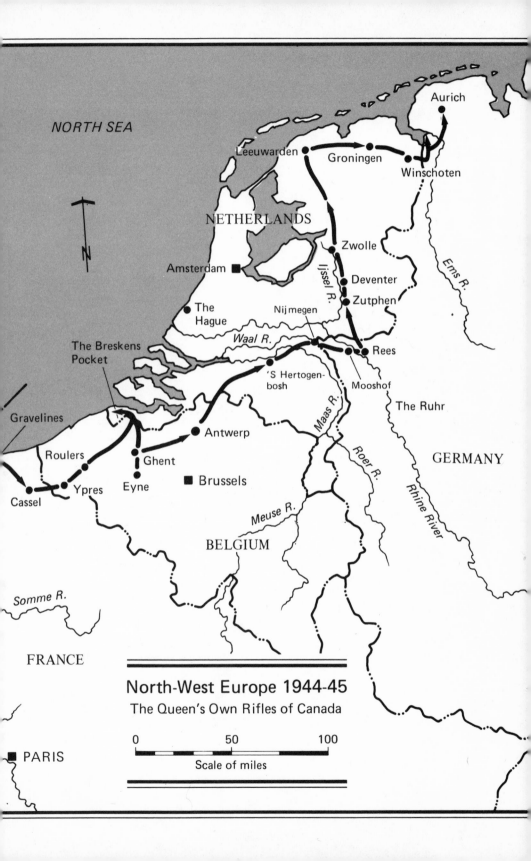

NORTH SEA

Aurich

Leeuwarden

Groningen

Winschoten

NETHERLANDS

Zwolle

Amsterdam ■

Deventer

Zutphen

IJssel R.

The
Hague

Nijmegen

Waal R.

Rees

The Breskens
Pocket

'S Hertogen-
bosch

Mooshof

The Ruhr

Ems R.

Gravelines

Antwerp

Roulers

Ghent

Maas R.

GERMANY

Roer R.

Cassel

Ypres

Eyne

■ Brussels

Meuse R.

Rhine River

BELGIUM

Somme R.

FRANCE

North-West Europe 1944-45

The Queen's Own Rifles of Canada

■ PARIS

0   50   100

Scale of miles

DUAL
ALLEGIANCE

This book is dedicated to my Canadian and Israeli comrades-in-arms with whom I shared so much

CONTENTS

PREFACE

In writing this book, I have drawn mainly on my own recollections of the events described herein. I have also drawn on my private files and archives, comprising letters, documents, and manuscripts going back thirty-five years.*

In the chapters concerning my experiences in the Second World War, I was greatly helped by Lt.-Col. Barnard's *History of the Queen's Own Rifles of Canada* and Lt.-Col. C. P. Stacey's *The Victory Campaign,* to which I referred very freely. Both of these gentlemen have been kind enough to read and comment on this section of my manuscript.

In the chapters dealing with the 1948 war, I owe a debt of gratitude to the late Yosef Eitan (Joe Eisen), a lifelong friend who supplied me with accurate data on the 7th Brigade. I am grateful to many others, too numerous to mention here, who gave me first-hand information regarding the various phases of the 1948 War of Independence. Many books have been written about that war, some of which contain certain inaccuracies (see the Appendix), but they have all been helpful to me as I checked dates, political background, and so on.

I would like to thank the Honourable Mr. Justice Harry Batshaw and Chancellor Meir W. Weisgall of the Weizmann Insti-

*Public Archives of Canada (MG 31 — G10) Dunkelman Collection

tute of Science and many others too numerous to list here for their encouragement and assistance in producing this book. I am grateful to my old comrade-in-arms Yitzhak Rabin, Prime Minister of Israel, for his generous Foreword, and to my wife, Yael, for her care in typing the manuscript, and for the many helpful corrections and comments she added while doing so. Finally my special thanks to Peretz Kidron for his assistance in assembling the final manuscript and to Douglas Gibson of Macmillan of Canada for the final editing.

B.D.

FOREWORD

by Yitzhak Rabin
(Prime Minister of Israel)

The time is probably not yet ripe to tell the full story of that unusual and dedicated group of men and women who went by the name of "Machal". They came to us when we most needed them, during those hard and uncertain days of our 1948 War of Independence.

Five regular Arab armies had invaded us on every side. Our total population was then hardly more than six hundred thousand. We were so outnumbered, outgunned, and outflanked that few experts were willing to give the reborn State of Israel more than a few weeks of life. The British had left behind total chaos, and essential services were at a total standstill.

We knew the stakes were incredibly high. Jewish history itself was in the balance. If we failed to defend ourselves, there would be no survivors, no Israel, no Jewish national future. For two thousand years we had waited for this moment in history when we would have our right recognized to self-determination in the Jewish homeland. When the battle was joined, we were already a decimated people with six million of our brethren destroyed in the Nazi holocaust.

So we fought back hard and defiantly, improvising our relatively small forces and meagre weapons as we went. Every able-bodied man, woman, and youngster joined the ranks in a war of national and personal survival.

We were not alone. As the word spread overseas, Jews in distant countries scrambled to volunteer. They were not mercenaries. They were Jewish patriots expecting no reward other than to see the battle through and the State of Israel secure. We called them "Machal", the Hebrew initials for *Mitnadvei Huz La'Aretz* — Volunteers from Abroad. By the time it was all over, some three thousand had joined us, veterans mainly of the Allied armies of the Second World War. Some were non-Jews who felt our battle for freedom was theirs too. They brought with them the skills that helped us put together the rudiments of an air force, an armoured corps, an artillery corps, and even a navy. Many gave their lives in the battle. Some came illegally, under assumed names, risking possible reprisal by their own governments if discovered. The contribution of this small band of men and women is a glorious chapter in the story of Israel's struggle for freedom.

Ben Dunkelman was a "Machal" volunteer. I first met him in 1948 when I was a young Palmach officer commanding the "Harel" Brigade. Jerusalem was under siege and I was under orders to reopen the road from the coastal plain and relieve the capital. Ben joined us in the battle. His particular expertise was heavy mortars and he worked hard training others in their use. His skills, which he had developed as an officer in the Canadian Army, helped clear many a mile of the besieged hilly highway.

His enterprise and bravery came to the attention of David Ben-Gurion, who was then Minister of Defence as well as Prime Minister. Ben Dunkelman was asked by Ben-Gurion to take command of the armoured Seventh Brigade which was made up mostly of captured tanks and a variety of other vehicles. Ben led the Seventh Brigade in the crucial fighting that freed most of Galilee. His tanks fought in the mountains of the far north and across into Lebanon as far as the Litani River from which they eventually withdrew. To this day a bridge along Israel's Northern Road that skirts the Lebanese frontier is named "Ben's

Bridge". It is Israel's way of acknowledging the exploits of a brave soldier and a proud Jew who came to his people's aid at a decisive crossroads in its history.

What follows is Ben Dunkelman's own story. It is not, as he himself attests, an official history of Israel's War of Independence. It is, rather, the personal narrative and perspective of one who shared with us his guts, his skills, his dedication, and his person in order to restore the name Israel to its rightful place on the world map.

Jerusalem, January 1976.

CHAPTER ONE

A Fight for Life

Their robes billowing around them, the group of Arabs marched up the hill towards us in a tightly packed knot. From the grim look on their faces it was clear that this was no social call; I knew that my policy forbidding them to enter our settlement to use the grass between our orange trees was not appreciated. Apparently they now intended to do something about it.

When they were about ten yards from us they stopped, allowing one man to step forward. He was a daunting figure, at least six feet four with shoulders to match. He stood there for a moment, assessing us with a confident smile. Then, without a word, he walked up to me and slowly put his hand first on my forehead, then on his. The message was unmistakable; it was either him or me.

As we began to circle one another in the red dust, I was much too preoccupied to reflect that this was a hell of a long way from Upper Canada College. By rights, like any other affluent young Toronto boy of eighteen in 1931, I should have been at school preparing for university or for the family business instead of fighting for my life in the dust of a Jewish settlement in the heart of Palestine. . . .

It was ironic that the people who were most directly responsible for my being there, my parents, were the ones who were most appalled by it. The regular barrage of letters insisting that I come back to Toronto at once made their opinion quite clear. They were responsible for my presence there indirectly, because they had made sure that I grew up aware of my Jewish heritage. Then, to their regret, on my eighteenth birthday they had presented me with the finest birthday present imaginable in 1931, a return ticket to Palestine via Europe, and five hundred dollars to spend.

I certainly made full use of that gift. The cruise from New York afforded all of the pleasures of a transatlantic summer voyage on a luxury liner and I flung myself wholeheartedly into them. Then there was Holland, and then a cruise up the Rhine. Under the combined influence of the heady scenery, some very high-spirited companions, and ample quantities of the fine local wines, I spent the cruise in a state of near-permanent intoxication. Germany was obviously a very fine place, and I was in a mellow mood as I began the next stage of my journey, a train ride to Genoa.

I shared my railway compartment with an affable young German named Heinrich, who made no objection when I addressed him as "Henry". We had a pleasant chat in English, meandering at random over many and various topics, as the train chugged southwards. At one point in the conversation, I happened to mention Hitler. "Oh, Hitler," said my companion disparagingly, "I know little about him. He will never be important in Germany." This pleased me. Then Heinrich added, as an afterthought: "But about the Jews — he is right!"

I was astounded. "Right?" I exclaimed indignantly. I'd heard about Hitler's ideas on Jews, and I couldn't comprehend what was so "right" about them. "I'll tell you," Heinrich explained in all earnestness. "After the war, two million Jews came to Berlin, from Galicia in Poland. Now they control all important business and industry in Berlin. Soon they will control all Germany. Hitler is right!"

I was flabbergasted! I tried to refute his statements: in the whole of Germany, I told him, there were no more than six hundred thousand Jews; most of them had lived in the country for generations; they were assimilated into German society and were "more German than the Germans".

He remained unconvinced. "It must be true," he pronounced with utter finality. "It *must* be true, because I read it in our newspaper."

I continued to press him. No, he admitted, there were no Jews in the little Bavarian hamlet where he lived. In fact he had never met a Jew in his life.

It was time for my bombshell. "I'm Jewish," I told him coldly.

At first, he refused to believe me. Later he grew terribly embarrassed. We both fell silent. There was nothing much left to say.

In Genoa, I found myself confronted by a choice. My funds would stretch to take me east to Palestine or west to Paris, but they would not allow me to do both. Normally Paris would have won hands down; I was a happy-go-lucky, fun-loving young man. But perhaps I was tired of Europe, whose castles and museums were beginning to pall on me. Perhaps it was Heinrich-Henry, who had shocked me with his innocent, matter-of-fact anti-Semitism. Or perhaps it had all begun much earlier, when I was a small child, listening in wonder as the grownups in Toronto talked long and seriously about "the land of our forefathers". In any case, whatever the motivation, my decision was impetuous and instinctive. That day in Genoa I sensed a sudden surge of curiosity about the country I had heard spoken of as a haven where the Jews would be safe from the Heinrichs of this world. I made my choice. Dismissing Paris from my mind, I went to book my passage. I was going to Palestine.

And so, ten months later, I found myself twisting and straining in the dust, locked in single combat with an Arab. It was a fierce, bloody fight where fists, feet, knees, elbows, and even heads came into play. But although I was only eighteen, I was six foot two and around two hundred pounds, and by now I could punch, wrestle, kick, butt, and gouge as well as any man. Gradually I began to gain the upper hand. Kneeling astride him, I began hitting him again and again, until his body went limp. Shakily, to the cheers of my fellow pioneers, I got to my feet and limped away, wiping blood from my face. Behind me I could hear the Arabs wordlessly picking up their champion and carrying him back down the hill.

It was the first time I had ever fought against someone who meant to kill me if he could: it was not to be the last.

CHAPTER TWO

Two Incidents

Two incidents from my childhood demonstrate the dual allegiance that has dominated my life and given this book its title. I am a Canadian and a Jew, with the strong loyalties that spring from both ties, loyalties that have shaped my life.

The first incident marked a significant moment in world history. I remember standing with my parents on Yonge Street, Toronto's main thoroughfare, watching the parade of soldiers returning victorious from the First World War. I was five years old, and had very little idea of the event's importance. But that didn't matter. I stood there waving a little Union Jack, utterly entranced by the spectacle: the endless lines of tough soldiers swinging past in perfect unison, some khaki-clad, some in kilts, the clump of their boots accompanied by the blare of regimental bands or the wild music of the pipes. Horses trotted by pulling lumbering guns, or bearing jingling cavalry, bright flags and pennants waved in the breeze, while all around me the huge crowd roared itself hoarse as Toronto cheered the heroes who had returned from the war to end all wars.

Traditionally, this book should now proceed to say that from that moment on I was determined to be a soldier, and was never happy until my ambition was achieved. Nothing could be further from the truth. Like all five-year-olds, I loved bands and a parade (I must confess that I still do) and admired the soldiers.

But I never, even then, wanted to *be* one. Only the way of fate has caused me, an idealistic but now-weary internationalist who at heart dislikes nationalism and all its trappings, including national armies, to spend the prime years of my life in uniform in wars fought between nations. I have worn the insignia of two armies but have always felt myself to be a soldier from necessity, not from choice. And since there were many other tasks awaiting me, I have always been quick to get back to civilian life as soon as possible. Perhaps the reason for this heresy is simply that I have seen too much front-line action ever to be dazzled by the romantic glories of soldiering.

But from the moment of that Toronto parade I have been sure of one thing: I am a Canadian, proud of Canada's heritage and proud — if need be — to fight for it.

The second incident took place two years later, at our lake-side cottage some distance north of Toronto. No bands played, no crowds were around to cheer. It was a cold, grey day and the loudest sound was of rain falling on the lake and on the sodden tennis court where I and my brothers and sisters huddled, waiting. I was seven years old and I was about to learn what it meant to be a Jew.

Our parents had told us about the anti-Jewish pogroms that had marked the Russian civil war. My mother, always a tireless charity worker, was working hard to find homes for the children orphaned in these massacres. My parents had volunteered to add one of the orphans to our family. Now, despite the chill and rain, my brother Joe and I, and our sisters Zelda and Ronny, were waiting patiently to meet our new brother.

Our long wait came to an end; as Mother and Dad drove up, we swarmed excitedly round the car. We fell back, awed into silence, as my mother helped out a pale, silent little figure, his pinched face dominated by a pair of enormous black eyes. He was utterly silent, and his eyes were blank and remote.

This was quite beyond our experience. When she had settled

Ernie into his room, Mother took us aside and tried to explain what had happened to Ernie to put him in this state: his parents had been killed before his eyes, and then he had been separated from the rest of his family. He had been sent halfway around the world, passed from one set of strangers to another, never knowing where he was or what was happening to him. He was still, she explained, in a state of shock.

So, to a lesser degree, were we. The little boy about my age who lay on his bed for hours on end with his face to the wall, ignoring our friendly advances, was a striking lesson to us. In a very real sense, seeing Ernie's suffering brought home to us what it meant to be a Jew in other parts of the world. The lesson learned in the two or three weeks that it took Ernie to thaw out and become a full member of our family, to our lasting delight and benefit, was something that I never forgot.

The family that Ernie had joined was a very happy one, and a very affluent one. My childhood home was a rambling English-style mansion, standing in a ninety-acre estate known as Sunnybrook Farm, on the outskirts of the city of Toronto. It was a very large house, with three storeys of living and servants' quarters on one side, while the opposite side contained two storeys of guest rooms, as well as a living room, a billiard room, and a library. These all centred on the large, airy morning room, whose great glass doors led out onto a broad patio facing the lawns. Adjoining it was an enormous hothouse, which included a permanent solarium, with palms, lemon trees, orchids, and exotic plants of all varieties, as well as a potting room where the flowers were prepared for the summer display outside. To the north, there was the hunt room, all in oak: a double cathedral ceiling rested on massive oak beams, the floor and walls were also of oak, and so was most of the exquisite period furniture, which clustered around a huge hunt table of great antiquity. Under the overhanging balcony, there was an alcove with an enormous fireplace, which could accommodate five-foot logs with ease. When it was cold, we'd gather there to enjoy the blaze.

Ours was a warm and cosy home; large as it was, it conveyed a lived-in feeling. Aside from our family, it was always full of guests, and the atmosphere was cheerful and friendly. Visitors found plenty to surprise and delight them: the bar, situated beneath the overhanging balcony, had a secret panel which opened up into a room into the basement, and there was a tunnel which ran under the potting sheds to the thickly wooded ravine below.

That ravine was part of the beautiful setting of the house. Three gardeners tended the thousand-yard drive, and the thirty-five acres of lawns and flower gardens which ran down to the banks of the Don River. The estate was a dreamland: a children's paradise, with plenty of space to roam and play and explore and hunt. At weekends, the family loved to ride through the ravines. Dad, Ernie, my sisters Zelda and Ronny, and I would all go out for long rides, splashing through the streams and following the winding trails which crisscrossed the property.

It was probably Sunnybrook that gave me my lifelong love of the outdoors. It gave me something else, too, thanks to my father's enthusiasm for farming, which led him to raise prize fowl on the estate and to keep ducks on a branch of the river, until the incursions of stray dogs put an end to them. Some of his agricultural interest rubbed off onto me, which was to stand me in good stead later.

All of this affluence was due to my father's business success, a rags-to-riches story that would have gladdened the heart of Horatio Alger. Dad used to tell of arriving in America from Poland as a small child, and being given a banana. Too proud to reveal that he had never seen anything of the kind before, he threw away the inside and bit bravely into the peel. This was typical of Dad; he was always ready for a plunge into the unknown. I have a photograph, taken when he was thirteen, that shows him standing in front of the shoe store he opened in

Brooklyn. Right from the start, his approach to business showed ingenuity and daring: he hit upon the brilliant idea of selling shoes on credit. Trade was brisk. All his friends came in for shoes. But, somehow, they never got around to paying for them, and he went bankrupt.

Later, when the family moved to Toronto, Dad went to work for his father, who by then was in business as a contractor who made buttonholes for clothing manufacturers. It was Dad's job to pick up the garments to be serviced. This took him on regular tours of Toronto's small tailoring shops, and he was profoundly affected by what he saw there: men, women, and children crowded into dreary, unventilated basements and firetrap backrooms, toiling from morning to night for a few cents an hour. These depressing sights made him resolve that if ever he had a business of his own, he'd never tolerate such sweatshop conditions.

But it wasn't only labour conditions that Dad observed on his tours of the workshops. In the course of time, he began to pay particular attention to one factory which specialized in producing uniforms. As Dad soon noticed, the proprietor, Harry Miller, was greatly helped in his work by his daughter Rose, who did her father's books. It did not escape Dad's attention that, in addition to possessing an excellent head for figures, Harry Miller's book-keeper was exceedingly attractive. After an eventful courtship, they were married in 1910.

Shortly before then Dad had taken the plunge and gone into business on his own, using $1,500 he had saved up to buy a small wholesale suit company. Business was bad, and Dad found himself in difficulties. But — as was his habit whenever he got into trouble — he adopted a totally new approach and followed it through with all the daring and vigour at his command. Since wholesaling had proved unprofitable, he decided to go straight to the customer, hoping to do better by retailing his product. Desperately short of cash, he nevertheless scraped together $25, which he offered as a prize to anyone who could suggest a good name for his company. A Toronto journalist won the prize, and, outside the tiny store he had rented, Dad put up the first "Tip Top Tailors" sign. The last of his money went into advertisements promising "Tailor-made suits — One price — Only $14.00!"

My father had hit upon the brilliant idea of selling clothes at a single price. Twenty suits were sold on the first day, and Tip Top Tailors was in business. Sales increased, allowing him to expand his operations; soon there were additional stores with the "Tip Top Tailors" sign. It wasn't long before he had bought out many of the manufacturers for whom Grandfather used to make buttonholes. From that first little retail store on Toronto's Yonge Street, Tip Top Tailors grew into an organization with sixty-five stores and three thousand dealers, the largest clothing chain in Canada.

CHAPTER THREE

Growing Up

Because of my father's wealth, as a boy growing up in Toronto I lacked nothing. Dad was occupied with the business and Mother always seemed to be engaged in charity work, so at first we were supervised at home by a governess. I am ashamed to admit that we made it a point of honour to get rid of our governesses as fast as possible; one unfortunate young woman was led such a dance that she left on the very first day.

Later, at private school my behaviour was not markedly better, and my academic achievements were, to put it kindly, on a par with Winston Churchill's. But on the sports field I came into my own. I played hockey and football with great zest, and since I grew to be unusually big and strong, with plenty of stamina, I was able to play through an entire football game without being relieved. Since our rather simple tactics obliged me to carry the ball every second play, "Stop Dunkelman" became the chief defensive tactic adopted by schools playing against Upper Canada College (or Jarvis, or Northern — I had a chequered academic career).

As it happened, my brother Joe and I were the only Jews in the first school we attended. Perhaps the fact that he, too, was big and strong had something to do with it, but as a boy I never encountered any overt anti-Semitism in that school or elsewhere. In fact, I had an absolutely carefree youth, playing all manner of sports during the school year, and sailing and swimming and fishing in nearby Lake Simcoe during the idyllic summers. I might very easily have turned into a spoiled young playboy, except that my mother would never have stood for it.

Mother was a whirlwind of energy, and communal work was her great passion. She was an officer of the Canadian Red Cross, where her humanitarian efforts earned her the Coronation Medal in 1937. But her energies were directed mostly into Jewish charities. In the Jewish community in Toronto she was treated with respect bordering on awe that was not always totally affectionate, as her nickname, "Madame Czarina", indicated. (It was, needless to say, never used in her presence.) She never shrank from confrontations. When a Reform rabbi permitted "Ave Maria" to be played at a meeting, Mother objected, and it was not long before the unfortunate rabbi had left Toronto. When the local newspaper, *The Jewish Review*, chose to follow an editorial line that displeased her, she founded a rival journal, *The Jewish Standard*. As its publisher she found a young journalist named Meir Weisgall as its editor, a man who was later to play an important role in my life.

When Mother discovered that the summer resorts around Toronto were turning into exclusive WASP enclaves that were placing restrictions on Jews buying land, another campaign was soon under way. In those days (even more than now) one of the symbols of social status in Toronto was a summer home and Mother was resolved that Jews were not going to be excluded. By way of a Gentile intermediary, she bought one hundred acres of land on Lake Simcoe and built a holiday resort of thirty cottages. The project was a great success and became known as one of the most beautiful resorts in Ontario. Mother named it "Balfour Beach" in honour of the British Foreign Secretary who signed the pro-Zionist Balfour Declaration.

The choice of name was not accidental. As long as I can remember her, Mother was an enthusiastic and active Zionist, with a deep commitment to Jewish colonization in Palestine. Much of this interest came to her from her father: Grandfather Miller was one of the earliest Zionists in America, and as a young girl Mother helped him in organizational work. But her Zionist fervour can perhaps be best explained by the fact that she herself might easily have been born in Palestine. Her mother — my Grandmother Miller — was born a Belkind, and was the only member of that family to head for the New World. If she hadn't married Grandfather, she might have joined the many other Belkinds who emigrated to Palestine, where they became prominent figures in the Jewish community then undergoing a process of rapid growth.

With the encouragement of my father, Mother made our home a transit station and hospitality centre for the Zionist leaders who were in Toronto to address meetings or seek help on some project. Our guests included the most prominent Zionist leaders of the time: Chaim Weizmann, Louis Lipsky, Stephen Wise, Shmaryahu Levin, and a host of others. They repaid our hospitality by giving us full and first-hand information about what was happening in Palestine, and in the Jewish world as a whole. Their accounts were heard by an unusually concerned and well-informed audience. Mother especially was highly knowledgeable—although she visited Palestine only three times in the course of her life, there wasn't a colony and village in the country which she didn't seem to know personally. She used to share in every triumph, and suffer with every setback, as though she were there in person, draining the swamps and planting the trees. By her concern and her sense of involvement, she helped to bridge the thousands of miles which divided Sunnybrook Farm from that mysterious "Land of Israel".

While the grownups talked, I used to sit at the side of the huge fireplace watching the flames dance and listening to the stories about Palestine, picking up the exotic place-names and trying to imagine what these towns and settlements looked like. I was a very impressionable child, and I drank in every word uttered by these imposing personages. One of them, Chaim Weizmann, then President of the World Zionist Organization, deeply impressed me with his description of a recent visit to South Africa, where he'd been taken to see the nature reserves, established to preserve the country's wild life. He startled us by pointing out the contrast between the care lavished on those animals, and the plight of the Jews. "Although the world has land set aside for animals," he concluded, "there is none for the Jews!"

I heard those words as a child, years before Nazi Germany launched its "final solution" to exterminate the Jewish people. Weizmann's prophetic warning made me keenly aware that the Jews faced extinction unless they, too, like the animals in South Africa, were protected by a "conservation program". Weizmann's message was clear: the Jews, too, needed land of their own. There would be many more seven-year-old Ernies unless the Jews gained a haven — in Palestine.

But from the adults' talk I gathered that there were many Jews who lacked an awareness of their perilous position and saw Palestine as unimportant. I remember Shmaryahu Levin coming to our house, after a visit to Germany, where he had tried in vain to arouse the German Jews to display their solidarity with the rest of the Jewish people. "The great majority of German Jews tell us they will not support Zionism," he said dejectedly. "They do not admit to any relationship with their fellow-Jews suffering in the pogroms in Eastern Europe. They are almost completely assimilated. When I appealed for help for world Jewry, their reply was: 'We're not Jews, we're Germans!' "

I listened to his words, and did my best to grasp their meaning, but this strange dichotomy between "Jew" and "German" was beyond my comprehension. I was simultaneously a Canadian and a Jew, and neither as a child nor as an adult did I find any conflict between the two. One allegiance did not contradict the other, and I held both, with a perfectly clear conscience. I had no sense of "divided loyalties". At Upper Canada College — which laid heavy stress on Canadian patriotism and loyalty to the King — I never considered myself to be an "outsider". I regarded myself as a Canadian, like my schoolmates; like them, I owed allegiance to the King.

At the same time, I wouldn't dream of permitting that allegiance to thrust aside my Jewish loyalties. And I was becoming increasingly determined that some day I would visit Palestine.

CHAPTER FOUR

A Change of Life-Style

After my encounter with Henry on the train to Genoa I made my fateful decision to forgo Paris and sail east to Palestine aboard the *Patria*. The journey across the Mediterranean was full of heady excitement for a youngster like me whose only educational accomplishment had been to acquire a love for the novels of Sir Walter Scott and the other great romantic writers.

In addition to a bewildering array of nationalities on board ship, there was even a detachment of the French Foreign Legion, travelling below in cramped conditions which seemed to me totally unsuitable for a force of glamorous heroes.

In the cheerful mix of people from many lands I found myself on very friendly terms with a young Palestinian Arab from Jaffa. He and I spent a lot of time together, exchanging confidences and feeling very much at ease with one another. But one day he said to me, half-jokingly, that we could be friends on the boat, but not in Palestine, where we would be enemies. The remark was made light-heartedly enough, but it came as a timely reminder that the spirit of international harmony on board the *Patria* could not supersede the bitter national conflict between Arab and Jew, which had already claimed many victims in Palestine.

That cruise also gave me a foretaste of the political and national complexities of the situation in Palestine and the Middle

East. For example, one Indian couple was quite astounded when I described myself as both a Zionist and a loyal British subject. Being Indian nationalists, in direct conflict with British colonial rule in India, they were quick to point out that Zionist ambitions for an autonomous Jewish state ran entirely counter to my British loyalties, since Palestine was being administered by the British. They had a point there, as I admitted: but I felt that by acts like the Balfour Declaration and their more co-operative attitude during the early years of their mandate, the British had been of greater help to the Jewish people than any other nation. (Later on in the thirties, as British policy became progressively more anti-Zionist—and even more so in the forties, when British policy conflicted violently with Jewish aspirations — I never permitted myself to forget the great initial contribution the British had made to the Zionist movement; that even held true in 1948, when I found myself being fired upon by British soldiers!)

These political discussions took up very little of the voyage. Most of the time was spent on enjoyment and relaxation, and the whole cruise remains in my mind as a very pleasant interlude. But it, too — like all good things — came to an end. The *Patria* docked at Alexandria, I bade farewell to my companions, and went ashore. Instantly I found my Canadian football training of use to me; getting through the throngs of importunate Egyptians required all the agility of a broken-field runner.

Egypt made a vivid impression on me. But despite my fascination, I cut short my visit in Alexandria and Cairo. I was keenly aware that Palestine lay near by, and that, after all, was the main objective of my trip. Eager to get there, I boarded the train out of Cairo.

Unless you have travelled through the desert on an Egyptian train you will not fully appreciate the discomfort of that bizarre journey. The track ran through the desert, along the northern coast of the Sinai Peninsula. The landscape was drab and monotonous, before it disappeared from sight when we ran into an appalling sandstorm, which caused the engine to break down. I was travelling third class, which was noisy and uncomfortable, and crowded with a motley assortment of British servicemen, Egyptians, and Sinai Bedouin. Toronto summers are hot and humid, but I had never experienced such intense heat as that which baked us as we sat, immobile, in the middle of the desert. My main diversion came from an Arab woman; she was travelling with her five daughters, for whom she showed great concern. When she asked me to take them under my protection, I was thrilled by such a romantic assignment, which I proudly carried out in the best traditions of mediaeval chivalry; Ivanhoe would have approved.

As the train, mysteriously revived, began to make its slow way across the desert, my excitement and anticipation grew. I was traversing the route which Moses and his followers had trudged for forty years. As we neared Palestine, I had a strange and mystical feeling of homecoming. Something similar probably happens to the overseas Irish when they return to their ancestral home on the Emerald Isle. Perhaps the feeling of the Jew for what its people have always called "The Land of Israel" is even stronger, for he has never felt completely at home in any country since the Dispersion.

I was no exception. At that time, I still entertained some doubts about the feasibility of the Zionist idea; but there was no doubt about my feelings for Palestine. The antiquated train made its way northwards, and as it chugged through the Judean hills towards Jerusalem, a great feeling of contentment and peace came over me.

Countless generations of Jews have dreamed of seeing the glories of Jerusalem, of breathing its pure mountain air, and of gazing across the hills which stretch in all directions, down to the Dead Sea and the coastal plain, with the Judean wilderness to the south and the fertile hills of Samaria to the north. I was fortunate enough to fulfil that dream; reality surpassed my expectation, and I was intoxicated.

In Jerusalem I arranged to go on a tour of the country with the Rosenbergs, a Toronto couple whom I knew well. We were lucky enough to obtain the services of a very famous guide named Yerushalmy. Before becoming a guide he had fought for the British in the First World War, serving in the Jewish Legion which formed part of General Allenby's forces when he pushed the Turks out of Palestine and the neighbouring countries. Yerushalmy was a good-looking man, and hardy and rugged into the bargain. Later in the tour, when our car was marooned in a sandbank and we found ourselves surrounded by a tense crowd of hostile Arabs, we greatly appreciated his obvious toughness, and his skill with the shotgun. Yerushalmy showed us around Jerusalem, taking us to all the hallowed shrines and points of interest which abound in the city, before leading us on the usual whirlwind tour of the country.

At that time, the total population of Palestine was about one million, and the Jews were a small minority, numbering no more than 160,000. But Jewish settlements were springing up all over the country — small and isolated, but veritable oases in a landscape which was otherwise largely barren wilderness. The colonies were well tended and green, standing out in contrast to the wasteland all around. The Arab villagers also tilled their land, of course, but they were terribly exploited by absentee landlords, disease-ridden, and tied to agricultural methods that were primitive and ineffective. It was not difficult to gauge the differences between the two peoples: the Jews cultivated only six per cent of the land, but they marketed fifty per cent of the country's agricultural produce.

As I surveyed these settlements, built up under the most difficult conditions, I was reminded of what Lawrence of Arabia had written to his mother: " . . . their settlements are like oases in the desert. The sooner the Jews farm it all, the better." Any scepticism I may have harboured about the feasibility of the Zionist dream was given a very convincing answer: it did seem possible for the country to absorb hundreds of thousands of immigrants and become a modern Jewish homeland.

It was a wonderful tour, and I enjoyed it immensely. Everywhere we went, we enjoyed the hospitality of the settlers, who did everything to make us feel at home. It was only later, when I was myself working in a settlement, that I realized how much their hospitality had cost them. Many of these people scarcely had enough to subsist upon, and they must have given up their own food for two or three days to feed the visitors "in a fitting manner".

The tour left me with a strange sensation. When I visited other countries, I was an ordinary tourist; I came, I saw interesting and picturesque places, and then I went on my way. My attitude towards Palestine was quite different. Here, too, as in Germany or Egypt, my curiosity was aroused, but it was not the idle curiosity of the spectator. The various sights I saw were more than merely interesting. They concerned me personally, giving me a sense of involvement such as I had never experienced before.

I began to ask myself all kinds of questions. I wondered what it felt like to be a pioneer, to take an active part in building up the country and cultivating its soil. I had heard about the hardships facing the settlers, and my tour showed me the arduous conditions they faced. I wondered what it was like to live like that, and endure hard physical labour in the blazing sun. All my life I had been accustomed to living well, with plenty of comfort and all the luxuries I could ask for. I had never experienced hardship or deprivation. But then, I had never experienced the kind of deep satisfaction which comes from tilling virgin soil, or the excitement of creating something from nothing, as these pioneers were doing.

I decided to answer those questions. At the end of the tour I was supposed to return to Canada with the Rosenbergs. Instead, I announced that I was going to stay, to go and work in one of the settlements.

I had no idea how to go about it. Instinctively, I followed the custom of the land, making use of my family ties. One of my mother's cousins had married a prominent leader of the Palestine Jewish community, a man called Yehoshua Hankin. I decided to go and see him, and enlist his aid.

Mr. Hankin was nearly seventy at the time, but agile and spry as a man thirty years younger. He was a fine-looking figure: with his white moustache and goatee, and a long mane of hair flowing down over his shoulders, he reminded me of pictures of Buffalo Bill. He was then engaged in land buying for the Jewish National Fund, and as his work required him to travel a great deal, he was one of the few Jews with a licence to carry a pistol. While I was accompanying him on a tour of the settlements, we passed a group of Arab horsemen along the way. I noticed him stiffen, as his hand slid underneath his coat.

Mr. Hankin listened sympathetically to my request, and promised his assistance in finding a colony where I could stay and work for a while. He proved very helpful, arranging for me to go to Tel Asher, a tiny settlement in the Sharon plain, thirty miles north of Tel Aviv. The village was in the coastal lowlands, and a very isolated position, with a number of hostile Arab villages perched above it in the Samarian hills. If it was a taste of pioneering I wanted, he couldn't have found me a better place.

My lightning tour of Palestine had given me a chance to get acquainted with various Jewish settlements. I knew that most of the colonies were at a rudimentary stage of development, and could not provide their members with much more than the basic necessities of life. Living quarters were Spartan, and the settlers made do with the very minimum of food and clothing. By contrast, the children of the kibbutzim were fed, clothed, housed, and educated in a lavish style. Nothing was too good for them, no sacrifice too great for this "generation of the future".

Some of the pioneers made the best of a bad situation by idealizing their frugal life-style; there was much talk of the virtues of poverty. They revelled in the freedom of their spirit, and the pioneering tasks they were performing, and the vision of the future they were building for their children.

Having seen other settlements, I came to Tel Asher with few illusions about the "luxury" I was likely to encounter. But even my modest expectations far exceeded what I found there. I thought I was coming to some kind of village. All I found was a windswept hill of red earth, with three small, box-like cottages perched at the top, surrounded by a few young orange groves, and all overlooked by a tall water-tower. I had hoped to find accommodation in some kind of cheap hotel or lodging house, but I quickly realized there was no point in even asking for anything of the kind: the whole colony consisted of no more than those three cement cottages and a bath-house.

The people of Tel Asher greeted me with great warmth, and did their best to make me feel at home. As for lodgings — they reassured me that I would have a place to sleep.

Sure enough, when the time came to go to bed, someone went outside and dragged in a straw mattress for me. I went over to help unfold it; as I bent over, I was knocked right across the room, landing with a crash against the far wall. This unexpected onslaught left me quite bewildered — till they killed and brought to me the scorpion which had just scuttled out of the mattress! Lepke, the man who had pushed me away with such scant ceremony, had saved me from a sting that could have had serious effects. It was a most dramatic — and fitting — welcome to Tel Asher.

After the mattress had been carefully scrutinized and pronounced scorpion-free, I lay down to sleep. But I didn't lie there long. That mattress may have been free of scorpions, but it fairly swarmed with bugs. As soon as they sensed my presence, they went on a bloodthirsty rampage, leaving me a mass of itching bumps. I spent the rest of the night scratching myself; needless to say, I got little sleep.

I finally dozed off for a short while, but I was wakened before dawn. It was time to go to work. Pulling myself to my feet, I gulped down a cup of tea in the pre-dawn gloom, and set off with the others to the orange groves. Like them, I was given a little package, which contained a meagre breakfast. Unlike them, I didn't think to guard it: no sooner had I hung the package on a branch and moved away a few paces than a crow swooped down and made off with it. The same thing happened the next day. In fact, I endured several breakfastless days until I learned to guard my precious little package of food.

Like most Israeli agriculture, orange growing has changed considerably since those days. Much of the work has been mechanized, and there is now extensive use of tractors and sophisticated agricultural machinery. But in the early thirties, almost everything had to be done by hand, and the only kind of "agricultural machinery" available was the turiya, a short-handled hoe with which we dug up the soil, removed weeds, and opened up irrigation channels. It was back-breaking work, because the hoe's short handle forced us to stoop all day, as we drove the blade into the hard earth.

This was totally unlike anything I had ever done before. I was eighteen years old, and quite soft; Mother's enormous meals and my luxury tour had left me stout and flabby. Looking around at the others, I was embarrassed by my physical state. I was strongly built and played lots of sports, but that had done little to prepare me for this strenuous, day-long drudgery. We all worked in the open, fully exposed; as the day wore on and the blazing sun of a Palestinian summer beat down upon me, the sweat poured off my body. Every muscle I had began to ache from the unusual effort. It was my hands which got the worst of it — the turiya handle had to be grasped firmly by the left hand, and allowed to slide through the right. As I brought it down, again and again, hour after hour, I felt the soft skin of my palms breaking out into painful blisters.

My physical sufferings were almost overshadowed by another kind of discomfort. As I hoed my row, trying desperately to keep up with my companions, I was acutely aware of the half-pitying, half-amused glances they were flinging at me over their shoulders. Their bodies were lean and tough; they had long adapted to this work, although initially it must have been as hard for them as it now was for me. With the natural feeling of superiority of the "old-timer" over the "greener", they must have got some satisfaction from watching this soft, fat, pampered rich boy trying to keep up. Seeing me sweat and suffer, they couldn't have expected me to last long at Tel Asher. In the meantime my distress provided them with some amusement. It was rough humour, almost cruel. It reflected a pride in their own strength as much as disdain for my weakness. But at the same time, there was a friendliness about it; indirectly, they were trying to help me by laughing at the difficulties and by needling me into overcoming them. Indeed, that is precisely what they succeeded in doing: I gritted my teeth and fought to stay with them.

After that first day's work, my body ached all over. Back in the cottage I flopped down on the floor to rest my tortured limbs. The blisters on my hands had burst, leaving a mass of raw flesh, and the pain, combined with a renewed onslaught by the ravenous bedbugs, again kept me awake much of the night. Eventually, I fell asleep.

In the middle of the night, I awoke in terror; something was crawling up and down my stomach and chest. After the encounter with the scorpion, my companions had described the various kinds of venomous insects and reptiles whose stings could cause great pain or even death. I didn't know what was now crawling about on me, and I lay there in a cold sweat, trying to decide what to do, and praying that it would crawl away. God knows how long I lay there in the pitch darkness before I finally decided to try to knock it off my chest. Slowly, very slowly, I raised my arm, then brought it down fast, trying to sweep whatever it was off my body. As my hand made contact, I felt a little jab in my finger. I was terrified; I was certain I could feel the poison starting to course through my body. Desperately, I grabbed my lantern, set it on the chair beside me, and shone it on my chest. Moments later in that welcome glare I saw a surprised little mouse climbing back onto me. I let out a great sigh of relief, and, thankful that I hadn't awakened any of my companions, rolled over and went back to sleep.

When I was shaken awake the next day, I lay there for a moment or two, struggling with the temptation to stay and give my tortured body a well-deserved rest. But I could imagine the mocking looks I'd see on my companions' faces if I failed to go out with them. With a sigh, I stretched my aching back muscles and stood up. Then, winding rags around my skinless palms, I went off to pick up my turiya. . . .

I shall never forget that first week at Tel Asher. Physically, I was in torment: the hard work, the sparse food, and the discomforts of my "bed" — all these were quite unlike anything I had ever had to endure. It was a long way from the leisurely comfort of Sunnybrook Farm. Only a few days earlier, I had been enjoying the luxurious life of a tourist, eating at good restaurants and staying at first-class hotels. It wasn't long since the heady dream of my Mediterranean adventure on the *Patria*. What a comedown!

The obvious and logical thing would have been to pick up my belongings and head for home, making use of the return ticket that was burning a hole in my pocket. There seemed to be nothing to hold me there: I had made no commitment to stay. Why didn't I get up and go? What kept me there?

First and foremost, I think it was my pride. It was a challenge for me, getting up at dawn and defying the heat and drudgery of long hours in the groves. I wasn't going to shy away from that challenge — especially when I imagined the derisive glances I'd meet if I were to admit defeat. Besides, my curiosity had been aroused; there were still many unanswered questions in my mind, and I'd be damned if I was going to let a little discomfort prevent me from finding out the answers.

CHAPTER FIVE

Tel Asher

After that horrific first week at Tel Asher, things began to get easier for me. I was gradually starting to toughen up. My muscles were getting used to the monotonous swing of the turiya, my once-soft hands had developed calluses, and I was growing accustomed to the heat. I was keeping up with the others, and I enjoyed my growing sense of equality with the "old-timers".

There were about twenty workers at Tel Asher. Most of them were from Poland or Russia (some of the latter had escaped from Siberia, where they had been exiled by the Soviet government for their Zionist activities). When they first arrived in Palestine, most of them had joined kibbutzim (collective settlements), but for various reasons they had found the collective life not suited to them. I'm not really surprised: they didn't fit into a kibbutz; they were a fascinating bunch of individualists, and argumentative to a degree I have never encountered, before or since.

Most of them were now trying to acquire farms of their own, while others were trying to resolve ideological differences with their former kibbutzim or political parties. In the meantime, they were working at Tel Asher, which was a company-owned settlement maintaining the orange groves of absentee landlords. Unlike a kibbutz, where property and income belonged to the collective, each worker at Tel Asher was paid individually, and then assessed for his share of the expenses.

Social life at Tel Asher was very active, though distinctly handicapped by the composition of the group: twenty men and one solitary girl! Her name was Rosa, and, as may be expected, she enjoyed considerable popularity. I never ceased to feel amazed at the energy of my fellow-workers, who could work hard all day and then walk to Kfar Saba (six miles in each direction) for a cup of tea. It was nothing for them to walk an hour to reach a neighbouring settlement, if they got to hear of a party where they'd have an opportunity to dance till the wee late hours.

All this was very much to my liking, and I quickly got into the spirit of the thing. I was beginning to find that life at Tel Asher was more than a painful challenge: there was a lot of fun to be had. Furthermore, when my companions saw that I was facing up to the difficulties, they began to treat me as one of them. I was eighteen years old, and the feeling that I had been *accepted* was one of the proudest I'd known. Originally, I planned to stay no longer than two weeks, but when the time came to leave, I decided to stay for another two weeks.

The work did not become less monotonous, but it brought its own satisfactions. I became quite proficient with the turiya, and I enjoyed my newly acquired skill. My physical condition was improving visibly: living on a frugal diet and working hard, I quickly shed a lot of surplus fat. Forty pounds lighter, deeply tanned, lean and hard—Mother would scarcely have recognized me!

At the end of the second two weeks, I again postponed my departure.

Day after day, I went out to the orange groves with the others. In time, I began to learn the tricks of the trade. For instance, I discovered how important it was to differentiate between the various types of soil, some of which are easier to dig than others. It was only then that I realized how my companions had exploited my ignorance when I was still "green", by giving me the harder patches. The discovery infuriated me, and I decided to get my own back.

After a training period building up my strength and improving my skill with the turiya, I set out to work my companions into the ground. On the appointed day I began to hoe in deadly earnest; soon I was well ahead of the others. This caused them serious concern: they were afraid that the foreman would expect them to keep up with the rapid tempo I was setting. In the end they were begging me to slow down! It was sweet revenge. Proudly aware of my newly acquired status as a pace-setter, I graciously acceded to their request. . . .

Once again, the time for my departure came around. Once again, I put it off—this time, without troubling to fix a new date. I was beginning to attract the attention of Gurevitch, the foreman; he took me under his wing, and began to teach me the finer skills of orange growing. He taught me how to graft the young trees and how to in-arch the older, ailing ones; he showed me how to do soil tests and how to lay out new groves (we planted hundreds of dunams of trees—oranges, lemons, and grapefruit). He taught me how to plan the irrigation channels, and that became my favourite job: it was a delight to find relief from the summer heat by standing ankle-deep in the cool stream. Every season had its own particular pleasures: there was spring, when the intoxicating scent of orange blossom filled the countryside; there was winter, when we had the deep satisfaction of picking the fruit we had tended all year.

From that, I went on to operating a bulldozer, which contoured and levelled off land for new groves; I also did some deep ploughing, my romantic soul thrilled by the thought that I was turning up land which had lain fallow for hundreds of years.

But not all of my experiences at work were as pleasant; there were dangers of all kinds lurking in the groves. In spring, we had to clean around the base of the tree trunks, removing the fungus-bearing mess of leaves and sand washed down by the winter rains. We did this work in pairs, to keep one another company in the lonely stretches of the grove. One day, I was paired with Michael, a fastidious character who invariably used a metal spatula to clean out his tree. I was too impatient for such niceties: I'd plunge my bare hand into the soft mess and simply claw it out. At one point, I went off for a moment to relieve myself, and Michael crossed over into my row, so that I wouldn't fall behind. It was just as well he did, or I wouldn't be telling this story. As Michael plunged his spatula into the base of that tree, it was struck by a deadly viper, of the variety Cleopatra used to commit suicide. If I had worked on that tree, the viper would certainly have struck my hand....

There were dangers of a more modern nature, too. Before our lands were ploughed up, we could easily trace the outline of First World War trenches, since the area was the scene of battles between the Turks and the Australians. One day we were digging holes for some new trees, when Chaim, who was working on the adjacent row, called me over to see some pretty egg-shaped metal objects he had just found. They were Mills bombs, but he didn't know that. Inquisitive about his finds, he pulled the pin on one of them. We should both have been blown to pieces. Fortunately, the pin was rusted and broke off in his hand, and the spring-loaded detonator was not set off.

Chaim was not as naïve as this incident might indicate. He was very sturdy and tough, and I was surprised to hear that, in his native Poland, he had been a "yeshiva bocher" (religious seminary student). I always used to believe that a yeshiva bocher was a pale and helpless weakling — and I was even more surprised when he told me how he and his fellow-students, with no military training of any kind, had organized self-defence groups to protect their community from pogroms — very unlike the stereotyped view of ghetto Jews submitting passively to humiliation or injury.

Chaim was typical of the Jewish pioneers in Palestine. I took a great liking to them from the start. Their temperament was very like mine, making it easy for us to find a common language. They were unlike many of the Jews I had known: these men were proud and uncompromising, bowing their heads before no one. Much as I was impressed by the country and its development, it was the people I really fell in love with — and at Tel Asher that love deepened.

In time, I got to know my fellow-workers very well, and some of them became close friends. One of these was Lepke—the man who had saved me from the scorpion on my first day there. He was a genuine character; a "ballegulleh", as a wagon-driver or teamster is called in Yiddish. Tel Asher was one of the few Jewish settlements where the language in use was Yiddish, rather than Hebrew. In the time I spent there, my Yiddish improved immeasurably, but my Hebrew remained at a rudimentary level. On one occasion, I thought I had an opportunity to learn Hebrew: this was when Bukalanik invited me to join him on a walking tour. Since I knew that he spoke fluent Hebrew, I thought he would teach me as we walked along. My hopes were dashed: Bukalanik was a well-educated man, with an unquenchable thirst for further knowledge, especially languages. Impatiently he brushed away my pleas to teach me Hebrew; instead, he insisted on speaking English throughout the tour. When we got back, his English had improved considerably; I, of course, knew no more Hebrew than when I had started.

Although it didn't help my Hebrew, that tour was a wonderful experience. This was nothing like the comfortable car drives I enjoyed with the Rosenbergs: we really roughed it. We covered much of central Palestine, going right off the beaten track, climbing through passes in the rocky hills, and cutting across open plains. Everywhere we went, we were made to feel at home, and we never lacked a place to stay the night. But it was Bukalanik who made that tour such a memorable experience. A lean, tough man, born in Bessarabia on the Russian-Romanian border, he was a great guide. Wherever we went, he seemed to know everything imaginable about the places we were passing— their geology, archeology, and history.

That tour was memorable for a number of reasons. For one, it led me to meet a man whose path was to cross mine at a number of important periods and who, until his recent death in 1975, remained a close friend and associate. This was Joe Eisen, a fellow-Canadian who came to settle in Palestine in 1930, when he was seventeen. In the course of time, Joe changed his name to Yosef Eitan, and under that name he will figure prominently in this narrative.

Yosef was of the tribe of red-haired Jews; his perfectly chis-elled features, his thick, matted hair, and his tall and burly frame all gave him the look of a Viking raider. He was a rare idealist: at the time I got to know him, he had recently arrived in Palestine as part of a group from the North American section of the Hashomer Hatzair (Young Guard) movement. They had come with the intention of establishing a kibbutz; indeed, not long after I met them, they were the first group from North America to found an independent kibbutz — Ein Hashofet. Their kib-butz, Ein Hashofet, formed part of the Hashomer Hatzair fed-eration, which, with the other kibbutz movements, was to pro-vide the bulk of the dedicated recruits who constituted the Palmach, the Jewish assault force which fought with such distinc-tion in the 1948 War of Independence.

It was around the time of that war that Yosef's path again crossed mine. In the meantime, he had served in the British Army during the Second World War, rising to the rank of major in the Jewish Brigade. In 1947 I met him in Canada, where he had been sent by Hagana command to work on arms procure-ment. Later, during the 1948 fighting he served under me in the 7th Brigade, where he became my chief of staff; subsequently, he took over from me as commander of the brigade. He was my host at the 7th Brigade reunion in 1973.

Throughout our long association, we were closely linked. I flatter myself that we were kindred spirits, and certainly we had a great deal in common. We were the same age, and came from the same country, and the latter fact especially singled us out. At that time — indeed, to this day — the majority of the Jews in Palestine were of Eastern European or Middle Eastern origin. The reason is not hard to find: the situation of the Jews in those countries was such that many of them sought a new home for themselves. The condition of the Jews in North America was far better. Consequently, the numbers of immigrants from those countries have always been small. Many American and Canadian Jewish immigrants have played an important role in the country's development, but they have never constituted more than a tiny percentage of the Jewish community in Palestine.

I was very keenly aware that my background was quite unlike that of my companions at Tel Asher. But nevertheless, despite these differences, despite the initial difficulties in communication through the absence of a common language, I did not find myself regarded as an outsider. After those first few weeks of "trial by turiya", once I showed I could put in a day's work like anyone else, and proved that I was able and willing to stick out the arduous conditions, I found myself accepted. As for my Canadian origins, I was simply another Jew, from yet another corner of the world. In fact, my North American background served to provide some amusement when I entertained my fellows by singing American songs, presented, to the best of my ability, in the manner of Al Jolson.

I had, of course, to answer many queries about the political situation in Canada and the United States, about the Jews there, and about the prospects of American support for the Zionist movement. This earnest approach to issues was very characteristic of my friends at Tel Asher. They were hell-raisers, and they would gladly dance half the night. But they were intelligent and well informed, and they displayed a burning interest in current

issues. Although there were endless differences of opinion between them, they were all firm supporters of the various labour
factions, and vigorous opponents of the right-wing parties. At
this time, I was making my first acquaintance with the complexities of the political scene, and if I encountered one end of
the spectrum at Tel Asher, I found another among my relatives,
the Kahanes.

I first made contact with the Kahanes shortly after my arrival
in the country. A sister of my Grandmother Miller married
Ephraim Kahane — a most remarkable character, who headed
an unusual family. Ephraim had left his native Austria after
fighting an officer who insulted his mother. He reached Palestine in original fashion, walking all the way across the desert
from Egypt. During the First World War, he and other members
of his family worked for British Intelligence, supplying information about the Turkish Army then occupying Palestine. He was
arrested, and only saved from execution in Jaffa when the city
was taken by Allenby's men. He was luckier than some of our
other relatives; Yehoshua and Mendel Hankin were arrested by
the Turks, who tortured them with the bastinado in an unsuc-
cessful attempt to break them, while Na'aman Belkind, Yisrael
Belkind's nephew, was hanged in Damascus for his role in the
spy-ring.

I often visited the Kahanes; I soon grew very close to them and
their four sons, especially the two younger sons, who were
nearer to me in age. Elyashiv was later to be of great assistance to
me in my land-buying ventures. Benyamin, whose room I
shared on my visits, was to meet a hero's death as a pilot in the
1948 War of Independence, when he used his unarmed Piper
Cub to decoy a squadron of Egyptian fighters away from a
column of Israeli infantry. By the time the Arab planes trapped
him and shot him down, they were short of fuel, and had to
return to base. The column was saved, but Benyamin paid with
his life. There is a monument to his memory at Eilat, on the Gulf
of Aqaba.

It was through the Kahanes that I made my first acquaintance with another aspect of the country's political life. The two main political groupings at that time were the right-wing Revisionists and the Histadrut (labour federation) parties. There was considerable enmity between them, which reached fever pitch at this time when Arlozoroff, a labour leader, was murdered on the Tel Aviv beach. The labour leaders suspected the Revisionists of instigating the murder; the Revisionists denied the charge hotly, and the debate raged loud and furious.

I did not yet fully understand the intricacies of the political scene, but I was highly distressed by this strife. Feeling that this was a time when the Jews of Palestine should stand united, I found an original way of demonstrating my opposition to this senseless dissension. Benyamin was a Revisionist, and I would sometimes accompany him to his meetings—wearing a cap with the emblem of Hapoel, the labour sports club! On one occasion, I did the same thing in reverse: I turned up at Tel Asher, which was solidly pro-labour, wearing a Revisionist cap. They wanted to lynch me. My well-meaning attempts to restore Jewish unity did not meet with much approval from either side. . . .

My venture into political mediation was not a shining success, but I had little else to complain of. I was definitely enjoying my life in Palestine. Almost without sensing it, I was undergoing a tremendous metamorphosis. Just a few months earlier, I'd been living in the lap of luxury. I had everything I could ask for — servants, cars, horses, spending money — and my only physical exertions were at sports. And now, here I was at Tel Asher, working long hours in the blazing sun, subsisting on a frugal diet which gave me less meat in a whole week than in a single one of Mother's meals!

My loss of material comforts did not make me unhappy — quite the contrary! To my famished palate, the skimpy meals of potatoes and leben (sour milk) tasted as delicious as anything conjured up by a French chef. I now slept as well on my straw mattress as on my springy bed at home. In Canada, I had unlimited pocket money, but there never seemed to be enough. Here, I was earning a princely twenty piastres daily (one Canadian dollar)—and I found all my needs lavishly supplied. I paid thirty piastres a month for my lodging, and another eight to nine a day for my food; I bought "Ophir" cigarettes at two piastres for a packet of thirty—leaving me with five to six piastres to squander! What more could I desire?

Let no one think that I dissipated all my earnings on riotous living: I *saved* as well! Within six months I had collected enough money to buy myself a donkey. I was overjoyed with my acquisition and had grandiose visions of galloping madly around the countryside, between my friends in Kfar Saba, Gan-Chaim, Gan-Hasharon — with an occasional visit to the nearby Arab town of Tulkarem for shishkabob.

Most of my dreams were shattered by little "Klotzky", whose vibrant sexual urges and single-minded persistence frustrated my plans and almost drove me out of my mind. On one occasion, I had a ticket for a symphony concert in Tel Aviv. On that precise day, there was a bus strike, but, undaunted, I decided to get to the concert on Klotzky's back. I set off bravely, and all went well, until I reached the main Tel Aviv road, which then was no more than a dirt track. As I rode south towards Tel·Aviv, little groups of Arabs passed by on their donkeys, headed north. This was fine—as long as the passing donkeys were males. But every now and then, when some cute little female ass passed in the opposite direction, all hell broke loose! First of all, Klotzky stopped, with his feet apart and his head down, braying his undying passion. With that, the struggle was on: Klotzky would twist like a pretzel, while I yanked at the reins in a desperate attempt to keep him from turning. In vain. As a lover, Klotzky was irrepressible, and away he would dash after his temptress, taking me away from my objective.

Not all my riding was as disastrous as that concert outing. Occasionally, Lepke would lend me his amazing Arab mare,

"Mediterranee". She could go like the wind and was as smooth as a rocking chair, and I loved to ride her. Lepke himself would ride her thirty miles to a race meet attended by the country's greatest racing stables. There she would contend successfully against all comers, regularly placing in the money. And then, the very next day, she was back in harness, pulling the plough or the wagon.

After a while I began to get letters from my parents, in which they announced that it was now time for me to return home. But I was having a wonderful time, enjoying myself as never before, and I had not the slightest desire to go back to Canada. I knew of all the comforts and luxuries which awaited me in Toronto, but they did not attract me at all. To my parents, this must have seemed incomprehensible; they probably thought that I lacked the fare-money, for they proceeded to send me a ticket. Gratefully, I cashed the ticket, and used the money to throw a party. Later, they sent me another ticket, and this time I found an even better use for the money — I bought a shotgun!

That gun served many purposes. For one thing, I loved to go hunting in the nearby swamps. On Saturday, my weekly day off, Lepke would lend me a mule, which I rode bareback. Lepke himself often accompanied me, as did the foreman of the neighbouring settlement of Gan-Chaim — a Belkind, distantly related to me. The three of us would compete against the Bedouin hunters, and when we bagged some wild duck, we took the opportunity to throw another party. During these hunting expeditions, I became friendly with the Bedouin, who openly admired my gun, a Krupp five-shot, capable of very rapid fire. This was the reason for the Bedouins' interest, and, perhaps, for their frequent invitations to me to join their "fantasia" festivities, where the highlight was the firing of every available fire-arm up at the sky. The idea was to make as much of a racket as possible, and clearly a five-shot possessed an impressive noise-making potential. Those "fantasias" were great fun, and I enjoyed them tremendously; they were a fitting preparation for the extraordinary fantasia many years later in honour of my wedding.

But however much enjoyment I got from that shotgun at "fantasias" and on hunting expeditions, I needed it for more serious purposes. By now, I was no longer working in the orange groves with a turiya. I had risen in the social scale. I was now a watchman — a "shomer".

Some six months or so after arranging for me to go to Tel Asher, Yehoshua Hankin found me standing before him once again. This time, the problem bothering me did not concern me alone. I was there to expound my views on the defence of Tel Asher — with a self-assurance quite remarkable (and not altogether praiseworthy) in an eighteen-year-old newcomer. It was unthinkable, I proclaimed, that we, the twenty or so Jewish workers at Tel Asher, should calmly lie down to sleep every night, leaving ourselves under the protection of an Arab guard. Something had to be done.

I had nothing personally against "Hawaja Haj", as our Moroccan guard was known. He was a good-looking man, and very friendly towards me, often letting me ride his fine black stallion. My companions told him that I was a "rich American", and he was deeply impressed. Thereafter, whenever I walked past his tent, he would invite me in for coffee, and make vigorous efforts to sell me one of his wives. Although I didn't take him up on the offer, this in no way diminished his demonstrations of affection for me. All the same, I objected to the idea of depending on an Arab to protect us. The system worked well enough at ordinary times, because our watchman was probably the biggest thief in the district; his rivals scrupulously steered clear of "his" pitch, thereby keeping us safe from small-scale thefts. But if the settlement were attacked in earnest, the attackers would be Arabs, and I didn't think we could depend on Haj to defend us in a pinch. And, as we all knew, the pinch could come at any time, since the British mandatory government was leaving the settlements in the countryside to fend for themselves.

I explained all this to Hankin. He obviously did not consider me presumptuous. He listened carefully, and then told me that our exposed position, near the Arab town of Tulkarem, and surrounded by Arab villages, did indeed call for a Jewish "shomer". But he warned me that a good shomer was not easy to come by, and we'd have to find one for ourselves.

We began to shop around for a shomer. Soon, we heard of a certain Yankele, a well-known shomer who had just come out of a British prison, where he had spent time for knocking in some-one's teeth "in the line of duty". I went to see him. He knew our district well, and expressed his willingness to take on the job, on condition that we found him an assistant. When I told him we couldn't find one, he replied quite cheerfully that I'd do! With this enthusiastic recommendation, I took up my duties in the prestigious role of assistant night-watchman at Tel Asher.

The shomer's job was to keep a lookout at night, and to protect the settlement from thieves or trespassers. Our relations with our Arab neighbours were friendly on the whole, and it didn't seem that guard duty presented much of a problem. Neverthe-less, I was surprised by the unorthodox manner in which Yan-kele tackled his assignment. His way of "going on guard" was to lay himself down to sleep on the table in our communal kitchen, and send me outside to keep an eye on things. When Arabs trespassed on our land, he would send me to kick them off, while he supervised the affair from the comfort of his table.

I was on my own. I had to do the best I knew, so I would grab a lance, jump onto Lepke's mare Mediterranee, and charge the intruders bareback, uttering Indian war-whoops. Perhaps the war-whoops were what did the trick or perhaps it was the lance; whatever it was, in most cases the intruders would run for it. But I didn't always have it so easy.

On one occasion, an Arab leaned inside the fence, and opened up the faucet to take a drink. He was a big fellow, and when I told him to make off (or words to that effect), he looked at me and drew himself up to his full height, saying "Ta'al!", meaning

"Come on!" I tied up my horse and clambered over the fence to him. As usual, I fought barehanded, quite relishing a little rough and tumble. The whole affair took on a different complexion when he produced a "shabariya" (dagger), at the same time grabbing me around the neck. At once I fell with a ju-jitsu break —but the trick didn't work with this fellow. I found myself on the ground, busy holding his knife-hand, while his other hand choked me. I managed to twist loose and kick him in the stomach. As he raised up, I grabbed him firmly by the testicles. "The Sergeant-Major", my boxing instructor at Upper Canada College, would have been ashamed of me; but I had little trouble with my opponent after that.

Till that time, there had been a kind of unwritten agreement whereby the Arabs were permitted to come into our groves and cut the grass growing between the trees. But I thought we should hold on to that grass, for use as fertilizer, or to sell for fodder. So I began to clamp down, and I wouldn't allow anyone to come in and cut it. That was the rule which provoked the fight with the Arab champion with which this book opens.

In time, the Arabs came to know me, and they began to steer clear of Tel Asher. Instead, they paid more frequent visits to the neighbouring groves, one of which was guarded by a man named Yehuda. On one occasion, when he was chasing off intruders, Yehuda was knifed. Obviously, this was a serious business, and the Arabs weren't just playing games. After that incident, I started going over to help him out; it wasn't long before his grove, too, was off-limits to the Arabs.

My stint as a watchman taught me a great deal about guerilla fighting. I would usually find myself outnumbered; if it came to shooting, my shotgun was inferior to the rifles the Arabs seemed to acquire with such ease, despite the official British restrictions that applied to Arabs and Jews. I had to learn to deal with the intruders singlehanded, employing stealth and surprise to balance out their advantages. One thing I discovered at this time was that, popular views notwithstanding, the Arabs were poor night-fighters. They dislike the darkness, and I could always use that fact to my advantage. Sixteen years later, when I was a combat commander in the Israeli Army, I was to remember this weakness.

However, long before I joined the Israeli Army, I was to put my combat skills to good use against an enemy far more formidable than the Arab armies. As a warning of what was in store for the world—and for me—the radio in the Tel Asher communal dining room sometimes boomed out the strange, blood-curdling sound of thousands of voices thundering "Sieg Heil!" It was a barbaric sound, primitive and inexplicably frightening; listening to it, I felt goose pimples on my skin, even though I knew the sound came from thousands of miles away.

But this was no more than a passing cloud. The Second World War was a long way ahead; the Nazis had yet to gain power in Germany. As for me — it was now a year since my arrival in Palestine, and I found life very satisfying.

CHAPTER SIX

Back and Forth

Every time I shared a meal with Asher Pierce, I came off second best. Asher was one of Dad's most unusual friends, a pioneer lumberman in Northern Ontario. When I was seventeen, we went fishing with him there, on the Martin River. It was a great trip: on the way up, Dad let me drive the family air-cooled Franklin, and on the river we had a wonderful time shooting the rapids, portaging upstream, and catching a great mess of pickerel, which our host cooked up as a chowder. Our exertions had given me quite an appetite, and I began to tuck in with all my might, expecting, as usual, to out-eat everyone else. But in Asher Pierce I had met my match: I watched in amazement as he calmly devoured over twenty large potatoes!

Two years later, in the summer of 1932, after I had spent a year in Israel, an unexpected invitation reached me at Tel Asher. Mr. and Mrs. Asher Pierce were staying at the King David Hotel in Jerusalem, and they asked me to join them for dinner. I was very pleased to accept: my only concern was my lack of proper clothes for such dignified surroundings. Looking forward to the meeting, I set off for Jerusalem, unaware of what was in store.

At dinner, while I was still adjusting to the dazzling white table linen, and the silver, and the strains of the orchestra in the background, my host went into action: he began to persuade me to accompany him back to Canada. He was both eloquent and insistent, and I found it hard to resist. What made it even harder was that I had no ordinary outsider to contend with: I was arguing with a man who had made a considerable contribution to the colonization of Palestine (he had founded Gan-Chaim, and "my" Tel Asher was named after him). I resisted to the best of my ability, but he just wouldn't take no for an answer. He simply went on at me until my powers of resistance ran out, and I gave my reluctant consent. I think he even managed to eat more than I did, once again.

The onslaught was not, of course, entirely spontaneous, but was merely a continuation of my parents' campaign to persuade their errant son to come home. Hearing of the Pierces' Palestine trip, Dad had seized the opportunity, and asked his old friend to bring me back. It was a smart move: in argument—as in eating— Asher Pierce was a hard man to beat. Forewarned about the strange things which happened to fare-money entrusted to my care, he insisted on buying my ticket himself—and topped it all by personally escorting me aboard the ship.

I returned to Toronto just over a year after I set off, considerably changed. I went off a flabby, pampered boy: I returned as a tough young man who had seen the world. I had laboured with my bare hands, enduring difficulties and hardships such as I never knew before. I had struck roots in a strange land and successfully waged a war of survival which sometimes required me — literally — to fight for my life.

After such a long separation, I was very happy to see my family once more. It was pleasant to be the centre of attention, with everyone curious to hear of my escapades: I became a much-sought-after expert on Palestine. As I told my stories, my listeners paid careful attention, displaying a deep and genuine concern for the Jewish Yishuv. But at the same time, there was a lack of comprehension, an unbridgeable gap. For all their interest, Palestine was not, it seemed, a land which personally affected my family and friends. To them, my trip was a wonderful adventure; they were thrilled by my stories, and probably proud of my romantic deeds as a pioneer and watchman in far-off Palestine. But that was all. Palestine was a fascinating episode — nothing more. They could not understand my personal attachment to the country, and when I pronounced my intentions of returning, I encountered looks of blank incomprehension.

It was my mother's attitude which surprised and perplexed me most. As I mentioned earlier, Mother was attached to Palestine in heart and soul. Not only were many of her relatives living there, most of her everyday life was spent in organizing help for the Yishuv. Everything that happened in Palestine was of interest to her. If ever there was a totally convinced and dedicated Zionist, it was my mother. And yet, when I went to live in Palestine, making strenuous efforts to strike roots there, Mother and Dad—both prominent members of the Zionist movement—did their utmost to bring me back to Canada. Later, whenever I wanted to go to Palestine, I always encountered opposition from my parents, Mother objecting no less than Dad. I found this hard to understand.

Perhaps it had something to do with the nature of Mother's own Zionist convictions. Perhaps her Zionism was no more than philanthropic, part of her active concern for unfortunate Jews, a charity providing a Jewish national haven for the homeless, while she, being neither persecuted nor homeless, felt no obligation to settle in Palestine herself.

But then — does a Zionist have an *obligation* to go and live in Palestine? I have the greatest respect for David Ben-Gurion and his contribution to the Jewish people, but I think he made a mistake when he dismissed the role of the Diaspora Zionist, claiming that it was the *duty* of a Zionist to move to Israel. The establishment of Israel—and, as history has shown, its continued existence — would have been impossible without the active support and encouragement of Diaspora Zionists. If Ben-Gurion's view had been generally accepted, Zionist workers and fundraisers like my mother would have become an extinct breed. Fortunately this particular theory never gained acceptance in the Jewish communities outside Israel, and as a result there are still countless thousands of Diaspora Jews who devote their time and energy and enthusiasm to the Zionist cause.

As a young man who had just returned "home" to Toronto, and yet felt "homesick" for Palestine, I was deeply puzzled by the apparent ambiguities of Mother's attitude. Now that I am older and have children of my own, I can perhaps better understand her reluctance to let me go to Palestine. As for myself, I have not lost the desire to live in Israel, nor have I given up hope of realizing that dream one day—as I proved by impulsively buying a villa outside Nathanya in 1975. But in the present climate of tension and danger prevailing in Israel, I have mixed feelings about taking my own children to live there.

Whatever she thought about settling in Palestine, there can be no doubt about the strength of Mother's attachment to that country, as she was to prove at the end of her days. When she was on her deathbed, she made me promise to have her buried in the then newly established State of Israel. I kept my word; her grave is in Degania, the first kibbutz. I have resolved to follow her example: wherever I live, I, too, hope to find my last resting place in the land of Israel.

But all this concerned the future; however much understanding I can feel now, at that time I wasn't much concerned with the feelings of others. I had enough on my hands, trying to cope with my own frustration and unhappiness over being back in Canada. My parents had succeeded in bringing me back to Toronto; to my father's relief, I began to work in the business. But I felt no desire to stay, and even less interest in Tip Top Tailors as a permanent occupation. Once more, I enjoyed the luxuries and comforts of my previous life. But that did little to sweeten the pill; as I told Dad more than once, I felt like a caged animal.

Looking back, I can see that the next ten years, until I got into the war, were the worst of my life. They could have been much worse, and certainly were much worse for my generation in Canada. Thousands of young men, thrown out of work by the Depression, spent "ten lost years" crisscrossing the country on freight trains, sleeping in hobo jungles, living on what they could beg, borrow, or steal, and always looking for non-existent jobs. It was a terrible time.

By comparison, my own life was unbelievably comfortable. Admittedly, since my father believed in his sons learning the business from the bottom up, I did lengthy stints on tough, dirty jobs in the warehouse and in the factory before I reached white-collar status. But I had a job—with very obvious prospects—and I had almost everything that money could buy.

But I was miserable. I could conceal it during the workday because I knew that the business was being hit hard by the Depression and needed my help. But in my off-hours I let myself go. My behaviour became very wild, as I partied till all hours and drove my car as if the roads were a private race-track. I began to drink heavily. Much of the stuff was bathtub home-brew, since Canada officially observed Prohibition, and I was lucky not to suffer any of the ill effects which sometimes attended home-brew drinking, like blindness or death. And I was lucky that my wild behaviour didn't put me in jail, or in a coffin.

But although I was letting myself go with bootleg liquor, I was careful to keep myself in shape. I took great pride in the powerful physique I'd developed in Palestine; I was lean and tough now, six foot two and two hundred pounds, and I felt no desire to revert to the flabby dumpling who had sailed off to Europe. However hard I worked during the day, whatever alcoholic excesses I indulged during my riotous evenings — I made it a habit to go to a gym daily. I boxed three rounds, skipped, hit the bag, did some weight-lifting, and wrestled with the professionals. It was a thorough professional work-out, and it kept me fit.

I managed to look after my body, but my spirits were low. The Depression, of course, had hit Toronto hard, but even at the best

of times it wasn't a city to set your heart singing. "A sanctimoni-
ous ice-box", Wyndham Lewis called it around about this time,
and he wasn't far wrong. (Happily, he wouldn't recognize the
city today.) Nothing could make me feel at home there—neither
my social dissipations, nor the material luxuries, nor my physical
training. I was miserable at being prevented from going back to
Palestine, and I watched eagerly for any chance which might
present itself to fulfil my dream. When, three years after my
return to Toronto, an opportunity arose, I grabbed it.

Mother's magazine, the *Standard,* was sponsoring a tour of
Palestine, for members of the Zionist organization — the first
such tour from Canada. As I was quick to point out, the organiz-
ers had little knowledge of conditions in Palestine. It would, I
argued, be advisable for someone of, say, my experience to go
ahead of the group, and make sure everything was all right. . . .
In addition, I promised to help conduct the tour, and show its
members around.

My reasoning was irresistible, and my parents had to acknowl-
edge the justice of my case. Jubilant, I packed my bags and set
off. This time, my trip went off in great style. As the advance
guard of a tour, I was treated royally, crossing the Mediterranean first class on the *Countess of Savoy,* the flagship of the Italina
Line. I arrived in Palestine for the second time on January 20,
1935.

This time, however, I planned to stay.

Before I left Toronto I had gone to Dad and explained that I
really wanted to settle in Palestine. To my surprise and delight,
he reluctantly promised to back me financially in getting established there.

After my very pleasant duties as a tour guide were over, I
sought out the men I wanted as colleagues for the project I had
in mind. One was Benny Adelman, a fellow-Canadian. The
others were Harry Jaffe, from South Africa, Joshua Hurwitz,
from New York, and Sammy Shapiro, from Chicago. They were
all old friends from my previous stay, all English-speakers, all

young and energetic, and they were perhaps romantic enough to share my crazy idea of buying land to start a new settlement in hostile territory.

In the 1929 riots, the Jewish settlement of Be'er Tuvia had been attacked by the neighbouring Arabs. The inhabitants were forced to withdraw, leaving the attackers to lay the colony waste, which they did with great thoroughness. This left the southern part of the coastal plain without a single Jewish settlement; I now proposed to buy land in that area and set about founding a new colony.

Considering the fate of Be'er Tuvia, that was a pretty fool-hardy resolve. But when I presented the idea to Benny and the others, I was highly gratified to find that they, like me, were inspired by a sense of adventure and a readiness to run risks. They were prepared to join me in buying land for the establishment of an agricultural co-operative of the type known as a "moshav"—and Joshua followed my example by persuading his father to provide financial backing.

I was very excited: this time I was in Palestine for good. Moreover, I was about to become a founding member of a new colony.

Although our contacts were good, buying the land turned out to be a far harder assignment than any of us had imagined. For example, one modest little plot of one hundred and twelve dunams (twenty-eight acres) had to be bought piecemeal from no fewer than sixteen Arab owners, some of whom sold us strips scarcely covering two dunams. Each deal was conducted separately, and each one involved much diplomatic activity, with long-drawn-out negotiations and hours of haggling. Sammy Seiger, a friend of my cousin Elyashiv Kahane, did most of the talking, sitting there calmly with the money stuffed into his boot, ready to be brought out at the precise moment when it was needed to clinch the deal.

Quite aside from the business at hand, I found this whole

operation a fascinating experience. Born and bred in Palestine, both Elyashiv and Sammy were well versed in Arab customs, and I watched the proceedings carefully, eager to get into the spirit of the elaborately courteous Eastern rituals and learn the local traditions of hospitality and socializing.

Everywhere we went, the Arabs were very kind to us, and their hospitality was lavish. On one occasion, they prepared a goose specially in our honour, and served us a particular delicacy: a soup covered with a thick skim of goose fat. Because of this skim, I didn't realize how hot it was, and poured it straight into my mouth. The heat almost took the skin off my tongue, and the pain was excruciating, but I did not make a sound, for fear of offending my kind hosts. I stood the test of Eastern politeness, but my mouth burned for a week.

The searches and negotiations went on for months, and in the end it all fell through. I was bitterly disappointed. I had woven many fond dreams of the settlement we would build, imagining us ploughing and planting, and making it into a flourishing colony, like the older villages.

But my disappointment was soon driven out by some very real bodily pain, inflicted upon me unintentionally, out of a misplaced sense of humour. The consequences were almost fatal for me — certainly they changed the entire course of my life.

It was Purim, the carnival festival, which perhaps explains why Elyashiv indulged in some horseplay. We were in a metal workshop when he baited the trap for me, showing me how to use the long-handled guillotine, which stood on a raised platform. After making a great show of pressing and straining to bring his full weight down on the handle, he stepped back and invited me to try my strength — while surreptitiously slipping in a pin to lock the mechanism. Never one to refuse a challenge, I seized the handle and exerted all my strength to force it down, but, of course, it didn't budge. As I strained, Elyashiv yanked the pin out, and the handle was suddenly released. I lunged downward, overbalanced, and found myself tumbling off the platform, gashing my leg on a jagged iron strip.

The iron was rusty, so I hurried to a doctor for some anti-tetanus shots. Unfortunately, it transpired that I was allergic to the serum, which provoked a violent reaction in my body. I began to swell up like a balloon. The swelling was internal, too; as my wind-pipe started to close up, I felt myself choking. It was a frightful feeling: a horrible death was only moments away.

It was whisky that saved me. I had a full bottle under the bed (my Toronto habits died hard) and, whenever I felt myself choking, I would fetch it out and swallow a slug. Whether the liquor relieved the swelling, freeing a passage for the air, or whether it just made me feel better and inspired me to fight for life, I don't know. I only know that I finally pulled through, and when I sat up, relieved at being able to breathe once more, the whisky bottle was on the floor, empty.

This incident occurred shortly after my parents arrived in Palestine with their tour group, and they made the most of the opportunity. Lying in bed, helpless and exhausted, I just didn't have the mental stamina to display my usual stubbornness. When Mother and Dad told me they were taking me home to Toronto — just for a few months, they reassured me, until I regained my health and strength — I was too weak to put up more than token resistance.

On my return I went to work in Tip Top Tailors again. Now, in 1935, in the heart of the Depression, things were even worse than before. Few people had the money to spend on new clothes, so sales continued to decline. The company was suffering losses on its current operations, and its reserves had been eaten up. Soon after, Dad had to sell off Sunnybrook Farm to help pay off his debts, but his finances were still tight. Not that the family suffered any real hardship — we always had enough for our current needs. We cut down on various marginal luxuries, and made savings wherever possible. The new town house which replaced Sunnybrook did not have the extensive gardens of its predecessor, so that we saved the staff and expense of their upkeep. And in a world where millions were enduring unemployment and hardship, we had no cause to complain. All the same, there was considerable concern over the state of the family business: it was the only important asset left, and saving it would require considerable effort.

Over the next four years I worked hard to do just that. Naturally, as I gained experience my authority grew, and I was able to introduce new ideas, such as decentralization, and the creation of a ladies' wear department, and one for sportswear. As the new ideas bore fruit, my authority increased.

I worked hard and played hard. I socialized a great deal, I went to parties, I raised a lot of hell. But I was tough enough to take it: there were many evenings when I would get high on bootlegged liquor, roll into bed at all hours — and be up promptly next morning, ready for a hard day's work.

On Fridays, straight after work, I'd jump into my car and drive ninety miles to Midland on Georgian Bay, to be with the light and comfort of my life — my beloved schooner, the *Dinny*.

The *Dinny* was built by a devoted sailor by the name of Cecil Schramm, who named her after his wife. Working with his own hands, helped by the local builders of Port Dover on Lake Erie, he spent years fashioning her, lavishing endless work and love on her. She was designed by Hand, a famous naval architect; Cecil Schramm double-welded her plates, an unusual procedure at that time. He had intended to live on the boat, but he was in for a bitter disappointment: when he took his wife out for a cruise on her namesake, she became violently seasick, and declared in no uncertain terms that she would not set foot on board the vessel again. Left with no other choice, her heartbroken husband put the boat up for sale, and I, still unencumbered by a spouse, was able to purchase her.

I fitted her out for cruising in Georgian Bay, installing an

old-fashioned wood-stove and a dining table which could seat
eight people comfortably. Thereafter, I spent every free moment on her during the summer. With the help of local
French-Canadian guides, I became familiar with the gorgeous
"30,000 Island" section of Georgian Bay, getting to know all the
channels of this unique body of water. It was a welcome relief
from my weekdays penned up in the city.

But that wasn't the only form of enjoyment the *Dinny* gave me.
With her interior so well fitted out, she was an ideal place for
parties, and we had plenty. Friends from other boats would join
me, and I would bring along my share of congenial company to
join in the revelry. Someone always brought a banjo or a guitar,
and we would play and sing. On a cold October evening, when
the thermometer was well below the freezing point and the wind
howled outside, that schooner cabin could be very snug, with the
wood-stove blazing, a glass of hot rum in my hand, and some fair
companion at my side. . . .

The *Dinny* did a lot to help me overcome my yearnings for
Palestine, but it wasn't my only "substitute". Since I wasn't there,
and couldn't take part in the efforts of the Yishuv in Palestine, I
did the next-best thing: I harnessed myself to Zionist work,
primarily in fund-raising and public relations.

Nowadays, almost all Jewish leaders and organizations call
themselves "Zionist", whatever they mean by that; the Zionist
movement finds support among all sections of the Jewish community, rich and poor. Things were different in the thirties,
when Zionism encountered opposition in Canada and elsewhere
from many Jewish groups and individuals, above all from the
more affluent, who were often also the most assimilated. At that
time, the bulk of Zionist support came from the poorer Jews —
the workers, clerks, office employees, and so on. This created a
major moral dilemma for me in my fund-raising work. Most of
my audiences consisted of working people, and it was their
support I had to enlist. However painful it was to take two or

three weeks' wages from a factory worker or stenographer, there was nothing else for it. Only much later, after the establishment of the State of Israel, did the wealthier sections of the community begin to pull their weight, making it possible to raise far larger sums than we ever dreamed of in those strenuous campaigns in the thirties.

During that time, as Nazi anti-Semitism went on the rampage and the situation of European Jewry grew increasingly perilous, there was great concern for the children growing up in such a hostile environment. While most Jews remained in Europe until it was too late to flee, many of them wanted to get their children out of harm's way. Youth Aliya was formed to cater to this need, by collecting children from European countries and sending them to Palestine, where they were lodged in kibbutzim and boarding schools.

As darker clouds loomed over Europe with every passing day, I threw myself into Youth Aliya work, often speaking for its appeal three or four times a week, organizing fund-raising affairs, and so on. It was perhaps the most important work I have ever done: when war came, bringing the nightmare of the Holocaust, thousands of children were in a safe haven.

CHAPTER SEVEN

Trying to Enlist

Volunteer? Didn't I know I was in an essential industry? Look at the plans I was making to set up a plant capable of turning out thirty-five thousand uniforms a week. Wasn't I going to help run it? Didn't I know how hard it would be on my father? The whole thing was "the height of irresponsibility"!

That was the reaction from my parents when I announced in 1939 that I planned to volunteer for armed service. They told me very forcefully that I was crazy to brush aside my exempt status, and they continued to oppose my plan with a stubbornness that matched my own. In time, Father even succeeded in arranging an offer from the Ordnance Corps that would have put me in charge of procurement of military supplies, a job with the starting rank of lieutenant-colonel. I wasn't interested; I no more wanted to spend the war as a desk officer than as a uniform manufacturer. My mind was made up. I wanted to get into the war.

From the outset anyone with half an eye could see that the war against the Axis powers was going to be a long and bitter one. If Canada and her allies were going to win, everyone was going to be needed. I was young and tough and as patriotic as the next man. Perhaps my Upper Canada College training with its proud reminders that in 1866 the school's pupils had actually borne arms in the defence of Canada against the Fenian raiders played its part. And perhaps that long-ago parade of soldiers on Yonge Street also had an effect.

Whatever the reason, it was quite clear to me that, as a loyal Canadian, it was my duty to volunteer to fight.

Besides, as a Jew I had a special score to settle with the Nazis. In 1939 no sane man could foresee the full extent of the horrors which Hitler's regime would unleash on the Jewish people, let alone the crazed scientific procedures which would evolve into the gas chambers and crematoria of the concentration camps. But already the anti-Semitic persecutions raging in Germany and the other countries dominated by the Nazis had made it clear that these men were the implacable foes of my people.

For all these very good reasons, it was clear to me that I should volunteer for military service.

In September 1939 I applied to join the Royal Canadian Navy. I chose the navy because I loved the sea, and thanks to the *Dinny* I had lots of sea-going experience. There was an additional, long-range reason for my choice. Palestine, with its long coastline, was clearly destined to become an important maritime country; some day, perhaps, the skills I would acquire in the RCN might prove to be of use there.

But if I had "Jewish reasons" for wanting to join the navy, the navy had its "Jewish reasons" for rejecting me. I was told they considered me over-qualified to serve as an ordinary seaman; as for taking me on as an officer—their quotas were full. Nevertheless, they promised to keep me on file, and notify me of any vacancy. Though disappointed at what I saw merely as an irritating delay, I was too naïve to question the explanations I'd been given. I went on with my work, expecting the navy's call to come any day.

Months passed, and still I hadn't heard from them. Then one day early in 1940 I received a call from an old friend—Maitland Steinkoph of Winnipeg. Naturally enough, conversation touched on the war and on our prospects for enlistment. I told him of my application to join the navy, and my hopes of an early summons. But he shattered my illusions, once and for all. He, too, had tried to join the navy, but a close personal friend engaged in naval recruitment had advised him in confidence that the navy would not accept Jewish officers. With its heavily conservative tradition, the navy obviously considered that a Jew was not suitable company in the wardroom.

It infuriated me that such habits of mind prevailed in a country supposedly at war against the Hitler regime and all that it represented. But I wasn't really surprised. Many RCN officers were drawn from the exclusive yachting circles, which were WASP-dominated and heavily tinged with racism. I was to encounter this again after the war, when I discovered that the existing yacht clubs were closed to Jewish applicants — which I dealt with by helping to found a Jewish yacht club.

But this, too, belonged to the future. At that time, early in 1940, I was primarily concerned with getting into the war. I had neither the time nor the motivation to make an issue out of the RCN's ban on Jews. I simply lost interest in joining the navy: I didn't want to fight alongside men who rejected me. (In time, the pressures and needs of war must have broken down the navy's conservative traditions; many months later, too late, I received my long-awaited call from the naval recruitment office.)

With the navy barred to me, I began to look around for another branch of the armed forces to join. I settled for the infantry, even though prospects of acceptance were not very encouraging.

This was the period of the "phoney war", and with almost no fighting occurring in Europe, the Canadian Army, ludicrously weak though it was, was in no hurry to expand its units. There seemed to be a hundred volunteers for every vacancy, and the units were very choosy. As a result, enlisting took on something of the character of trying to join an exclusive club. But at long last, as a result of considerable string-pulling, I succeeded in enlisting in the 2nd Battalion of the Queen's Own Rifles.

At that time, the Queen's Own, like other militia regiments, was only partly activated: the 1st Battalion was on active service, while the 2nd remained in reserve, with the men doing training on a part-time basis. Accordingly, I divided my time between Tip Top Tailors — where I was trying to get the staff organized to function effectively in my absence — and the army, where I was learning the ropes in the same way I first got acquainted with the business: from the bottom up. In the course of my part-time soldiering, I was a rifleman, was sent to NCOS' school, and graduated with corporal's stripes; later, I was promoted to sergeant, and served as a company sergeant-major.

All this was a very long-drawn-out and frustrating process. It was the summer of 1940, and the war had taken a serious turn. France had fallen and only the tattered remnants of the British and Commonwealth troops who had got off the beach at Dunkirk still stood in arms against Hitler. The whole world's future was in the balance and I was spending my evenings as a soldier teaching others how to salute, and other tasks equally vital to winning the war. I wanted to get into active duty: I wanted intensive training, to prepare me for combat. Instead, the months were passing by, and I was still leading a schizophrenic life as a business executive by day and a soldier by night. It seemed that I would never get into the war. Finally, after six months as an NCO, I was recommended for an officers' course. This came as a great relief, as I expected an immediate summons. But another three or four months elapsed before I was called up and admitted to the course at Brockville, two hundred miles east of Toronto.

If it was real, full-time, intensive training I wanted, that course at Brockville satisfied every possible wish! It should be remembered that, at twenty-eight, I was an old man to start a career as an infantry officer. The other participants were much younger — the average age must have been around twenty-two. What was worse, I was out of condition, and my weight had crept up to around 240 pounds. The course was not designed for out-of-shape fatties; it was a test of endurance as much as anything else. We were on the double, jogging from early morning till late at night, with long route marches nearly every day. There were times when I wondered if I was going to survive (which brought back rueful memories of Tel Asher), but I quickly toughened up again, and was in good shape by the end of the course.

A further test was provided by the weather. Winter in that part of Canada is always cold, but some winters are colder than others. That winter was unspeakable. One of my worst experiences as a soldier—and I include the hell of front-line combat—was guard duty at Brockville on nights where the temperature dropped to thirty or forty degrees Fahrenheit below zero. As sentries, we were absolutely forbidden to move a muscle (so as not to give away our position to the enemy), and with nothing more on our feet than regulation leather boots, it wasn't long before our legs froze. That was bad enough. Thawing out afterwards was sheer agony.

Despite the hardships (or perhaps because of them, I don't know), it was an excellent training for infantry officers. After three months, I graduated as a second lieutenant, and went on to Camp Borden for advanced officers' training. Borden was one of the army's permanent camps, situated only sixty miles north of Toronto. For us "one-pip wonders", conditions there were positively luxurious compared to Brockville and I enjoyed our training, from which I emerged a full lieutenant of the Canadian Army!

Every officer was expected to spend some time as an instructor, and I was now posted to Cornwall basic-training centre. CABT #31, as it was termed officially, gave me just about the most fun I had ever had in my life. If I had been six years younger— and there hadn't been a war on—I would have been well content to spend my remaining youth there.

Cornwall is about fifty miles west of Montreal, on the border of Ontario and Quebec. The local population is a mixture of

French Canadians and Scottish settlers, and many of the camp's permanent personnel were local people. The commanding officer, Colonel Rudy Larose (later Sergeant-at-Arms of the House of Commons in Ottawa), was like a character from a history of pre-Revolutionary France, an officer and gentleman of the old school. He believed in living in style. Our cuisine was second to none in the land — not surprisingly, since Rudy had arranged for the posting of the former chef of Ottawa's grandest hotel, the Château Laurier. My weight soared. But eating was not my only recreation: the civilian population was extremely friendly, we officers were very popular with the local ladies, and I managed to have lots of fun.

I was in charge of training so-called "problem platoons". These usually consisted of men of supposedly low intelligence, who had been classified as unsuitable material. I found that most of these men did not have low IQs, they simply lacked a formal education. Many of them were Indians or backwoodsmen who had received little schooling, but there was no reason why they should not make excellent infantrymen. Thanks to the good relationships I was able to establish, they went through their training successfully, and I even managed to keep them out of trouble — perhaps my main feat, as they were a pretty wild bunch, especially when they got hold of liquor. I had my own system for keeping them out of jail: if one of them wanted to go to town for some fun, I'd ask for two volunteers to accompany him. The "escorts" were on their honour to stay sober, guard their charge from the police, and make sure he got back to camp.

I also had "special platoons" from the opposite end of the spectrum: men with exceptionally high IQs. Taking them through the same basic training was an interesting contrast. I once trained a platoon of signallers—an excellent bunch of men, all of whom were "officer material". Assisted by the best NCOs in the camp, I gave this platoon intensive training, which rapidly took them through the basic course and advanced training, too.

This was around the time of Pearl Harbor, when the United States entered the war. The Americans asked for Canadian soldiers to come down and put on exhibitions for them, to help boost morale and back up their draft. I went down to New York State with the crack platoon of signallers. All of them tackled the assignment with enthusiasm — Canadians always enjoy showing Americans how things should be done — and they put on a most impressive show. With only about ten weeks' training behind them, they demonstrated a battle drill, staging a mock attack with smoke and blank fire. We rounded it all off with some parade-ground drill, headed by a pipe band. We made a hell of an impression. Our American hosts were open-mouthed with admiration, their announcer going into raptures over our precision and skill. We did not go out of our way to disabuse them of the notion that this was just an average Canadian platoon.

I was only supposed to spend three months at Cornwall, but I made the mistake of performing my duties so thoroughly that Colonel Larose came to consider me indispensable. I have the sneaking suspicion that his reasons were not purely military. On top of my official duties, I had the extra-curricular role of leading sing-songs in the mess parties. If there was one thing Colonel Larose liked, it was a party; consequently, he tried to retain my musical services on a permanent basis by appointing me camp intelligence officer — which made it much harder for me to get out of there later on.

But this job of intelligence officer soon created a great deal of tension between the colonel and me. It was part of my duty to report on the state of morale in the camp; in doing so, I ventured to stir up an issue which many considered taboo, and on which Colonel Larose, as a French Canadian, was particularly touchy. Although conscription was in force at that time, it only applied to service in Canada; only volunteers were ever sent abroad. The volunteers were produced by lining up the men on the parade ground, with bands playing and banners flying, and bombarding them with rousing patriotic speeches, which culminated in a stirring call for volunteers for overseas service. Aside from its other defects, this procedure created considerable tension between French- and English-speaking soldiers. Like all other citizens, French Canadians were conscripted into the army. But, for reasons rooted deep in Canadian history, they displayed little enthusiasm for the war against the Germans (several Quebec men confided to English-speaking colleagues, I'm not sure how seriously, that they wanted the training mainly to prepare for the forthcoming fight against Ontario). As a result, few of our French-Canadian recruits volunteered for service overseas, and the Ontario men were rightly resentful of this fact.

I, too, found it intolerable that some men were going abroad to face danger, while others, equally fit and capable, stayed at home. My opinions were very forcefully reflected in my intelligence reports, which, in effect, preached for an extension of conscription to overseas duty. Like other French Canadians, Colonel Larose was opposed to such a move, and he called me in for a dressing down. However, to his indignation, I refused to withdraw my reports. My opinions on the subject grew even stronger later on, during the European campaign, when the "voluntary" system left the Canadian forces so short of replacements that combat units suffered from a chronic lack of trained manpower.

Aside from that little tussle with Colonel Larose, I got myself involved in another conflict, which I helped bring to a successful conclusion. On first reaching Cornwall, I found that the food dished out to the men was literally inedible. It wasn't for lack of materials — in fact, there was an over-abundance — and the quality was fine, since all ranks, officers and men, drew the same basic ration. The fault lay in the way the food was distributed and prepared, and the results were abominable.

The other junior officers and I got together and decided to do something about it. Whenever one of us was duty officer, he would raise hell in the men's kitchen and the quartermaster's stores, and his duty officer's report would detail every defect and shortcoming. In addition, we took to eating our meals with the men. The commanding officer, the quartermaster, and the cooks got the message: within a short time, the men's food was almost as good as that served in the officers' mess: delicious steaks, roasts, and stews, with fresh fish and vegetables.

After that, care for my men's food became one of my prime concerns in any unit I joined—and this, no doubt, was one of the reasons why many soldiers were happy to serve under my command. It wasn't that I followed Napoleon's famous adage about an army marching on its stomach—I simply like good food, and I hate to see it spoiled. I readily adopted the Canadian Army's tradition whereby a good officer doesn't touch his food before ensuring that his men are fed, and in the field our rations were always the same.

Throughout my time with the Canadian Army, I enjoyed excellent relations with my fellow soldiers, of whatever rank. This began right from the start of my service, when I was a rifleman, and, later, an NCO. My background was quite unlike that of most of my fellow-soldiers. Only a short time before, I had been a leading executive in a large company, with thousands of employees under my direction; my income was considerable, and I enjoyed a very affluent life-style. But my experiences in Palestine had taught me to rough it and to adapt to very different conditions; and neither my wealthy family upbringing nor my position at Tip Top Tailors had ever made me put on airs. I never saw myself as "superior", nor did I regard the company's employees as "inferior"—on the contrary, I was full of wonder and admiration for their skills. All this made it very easy for me to adapt to the army. I had no difficulty in fitting in and staying on friendly terms with my fellow soldiers and NCOs.

I continued to maintain cordial relationships with my subordinates when I became an officer. In this I was closely following the traditions of the Queen's Own Rifles, which tried to create a close camaraderie between officers and men by insisting that its officers come up through the ranks (in sharp contrast with other regiments which would not accept officers who came up from their own ranks). I tried to ensure that my men were well looked after, which extended beyond seeing that their stomachs were filled. It isn't only bad food that can make a soldier's life a misery. When I was an instructor at Cornwall, I served as "soldier's friend", helping the men to deal with personal problems. I advised them on marital and financial and legal entanglements, and if they got into trouble with the civilian courts, I tried to defend them. In matters of military transgressions, I usually avoided laying charges, preferring to deal with disciplinary problems by work punishments. Although the culprits did not enjoy the chores they were given, they were usually grateful to me for sparing them from a spell in jail. My care for my subordinates was very richly rewarded. I felt that I was liked and respected by the men under my command.

In view of the treatment I'd had from the navy, it is interesting to note that I never felt any hostility towards me as a Jew while I was in the army. On the contrary, any discrimination usually worked in my favour: my fellow-soldiers seemed to go out of their way to treat me better. But I did encounter one anti-Semitic incident. It occurred when I was in military hospital, recovering from mumps. We were listening to a news broadcast, which, for the first time, officially verified that the Nazis were conducting large-scale massacres of Jews in German-occupied Europe.

As the announcer reported that the massacres had already claimed over a million victims, there was a deathly hush throughout the ward. Suddenly, the silence was broken by a raucous voice from the adjacent ward: "Well," the man exclaimed, his words clearly audible throughout the hospital, "that's one goddamned good thing Hitler's done. I wish he'd come to Toronto to wipe out the Jews there!"

The words went through me like a knife. I came from Toronto and my whole family lived there. What that man said was a direct personal affront of the worst possible kind. I hurled myself out of my bed and stormed into the next ward.

"Who said that?" I roared.

Defiantly, one of the men said: "I did!"

I stalked over to him. "I'm going to kill you," I said, and that was precisely what I intended to do. Just as I was reaching out for him and his eyes were almost popping out of his face in terror, I took hold of myself. "No," I told him, through clenched teeth. "You're not worth my while. I've got a job to do, and if I kill you —or a lot of Nazi bastards like you—I won't be allowed to do it." With that, I turned on my heel, and marched back to my bed, still shaking with rage. It was a long time before anyone broke the silence.

CHAPTER EIGHT

The Queen's Own Prepares

Throughout the war years, the Atlantic was a perilous place, heavily infested with German U-boats. Thousands of brave men lost their lives making that hazardous crossing. When I crossed it in March 1943 I contracted the mumps.

It was a miserable voyage. From its state of grace as a pre-war luxury liner the *Queen Elizabeth* had fallen to become a troopship; she was still a proud lady, so swift that she needed no escort, but nevertheless in her new role she had been designed simply to carry the largest possible number of men. The resulting overcrowding was literally claustrophobic. For example, there were twelve of us officers crammed like sardines into what had once been a cabin for four. Our conditions were still better than those of the men, billeted below in holds which had been converted into enormous dormitories. I remembered my voyage across the Mediterranean on the *Patria,* and my indignation when I saw how those Foreign Legionnaires were quartered. It was my turn now. . . .

To cap it all, a mumps epidemic broke out on the packed vessel, and one of the dining messes soon turned into something like the Atlanta hospital shown in *Gone with the Wind.* There were bodies everywhere, and overworked and overtired doctors hurrying from bed to bed. I was lucky to escape that particular horror, and at the end of the voyage was able to congratulate myself on staying healthy, since no symptoms of mumps had appeared.

Our arrival in England was a great relief after our cramped transatlantic voyage. We were stationed at Aldershot, quartered in barracks of great antiquity—they had housed the soldiers who fought in the Crimea, and looked it—but at least there was lots of elbow room. There was nothing for us to do during the first few days, so we fell into the role of tourists, making the rounds of the local pubs and visiting a music hall or two. It was an unspectacular beginning to our mission to save the world.

After a week, we were ordered to report to the Bordon battle school close by, where the course was notoriously difficult: right from the start, participants were expected to run twenty to thirty miles with battle kit. As usual, dammit, I had allowed myself to get out of shape — and the final round of farewell parties in Canada hadn't improved matters. On top of that, my attack of mumps had ended its incubation period, and I was beginning to feel unwell.

I must have been a pitiful sight that first day at Bordon, as I struggled to keep up with my squad. Military instructors are not renowned for their tender-hearted compassion, but this time the officer in charge was sympathetic since he could see that something was wrong, and sent me to be examined. Although I was obviously unwell, and my jowls were beginning to swell up, the doctor was unimpressed. He accused me of trying to shirk the battle course, and brusquely ordered me to return to duty. The next day was agony. I staggered around the course in a daze, periodically throwing up and wishing that there were some Germans around to put me out of my misery. This time the super-patriot doctor diagnosed mumps, and had me sent to an isolation hospital. By now the swelling had spread over my whole body; my testicles, too, were painfully affected, arousing fears of sterility (which my six children subsequently proved to have been exaggerated).

Overcoming the mumps — and the anti-Semitic incident described in the previous chapter—I was posted back to Aldershot, where I formed part of a pool of hundreds of officers, waiting eagerly to join their units in the field. The postings were on a system of rotation: each officer spent some time with his unit, and then went back to his holding depot, while he was replaced by another man. This system engendered keen competition among the officers, who vied with each other to gain and hold field postings.

On my first active posting to the battalion, I joined A Company, as commander of Number 7 Platoon. I was pleased with my men, a tough bunch of hard-rock miners from the North. I thought that this was a permanent posting, but my hopes were soon dashed, when, after only a few weeks, I was ordered to report to an infantry school to serve as a small-arms instructor. Rumour had it (in the Canadian Army, like any army, rumour was a major part of our life) that, once attached there, I would never be able to leave again. I went to my commanding officer, "Jock" Spragge, begging him to get me out of this assignment: I wanted to remain with the active unit, not in some school. He was very sympathetic, but there was nothing he could do about the posting. However, he gave me some good advice: when I got to the infantry school, he suggested that I play it as dumb as possible. . . .

Because no movie camera was present at the subsequent interview, the world has lost one of the great comic episodes of all time. Before the interview, I prepared myself with great care; so when the colonel, a brisk, no-nonsense regular, looked up to greet his new small-arms instructor, he saw across his desk an astonishingly rumpled figure, standing at a bizarre approximation of attention. On the slovenly new officer's slack-jawed face was a look of great earnestness.

The earnestness was very important. I am naturally fairly slow-spoken, and when the occasion demands I can rival any village idiot — and it is obviously difficult to interrupt someone who is earnestly doing his inarticulate best. Haltingly and with much furrowing of my brow, I confessed to the colonel that, unfortunately, I was "not mechanically inclined", and consequently wondered whether I would make a good instructor. When his crisp questions about such knotty problems as what city I came from required ten seconds of earnest thought before an answer could be produced, he was visibly unimpressed. Clearly, he had been stuck with a slovenly, undisciplined half-wit.

The creaking army machinery went into action with unprecedented speed. I was pronounced unsuitable and whisked out of the camp that same day, back to my battalion. I was overjoyed.

By this time, the 1st Battalion of the Queen's Own had been on active service for three years. They were a superbly led and trained body of volunteers, proud of belonging to Canada's senior infantry regiment. That continuing pride will perhaps excuse my noting here that in the forthcoming European campaign they were to prove themselves one of the best assault units in the Allied armies. On D-day, the Queen's Own formed part of the 8th Brigade, driving seven miles inland while the Americans failed to get off the beaches on our right flanks; the British on the left were pinned down a few miles inland. After that, in the thrust along the French coast, nearly every enemy fortress was reduced by the 3rd Canadian Infantry Division, with the Queen's Own often in the position of honour at the head. It was the same in the drive through Holland and on into Germany: soldiers of the Queen's Own were the first Allied troops to reach the Rhine in the assault on the Siegfried Line after helping to clear the Scheldt Estuary, and they played a decisive role helping to breach the Schlieffen Line, by their successful assault on Mooshof and the Balberger Wald.

In the meantime, the war had started to swing our way, and an Allied invasion of Europe was only a matter of time. We were now in training for that invasion. The doctrine which governed our training — and, later, our combat role — made us, the infantry, into the monarchs of the battlefield. We infantry officers learned to handle the supporting arms, which were placed under our command. In action this procedure proved highly effective, as we co-ordinated the artillery, air, and armour support from our vantage point in the front line.

Back with the battalion once more, I took over the mortar platoon, and went off to a course for mortar officers at the famous English battle school at Barnard Castle. The participants were picked from combat units throughout the British Army. Most of my companions had seen action in various theatres of war: there were Desert Rats, veterans of battles against Rommel in North Africa, officers fresh from the Italian campaign, Chindits who had served in Burma where the mortars had to be carried through the jungle on mules, and officers from many famous Canadian, British, and Allied regiments.

It was a six-week course of combat training, where conditions were deliberately made harder than on the battlefield. The aim was to weed out those who couldn't take it, and the casualty rate was high; one officer complained that he was being made to run more in one day than in a whole year of action in the desert. But by now I was in good condition, and I stood up to the rigorous training — until the last day.

On the final day, we tackled the famous Barnard Castle obstacle course, a series of obstacles and barriers which were notoriously difficult to surmount. One of the most difficult of these was a fifteen-foot-high bridge, bordered by barbed wire. Because of my weight, I was excused from taking this jump, but I cockily thought I could make it. As I crashed to the ground I felt my right ankle go.

In terrible pain, I was rushed to hospital, where I learned that I had, indeed, broken my ankle. On top of the physical suffering, I now had to face a further worry. I was afraid that the accident would make me forfeit my chance of joining the battalion when it went into combat—and so it might, if I hadn't been lucky enough to fall into the hands of an excellent doctor, one of the best bone surgeons in Britain, with ideas far ahead of his time. I was to be one of his guinea pigs.

After examining my ankle, he strapped it up with a walking cast and announced that I was to start walking immediately. And then, to show that he *meant* immediately, he ordered: "Now—up on your toes! Up! Up! Up!"

I couldn't believe my ears. I thought that we were supposed to be fighting against crazy doctors, not obeying them, but he was so insistent that I gave it a try, forcing myself up a fraction. I fell on my bed, almost passing out from the pain that surged up from my ankle. I lay there in a cold sweat; "I just can't put my weight on it," I told him.

"You must," was his reply. "Tomorrow I'll show you men who have been lying in bed for six months—their ankles have still not healed because they have been immobile for so long." And he did, and I walked, and my ankle healed miraculously quickly.

Other amazing things were going on in that hospital, too. I was one of the lucky ones. My companions included British seamen whose bodies had been hideously scarred by scalding steam or blazing oil, but who were miraculously being patched together again. Even more miraculously, there were men wounded on the beaches of Anzio who arrived with their bodies still encased in the casts applied on the battlefield almost two weeks before. When the staff removed the cast from, say, a mangled leg, the stench of the festering mass would almost knock you over. But Nature's own concoctions were healing the wounds—a process that brought astonished researchers to the hospital to study it.

After a few weeks in hospital, the doctor put me into a light cast, and sent me back to the battalion. His prognosis proved correct; with several more weeks of exercise and therapy, my ankle healed up completely. Although I limped painfully for some time, I was mobile.

My posting with the battalion's mortar platoon was a permanent one—in other words, as an officer with specialized training I was no longer in danger of being rotated out. My command of the mortar platoon was a serious matter, and deserves a few words of explanation. Infantry mortars can give really close, precise support to assaulting troops or armour; they are highly effective weapons. They are light and mobile, and can accompany an infantryman almost anywhere he goes. Because of their high trajectory, they can shoot over and into almost anything and everything. A sergeant in the Queen's Own, Sergeant Corrigan, was to prove that when he dropped a mortar bomb into the magazine of one of the main German ammunition magazines in Boulogne, blowing it sky-high. . . .

The mortar platoon numbered seven sergeants, six corporals, and twenty riflemen. They were a fine group of men, highly trained and skilled. Every single one of them, from the sergeant section commander down to the carrier drivers, was a specialist, and almost any one of them could have taken over command of the platoon if necessary. They were the neatest, and the toughest, group of men I'd ever seen. As I took over command, I promised myself I would do everything in my power to prove worthy of leading them.

The sergeants of the Queen's Own are a very special breed of men, and I am proud of once having been a sergeant in the 2nd Battalion. (Later, in Holland, I was made an honorary member of the sergeants' mess; as a special testimony to our close comradeship, I was given a member's ring—the only one I have ever worn.)

The sergeants of my platoon were, as I expected, an impressive bunch. Roly Guiton, the senior sergeant, was a dapper, handsome man who had shoulders as broad as a barn door and was reputed to be the toughest brawler in the regiment. Sergeants Styles and Sullivan were also clean-cut, fine-looking men. "Papa" Warner and Clute were senior sergeants, much respected by everyone in the battalion; both of them were big and raw-boned, while Sergeant Sully had the appearance of an old-fashioned prize-fighter, tough and burly, with his broken nose askew.

In my first few days with the platoon, the sergeants and I looked each other over. I was the officer in command, and they were expected to obey my orders. At the same time, I knew that I could do little without their co-operation. The question was, what would be the price of that co-operation? Would they go by the old adage that officers come and go, but sergeants go on forever — or would we get along? Clearly, this contest would determine my success in leading the platoon.

It was only when I got back from the Barnard Castle combat school, still hobbling, that the decisive trial of strength began. The mortar officers' course had taught me an entirely new approach to the use of our weapons, and I was eager to introduce the innovative battle drills I had just learned. The sergeants, however, were obviously reluctant to give up the familiar routine, and adopted a rather unaccommodating attitude. I just couldn't get their full co-operation, and I suspect that they, being skilled specialists, were resentful at having to adapt to the ideas of a comparative newcomer like myself. To make matters worse, I insisted on taking the platoon on a regular series of route marches, carrying our mortars and bombs on our backs, forty pounds in addition to our regular equipment. This was tough going, and produced a lot of bellyaching.

There were minor incidents all the time: the sergeants were certain that I couldn't force my ideas on them, they knew that they were indispensable, and they were constantly probing and testing, trying to find out how far they could go with me.

One day, while I stood awkwardly in front of the formed-up platoon the seven sergeants strolled onto parade two minutes late. They were headed by Guiton, clearly trying to remind me who was the boss. I accepted the challenge. It was only a few weeks before D-day, and I knew that I was taking the risk of losing the seven best sergeants in the Canadian Army; but I couldn't take the even greater risk of going into action with two masters at the helm. I put them all on charge.

Anxiously, I awaited the outcome of my gamble. To my relief, Colonel Jock Spragge, the battalion commander, backed me up; to my even greater relief, Brigadier Blackader, the brigade commander, decided to let them off with a reprimand. I had passed an important hurdle: my authority in the platoon was never challenged again. From that time on, the sergeants, like the rest of the platoon, gave me their most loyal support, and we worked together as a team, in true harmony and mutual respect. It wasn't long before their friendship and loyalty to me were put to a most convincing test.

It happened only a few days later, when my sergeants got together with their colleagues of the anti-tank platoon, and decided to have a party. They invited me and the anti-tank platoon commander, Don Hogarth, a very good friend of mine. Don, then a lieutenant like me, was a tough, hulking man, very handsome even though he had recently been badly scarred in a jeep accident. He was going to be scarred a little worse before the night was out.

The party began with great gusto, and we were all soon in very high spirits. Things were going extremely well when, without any apparent warning, Roly Guiton and Don Hogarth started squaring off for a fight. It was a very dicey situation, because if they had begun, all the other sergeants would have joined in — and I wouldn't have kept my hands in my pockets, either. And since we were in a pub in the middle of Aldershot, with MPs all around, a drunken brawl would have resulted in court-martials for the whole lot of us. Who knows where that would have ended?

I tried to restore the peace, stepping in between Don and Roly and trying to pacify them, but I had no success. The situation was desperate, and it called for desperate remedies, so I turned to Don and accused him of having insulted one of my sergeants — and invited him outside to settle things with me. My calculation was that while a fight between an NCO and an officer was an extremely serious matter, it wouldn't be quite so bad if those involved were two officers of the same rank.

We stepped out into the blackout. The fourteen sergeants of the two platoons formed a protective screen around us to ward off the police. It was a most effective defence: they must have been about the toughest group of men on earth. Safe from any unwelcome intervention, Don and I stood toe to toe and slugged it out. We were both pickled to the gills.

The blows flew back and forth, neither of us pulling his punches. Don's were landing painfully enough, and I don't think he could have been enjoying mine either. He was really swinging wildly, although he slowed down a bit after hitting the wall of the pub several times. Occasionally, he would make a grab for me, and we'd tumble to the ground, still banging away at each other, and bellowing all kinds of bloodcurdling threats. I had done a lot of boxing and wrestling, and with my 240 pounds against his 200, I had a clear advantage over him.

This must have gone on for quite a long time, since we were both close to being indestructible. Finally, I remember my sergeants pulling me off him when I was banging his head on the pavement. My sergeants propped me up and led me back to my quarters, where they rolled me into bed to sleep it off. They must have remained on the watch, because, later that night, I was awakened by Don's bellowing as they stopped him from coming in at me with a club.

The next day, Don and I were the very best of friends.

In time the battalion went up to Inverary, in the Highlands of Scotland, to practise landing drills with the navy. We learned to co-ordinate landing craft, and we even practised firing our mortars from these unstable little vessels, acquiring a thorough knowledge of amphibious operations that was to earn the 3rd Canadian Infantry Division, to which the Queen's Own belonged, the nickname "Water Rats". On one occasion my men and I almost became dead water rats when in the heat of a fake assault I gave the order "Up!" (decreasing the range) when I meant to increase the range. By the time I realized my mistake— along with everyone else in the landing craft—the bombs were in the air, and we were sailing ahead in underneath them. It was an impressive display of discipline for troops who had never been under fire. Everyone merely glared at me, until the bombs dropped harmlessly into the water just ahead of us.

That wasn't the only unusual thing we did with our mortars. I took a deep interest in these weapons, which struck me as potentially very useful, although they had two major problems. It took a comparatively long time to get a mortar battery ready for firing, and when it began to shoot, aiming and range-finding techniques were rudimentary. I looked for ways to correct these shortcomings.

Setting up the battery involved some time-consuming preliminaries, which were considered essential for effective aiming techniques. The commander had to establish a base-plate position for the mortars and find a suitable spot for an OP (observation post). He then had to pinpoint an auxiliary aiming post—a kind of agreed reference point, for directing the battery's fire. All these positions were determined by reconnaissance on foot, which took a long time.

I decided to shorten this whole process, by cutting out the footwork and using a map to fix the various positions. A careful look at my large-scale map was an effective way of finding the most suitable point for each of them, and it speeded things up considerably. Using these methods, I'd have my mortars ready for firing within ten minutes, when the time laid down in the instruction manual was one hour!

I took the use of maps one step further, to improve aiming techniques. Hitherto, mortars were ranged in, which is a polite euphemism for lobbing a shell in the general direction of the target and watching where it comes down: if it falls to the left, you tilt the mortar to the right, and if it falls short, you lower the barrel a bit. Experienced crews could do this quite quickly and effectively, but the method was defective; its main drawback was that it gave the enemy ample notice that the mortars were zeroing in on him, leaving him time to take cover or shift his positions. I took my problem to Ellie Dalton, the commander of support company, who had once commanded the mortar platoon. At my request, he arranged for me to acquire the necessary training with artillery. I carefully learned the artillerymen's techniques of mathematical sighting with the aid of map coordinates. Again using artillery techniques, I would radio or phone corrections from the OP, using map references to adjust the aim.

The whole concept was very simple, needing nothing more than a good knowledge of how to use maps. I sold the idea to our infantry officers, who learned how to direct our mortar fire at the objectives of their choice; all they had to do was give us the necessary map references, and we would zero in with our bombs, straight on target, with a minimum of ranging shots, hitting the enemy without giving him the slightest warning of what was in store for him. Sometimes, we would get a map reference and have ten or twenty rounds in the air before the Germans knew they were under fire. As each bomb had a swath of a hundred yards, the effect was deadly. We were soon to put these techniques to good use.

CHAPTER NINE

Marking Time in England

I spent over a year in England, prior to the invasion of Europe. Like every other Canadian, there were moments when I was sick and tired of training and retraining, and of running all over England in the rain. But in the course of that time, I saw our battalion—like the rest of the Canadian and other Allied units— reaching an ever higher pitch of training and proficiency, and acquiring a growing belief in its ability to smash the German Army when the moment came. We were ready, poised for the decisive lunge across the Channel and into Europe.

But men are not steel springs: they cannot maintain that kind of tension for long periods of time without some release. The prolonged period of training, the endless waiting, the awareness that the invasion was drawing near — together with the uncertainty about its precise date and what it held in store for each of us — all these combined to keep us under high pressure; and, as is only natural, we looked around for ways of letting off steam.

Whenever there was a chance, we would go off for a little relaxation. In the evenings, we visited the pubs in the little English towns and villages where we were stationed. We usually found ourselves very hospitably received, since the English civilian population generally liked the Canadians, and there was always convivial company for a quiet drink and a chat. But that wasn't exactly the kind of relaxation we young men were seeking, and we'd seize any opportunity to head for one of the larger towns. I took advantage of any free evening to hop on a motor-bike and ride thirty or forty miles through the blackout to Brighton, or some other town where there was lots of amuse-ment to be had, as well as unlimited quantities of very fine Irish whisky.

The ride *into* town wasn't too bad; the bike's headlights were painted over in conformance with blackout regulations, but I was a good rider; I had spent a week training as a dispatch rider, careening at full throttle across the bumpy gorse and heather, and anyone who survives that must have a pretty good idea of motorbike riding. On the way back from Brighton, however, after I had stoked up on sizable quantities of liquor, it was an entirely different story. On one occasion, I gave a lift back to camp to Rifleman Simpson, a batman of B Company who served in our mess. It was an eventful ride; I was far from sober, and, riding through the pitch dark, we took some spills, although no damage was done. Simpson was thrilled by the experience, and later entertained the officers' mess with a full account of our adventures on the road.

This was rather unfortunate, for his story was heard with keen interest by no other than my company commander, Ellie Dalton, who then turned to me and notified me in very clear terms that I was to stay off the motorbike—"Grounded until further notice!" was the way he put it. I suspect that the ban stemmed less from a tender concern for my welfare than from Ellie's fear that my joyriding might leave him without an experienced mortar of-ficer.

Ellie and his brother, Charley, were both company comman-ders in the battalion. In addition to being fine soldiers (inevita-bly, they were referred to as "the Dalton Gang", after the famous outlaws), they were also excellent company. They were born raconteurs; each of them was ready to tell a string of stories at the drop of a hat. In fact, they claimed that a Dalton's story-telling abilities were tested at birth; if it failed the test, it was strangled.

Good company was also provided by the other high-spirited young officers: Dave Owen, Dave Mills, Hank Elliot, Ken Mac-Leod, and many others. Most of us had come through officers' school together, or shared postings at various times, and we enjoyed going out together for some fun. For many of these wonderful young men, that fun might prove to be their last fling on this earth. We were all aware of that likelihood, which added a special urgency to our searches for pleasure. Our senior officers understood our feelings, and displayed much patience with our merry-making. But all the same, they were concerned about us getting ourselves into serious trouble, and thus becoming un-available when the battalion went into action. I remember one occasion when our battalion commander, Jock Spragge, drove down to Brighton to pick up Ken MacLeod and me before we got ourselves into a jam.

In our turn, we junior officers did the same with our own men — partly because we wanted to save them from trouble and suffering, and partly because we wanted to ensure a full com-plement of trained soldiers in the platoons we commanded. A certain London pub, the "Lord High", was, unofficially, "off limits" to officers. This had nothing to do with army regulations; the men regarded this as their own, and they didn't want any officer butting in. If one dared to show his face there, as likely as not he'd get it punched. But I didn't let this deter me, and I'd often go there in search of some man from my platoon who was missing and in danger of getting himself into trouble.

If I couldn't find the missing man in the pubs, I made my way to the Bow Street police station, where he might be lodged after being found "drunk and disorderly", or engaged in some wild brawl. I always felt a slight thrill when I walked into that famous police station, which features prominently in so many familiar detective stories. My pleasure was not shared by the English policemen, who treated me with a singular lack of courtesy when I came looking for my men. I can't blame them: by this time, they must have been pretty tired of the Canadians and their shenanigans.

Ordinary English civilians, on the other hand, were usually friendly and hospitable, displaying a great measure of patience with our horseplay. Not that we did them any harm. Any violence we got up to was usually kept among ourselves; unlike other Allied soldiers, Canadians rarely got into fights with English civilians. But a group of our soldiers out on a spree would sometimes wreak considerable havoc—which the British took in surprisingly good part. In return, we would try to repay them for their kindness. I remember the Christmas of 1943, when we put on a show for the children of Bournemouth. My non-Christian origins didn't excuse me from active participation: in fact, I was honoured with the role of Santa Claus. I dressed up very elaborately, with white whiskers and all; uttering deep "Ho-ho-ho, Ha-ha-ha" sounds, I felt that I was putting on a most convincing performance. Suddenly, without warning, a little boy in the front row let out a piercing shout, clearly audible throughout the hall: "'E ain't San'a Claus! Look't 'is boots—'e's a Can-ide-yun!" We must assume that his knowledge of Canadian boots was gained innocently, although some of my colleagues' accounts of their conquests among the fair sex in England causes me to wonder.

Needless to say, we took some interest in the English girls. In an attempt to minimize unfortunate liaisons with English ladies of easy virtue (or husbands overseas), some women's welfare organizations made well-meaning attempts to organize "blind dates" for us. The young ladies who turned up were pleasant enough, in their own way, and did their best to entertain us. But they were not exactly what we'd been praying for....

On my last leave before D-day, I woke up to find myself in an unfamiliar room with a girl I couldn't remember. I was a little dazed, hung-over, and somewhat suspicious: at that time, field security was being tightened up to preserve the secrecy of the invasion plans. Under the influence of the spy scare, I became afraid that she'd been taking advantage of my befuddled state to extract information from me, and behaved rather coldly towards her, although she was very beautiful, and very affectionate. All the same, she insisted on coming down to the station with me, to see me off. It was a touching gesture on her part. Likely as not, she guessed that this was my last leave before going into combat, and she sensed correctly how much it meant to me to have someone send me on my way.

In those last few days before D-day, the Allied Supreme Commander, General Dwight Eisenhower, honoured us with a visit. After we had spent hours preparing and waiting for him, he finally arrived; his inspection of the battalion was brief and ended with a short speech. At that time, Eisenhower was touring the units scheduled to take part in the invasion; I don't remember the precise wording, but the gist of it was as follows:

"I envy you men: you're more or less at the bottom of the ladder. You're young, and have your whole career as soldiers ahead of you. You're going out on an exciting adventure — and there's no limit on how far you can go. There will be unlimited opportunity for advancement. As for me — I've gone as far as I can — I'm supreme commander, and you can't get any higher than that." Or words to that effect.

Within a few weeks, many of his young listeners were dead or maimed for life; General Dwight Eisenhower went on to become President of the United States of America.

Stirring speeches were all very well, but an even more important part of our training for D-day consisted of getting used to the LCT (landing craft tank) which was to carry our mortar unit across the Channel. It took some getting used to, since it was perhaps the most uncomfortable vessel invented since the dug-out canoe. To be fair, our comfort was the last thing the designer had in mind; the LCT was a flat-bottomed barge designed to take three tanks in the centre of the deck, flanked on all sides by carriers — with not an inch to spare. We had to crowd into the carriers and make ourselves as comfortable as possible.

We spent many days in training on board our hated LCT and we were always about as comfortable as dice in a cup. Every little wave tossed the flat-bottomed boat around like a cork, and we, in turn, were tossed around, becoming a mass of bruises as we were smashed against the armour-plated sides of our carrier. Naturally, we were completely exposed to the elements, and for days on end we subsisted miserably on cold rations.

Our personal equipment did include some tiny portable stoves, operating on "canned heat". But, surrounded by gasoline and ammunition, we couldn't light them on the LCT. Nevertheless, some of the men, ever resourceful, did find a use for the "canned heat".

There was always a lot of seasickness on board the LCT, and even my long years of small-boat sailing didn't stop me from feeling queasy at times. But one day, on the exercise immediately preceding the actual invasion, I noted that there seemed to be an unusually large number of men with their heads over the side. I had no idea of the reason, until, after holding the legs of one of my sergeants as he was emptying his guts into the sea, I demanded to know what the hell was going on. He admitted that in addition to the usual cold meat stew (always bad for the stomach) and the cork-like bobbing of the boat (always even worse for the stomach), his insides were rebelling against a high-octane pick-me-up made of alcohol squeezed from the "canned heat" and "purified" by filtering through a sock! The fact that men were prepared to go to such suicidal lengths to relieve their misery is some indication of the sorry state we were in after days on that bucking bull-pen. In the end, we reached a stage of numbness where we could barely think of what awaited us on the other side

1. The Dunkelman family poses beneath mother's watchful eye; the dashing young B.D. stands directly in front of her.

2. The library at "Kibbutz Dunkelman" with the billiard room beyond it.

3. Young Ben Dunkelman, in his Upper Canada College blazer, armed to deal with quarrelsome playmates.

4. Four years later, young B.D. in his Tel Asher uniform, armed to deal with Arab intruders.

5. B.D. ploughing at Tel Asher, with Mediterranee, the race horse.

6. Grafting orange trees.

7. Tending young Toronto blossoms.

8. The *Dinny* speeds across Georgian Bay, with B.D. at the helm.

9. Father, Ronny, Zelda, and B.D. strolling on the boardwalk at Atlantic City in 1936.

10. 1942 Training Camp in Cornwall, Ontario. Lieutenant Dunkelman, proud of his prizewinning platoon, beams from his position to the right of Lieutenant-Colonel Rudy Larose.

11. "One-pip wonder" Second Lieutenant Dunkelman of the Queen's Own Rifles of Canada.

of the Channel—perhaps, for once, the army knew what it was doing.

At the same time, all of us, officers and men, shared a great sense of anticipation. We knew that we would have the privilege of taking part in a unique historic event. Despite all the discomfort, I wouldn't have traded my place on the LCT for anything in the world. We waited excitedly for the day when we would get the long-awaited order.

CHAPTER TEN

D-Day and Beyond

Then, one day, the order came. I was dizzy and sick with tension when I found my hands closing over a big roll of maps, which, unlike their predecessors, were overprinted with real names. This was it—we were on our way. As I unrolled the maps, I was horrified to feel them ripping from the bottom. This was no great mishap, but in my distracted state of mind, it magnified itself into a major tragedy.

Throughout the crossing, the Channel was tossing wildly. As our LCT splashed its way across, pitching and rolling worse than ever before, the thought uppermost in my mind was the fear that this stormy weather would cause the invasion to be postponed. I knew that any postponement would be a long one, for weather and tide conditions were rarely suitable. But, before long, I was too numbed and brutalized by the prolonged ordeal of the crossing to consider—or fear—what we were about to face on the beaches.

If anything could make us forget our discomfort, it was the awesome sight which met our eyes all around. In every direction, as far as the horizon, the sea was alive with vessels of every conceivable type and size, from mighty warships and aircraft carriers down to tiny infantry landing craft. The sky above us was black with skeins of aircraft droning their way towards France. All the while, we knew, a stupendous hail of shells and bombs was pouring down on German positions in the landing areas. All of us desperately hoped that no enemy troops would survive the battering and be fit to oppose our landing.

The thick concrete fortifications of the coastal defences spoiled our hopes. As A and B Companies hit the beaches, they ran into heavy enfilade fire. They didn't pause: clambering over the sea wall, they swept across the open sand and stormed the German positions, silencing the deadly 88s and machine guns which were raking the beach. This first engagement was fierce and costly. Both company commanders were wounded (Ellie Dalton commanded A Company, and B was under his brother Charley), and B Company lost almost half its men in that initial dash over the sand. The only officer left in B Company was Lieutenant Hank Elliot. He now took over command, while a corporal headed the remnants of A Company. Together, the two companies silenced the remaining strongpoints on the coast, and then pushed on inland.

When the second wave of the battalion went ashore, we were in the first LCT to hit the beach. It was H + 45 (45 minutes after the first assault wave had landed) and we were bringing in the first infantry-support weapons and vehicles. Our vessels carried three Sherman tanks from the Fort Garry Horse, and twelve carriers from our battalion (two from B Company headquarters, five from the light-machine-gun platoon, and five from my mortar platoon). My carrier was the first one off from the mortar platoon following the tanks and carriers of B Company and it had to make a sharp turn to avoid an obstacle at the water's edge. The driver of the second mortar vehicle was a little slower; he ran his carrier into the obstacle and it overturned in the water. This could have been serious, but fortunately its occupants escaped unhurt, and we were able to salvage the equipment. Aside from that, we got ashore without mishap.

Apart from an occasional sniper's bullet, we did not encounter enemy fire on the beach: A and B Companies had done a good job. We were ready to move forward, but we now ran into a serious snag: the plan called for the engineers to blow an opening in the sea wall and clear other obstacles from the path of our vehicles. The rough seas, however, had prevented the engineers from landing their tanks; they hadn't pierced the sea wall, and we had no way of getting through with our vehicles. We were safe enough behind the wall, but we weren't making much of a contribution to the war effort. I went to find my company commander, Captain Tony Cottrell, who was the beach officer. He had been wounded by a mortar shell which had landed so close that it blew the pack off his back. Now, all bandaged and strapped up, he managed to carry on with his task. There was little he could do to help me at that moment: he had no solution for the sea wall, and he didn't know where to locate the headquarters of C Company.

Finding a narrow gap in the sea wall, I crawled through and set off to locate the commander of C Company, to find out how we could help him in his advance. There were route markers along a ditch on the landward side of the wall. I crawled along the ditch, nervously aware that I was now exposed to snipers, and there could be mines about. Creeping along, I didn't see any of our men until I encountered one of the battalion's sergeants — Jamieson — sprawled on the ground. He had been shot through the neck by a sniper. It was a terrible wound; I was sure (wrongly, as it fortunately turned out) that it was fatal. I did what I could for him and crawled on. It was a welcome, of sorts, to the war.

Within ten yards I received another welcome when I felt what seemed like a mighty kick in the leg. The sniper who got Jamieson must have spotted me: his bullet had whizzed past my head and grazed the heel of my boot, leaving a bright scar down the black leather. A narrow escape — the first of many — and I got out of there fast.

Still I saw no one, and with a growing sense of desperation I crawled another hundred yards or so, till I came to a path inland. I followed it a considerable distance, but without finding our troops, who seemed to have disappeared into thin air. Retracing my steps, I crawled back along the path (my heel reminding me that my old route had certain disadvantages) to another narrow gap in the sea wall. I was now back on the beach, but a considerable distance to the north of my platoon. I had been running and crawling over hundreds of yards of slithery sand, and only my rigorous training carried me through.

I staggered back to the platoon, having found no opening in the sea wall other than a gap wide enough for a man but too narrow for the vehicles. I began to consider leaving the carriers on the beach, and advancing with our mortars on our backs, as we were trained to do; it seemed the only way we could get up forward to support the assault companies. At this point, however, Tony Cottrell appeared again with the good news that the engineers were about to blow a path through the obstacles. With the Shermans leading the way, we now moved off the beach and raced ahead to join up with the assault companies.

The town of Bernières-sur-Mer was cleared in house-to-house fighting; with its occupation, A and B Companies had reached their objective. C and D Companies now leapfrogged beyond them, thrusting on inland. As we made our way along the sunken roads, flanked by ancient hedgerows, we found ourselves encountering next to no resistance.

By now, there was a mass of vehicles of every type on the sunken road, all concealed from the enemy on our flanks by high rows of hedges. I kept looking up nervously, expecting enemy aircraft at any moment. I just could not understand how our air force could provide such cover, which seemed too good to be true. I was puzzled, too, by the lack of any preplanned German defensive fire on this, the one road leading from the beach. The guns close by had been taken out by our own troops and I could only presume that the pre-assault naval bombardment and air force bombings had done a superlative job in knocking out the enemy artillery. Otherwise, of course, we would have been sitting ducks.

As we moved slowly along the road, we filed past a figure lying in the ditch alongside the road. He was one of our boys, lying on his stomach, as if in sleep, his fair head resting on the sleeve of one arm. His other arm stretched out before him, revealing his service stripes: three red and one silver. He had been training for four years and now, after a few hours of action, his job was finished. I could only stare and think of the futility of it all.

The Queen's Own Rifles had suffered the heaviest casualties of any unit in the Canadian Army that day—sixty-three killed or died of wounds, twenty others wounded or injured in battle. At 1730, D Company, under the command of Major Neil Gordon, took the battalion's final objective — the village of Anisy, seven miles inland.

With the occupation of Anisy, the Queen's Own had attained all its D-day objectives. To my knowledge, it was one of the few assault units of the invasion force to do so; at the same time, the Americans were still pinned down on their beachheads on our right flank, while the British achieved only limited success. In clearing the beaches, our battalion did an exceptionally thorough job, as Chester Wilmot testifies in *The Struggle for Europe*: "So fast did the Queen's Own move . . . when the Régiment de la Chaudière landed fifteen minutes later, the only fire on the beach was coming from snipers." The battalion had fulfilled all its tasks — but the price had been a heavy one.

My platoon was lucky that day, which was a happy omen for the future. The only injury was suffered by my batman, Francis, and ironically it was not caused by enemy action: he was hit in the kidneys by a clod of earth flung up when we used explosives to dig out mortar positions. I wanted to have him evacuated, but he refused to go. He was in great pain, however, and since I had inadvertently caused his injury with the explosives, I had to make amends: instead of Francis digging the slit-trench we shared, I had to do it myself.

Francis was a fine figure of a man. A full-blooded Huron Indian, the son of a chief, he was tall, with piercing black eyes, bronze skin, and big black moustache. His scalp was shaven, with only a narrow scalp-lock left in the centre. He was a primitive man, a grim, unsmiling warrior who volunteered for the Canadian Army after serving for many years with the United States Army, where he reportedly ran afoul of the law. Despite his injured kidneys, I almost had to use force to stop him from slipping out that night in search of German scalps.

Our exposed position that night was an unusual one for the mortar platoon. Normally the mortars would be sited in as safe a position as possible, preferably in a gully about five hundred yards behind the lines, with telephonic connections to the observation posts forward which controlled their fire. In the present exposed position, the mortars had to be well dug in and concealed. This required an enormous hole; hence the blasting which had produced Francis's injury. The rough craters formed by the blasting then had to be laboriously cleaned out with pick and shovel and the six mortar carriers concealed near by. Meanwhile, since we were with the foremost troops, expecting a counter-attack at any moment, an all-round defensive position had been planned and the men had to dig their own personal slit-trenches.

Only former soldiers know how much time foot soldiers on active service spend digging. Perhaps my other readers might care, as an experiment, to try digging a five-foot-deep hole in the garden with a friend, making it six feet long by two feet wide. To make the experiment more realistic, they should use a pick and shovel they have carried around all day and select hard, rocky ground. And, as you dig, bear in mind that this was normally a minor part of the day's work, something you did at the end of a hard day's fighting, which often included digging as many as ten or twelve shallower versions as you moved forward or changed positions.

That was the case with me on D-day, and I found the job exhausting. Then, still caked with dust, I took turns all night with Francis in peering out into the darkness for signs of the enemy.

That first night ashore was not altogether uneventful. Jock Spragge, our battalion commander, had turned in when he was wakened and anxiously informed that German paratroopers had landed near by. "If you can't handle them, let me know!" said he, and promptly went back to sleep. The paratroopers didn't come near us. As for me, Major Al Nickson, the commander of C Company, put my platoon on stand-to, and forgot to stand us down. When dawn came, I went over to his trench and found him fast asleep. I woke him up and pointed out his oversight, in somewhat aggrieved tones. He regarded it as a hell of a joke; I didn't think so at the time.

We were repaid next day for the discomforts of that sleepless night when a Frenchwoman—right up in the front line—defied our shouts to stay under cover, and ran to her home, whence she returned some time later to present us with a delicious dish of rabbit she'd just cooked up. This was typical of the welcome we got from the French civilians, who turned out everywhere to cheer us, even while battles were in progress and bullets and shells were whizzing all around. The Allied command had warned them to stay inside, as much to protect us from disguised Germans as to ensure their safety. When "cleaning out" a village, we had orders to shoot at anything that moved, and, of course, when enemy were known to be around we did just that. But we held our fire when entering the populated areas.

I have heard other disillusioned accounts of the ungrateful way in which the French treated their liberators. But my own experience was that they would go to great lengths to express their gratitude to us. Later, while we were under heavy bombardment outside Calais, one man, with a fine sense of occasion, sprinted through the bursting shells to bring us a cobweb-trailing bottle of the finest champagne I've ever tasted.

We remained in the front line for five days, and then, on the morning of June 11, were ordered to pull back to a rear rest area. This was welcome news: after the ordeal of the crossing, and five days in combat with little more than a few hours' sleep each night, we were exhausted. As we drove along, we were in good spirits, eagerly looking forward to our rest.

We should have known better — and in time, as our bad luck held, we became more sceptical about promised rests and leave. When we reached the rear area, and were about to dismount from the carriers, the order came through to turn around and head straight back to the front: there was a German counter-attack in the offing! It was a great disappointment to forfeit our long-awaited rest, but there was nothing else to do. We turned the carriers around, and back we went.

Our command was hurriedly preparing a combined armour-infantry assault to forestall the German counter-attack, and as soon as I arrived back at the front, I was ordered out into no-man's-land on reconnaissance. Together with the artillery's forward observation officers (foos), I was to set up a forward observation post and a fire plan to support the assault. By happy chance, I ran into an old friend, now serving as mortar officer in the Regina Rifles, who proposed that his mortar platoon combine forces with mine. We set up our op in a farmhouse, ahead of the Regina Rifles positions, where we were under enemy observation and sporadic sniping; one bullet went through the window at forehead height at the precise moment that I was bending down to consult my map, an event which interfered with my concentration.

After preparing the fire plan I ran back to meet our attacking forces at the start line to co-ordinate our fire with their assault. Our attack was to be a joint tanks and infantry affair, the infantry consisting of our D Company, under Neil Gordon, one of the best officers we ever had. As I stood waiting at the start line something occurred which made it clear that this assault was getting completely out of our control. The tanks—a squadron of 1st Hussars — came thundering up to the start line with infantrymen of D Company clinging on — and then, to my amazement, instead of halting to work out the final details and permit the infantry to dismount, they proceeded to charge through the start line, without even slowing down. At first I assumed that the tank commander had crossed the start line by mistake and would return to begin the attack properly, with the infantry on foot; but as the seconds ticked away and the column continued to advance over the hill it began to look as if he had never heard of the word "co-ordinate"! We were ready to lay down fire from our two mortar platoons, as well as from two regiments of artillery—and here he was, charging at the enemy unsupported. Effective supporting fire was out of the question now, because we didn't know the precise advance route, and were afraid of hitting our own men. They were on their own.

The assault force ran straight into a German Panzer division, "Tigers" equipped with 88 mm cannon, which completely outgunned our Shermans. In their contemptuous manner, the Germans used to refer to the Sherman as "the Ronson lighter"—as they said, one spark and it lights up. Certainly, within a few moments of that foolhardy charge across the start line, many of the tanks had been hit and were ablaze in the cornfields. I ran ahead to see if I could work out where our attack was going and met Neil Gordon returning, his face swathed in heavy bandages, after being shot through both cheeks. He was unable to speak, though it was unclear whether this was caused by his injury or his sorrow—most of D Company, a fine body of men, had been lost in the first few terrible moments of the attack.

Although our attack was a failure, we gave the enemy something to think about; indeed, I have never witnessed a battle of this intensity, before or since. Much of the damage was done by one of our lieutenants, George Bean, who despite being wounded twice in the initial assault gathered together Sergeant Scrutton and a little force with seven riflemen and two tanks. With them he succeeded in breaking right through the enemy lines, and entering the village of Le Mesnil-Patry, where for a time they wreaked havoc among the astonished enemy forces. When Bean was wounded again, Sergeant Scrutton gathered the little band of survivors together and they made good their withdrawal. George Bean was awarded the Military Cross and Sergeant Scrutton the Military Medal for their roles in this heroic action.

Although I hadn't been given the opportunity to co-ordinate a fire plan with the assault, I gave what covering fire I could with my mortars. Noticing some haystacks which I suspected of concealing Panzers, I set the hay ablaze with phosphorus bombs, and the eruptions from the haystacks as the tank crews desperately baled out showed that my hunch had been correct. Now, as I witnessed the sorry debacle of our retreat, I ordered the mortars to step up their fire, to cover the retreat and block any German attempts at pursuit.

An Indian scout of the Regina Rifles was with us in the OP, scanning the country ahead. Suddenly he stiffened and pointed out a German helmet in the cornfield. Although he'd spotted it with his own eyes, unaided, I had trouble finding it with my binoculars, since it was a full fifteen hundred yards away. Yes, there was indeed a German helmet visible there—perhaps there might be a few others around.

Calling up the mortars on the field telephone, I ordered a few rounds dropped there. The bombs landed, with startling results. Hundreds of German infantrymen rose to their feet and began running in all directions. That single helmet had given away a large concentration of enemy infantry, massing for the attack. This was my opportunity: I called in every available mortar, and within seconds there were hundreds of bombs in the air. It was a mixture of high explosive with phosphorus incendiary shells, and the effect must have been devastating. Within a few minutes, that unit no longer constituted a fighting force — it had been blown sky-high.

Our mortar fire had completely disorganized the German counter-attack, and the enemy had suffered enormous casualties in the course of the attack. In fact this sector gave us no further trouble, and on June 16–17 Le Mesnil-Patry was occupied without a shot being fired. The British found fourteen knocked-out German tanks and over two thousand German dead in the fields and ditches. But at the time we were unaware of the full extent of the damage we had inflicted, and I was concerned with getting the mortar crews to cease firing and prepare to withdraw. As my carrier drove through a narrow village street, we came under heavy fire; the Panzers were trying to inflict further casualties on our retreating tanks. Our Shermans floundered and churned, trying to get out of the line of fire, and we, too, did our best to get away. Suddenly, there was an explosion above my head as an 88 shell hit the side of a building close by. I found myself being blasted right out of the carrier, and when I hit the ground my uniform burst into flames. As it burned, I lay there helpless: I was paralysed from the waist downwards. I looked up, seeking help. To my amazement, my eyes encountered the fixed stares of my men, who sat there stunned by the blast, too dazed to come to my aid.

To make matters worse, my helmet had been lifted right off by the explosion, and then pulled back by the strap, giving me a stunning blow on the head. Incredible as it may sound, the thought that flashed through my mind at that moment was: "If I live through this, I'll never wear a helmet again!" (I haven't.) All this must have taken no longer than a split second. I pulled myself together and managed to get my arms working enough to beat out the flames before they did any serious damage. As I was doing so, I saw someone else near me, lying on the ground, ablaze. I was still paralysed and there was nothing I could do for him: I just watched, helpless and horrified, as he burned and burned.... Finally, my body began to function again, and I pulled myself to my feet. It was a terrible scene, with the badly mutilated bodies of the dead and wounded all around, and it took us a long time to sort things out.

When we had a chance to catch our breath, it became clear that we had halted a determined German thrust which committed some of their élite SS units to a desperate attempt to push us back onto the beaches. Our attack may have been costly to us (D Company lost over 100 of their 135-man complement) but, as General Guy Simonds later noted, the action "put a Panzer division on the skids". But I knew that we could have attained a far greater success if the supporting arms had been properly co-ordinated. It is my firm opinion that we would have done much better if the armour had been under the command of the infantry — instead of vice versa.

A few days later, I was sent out on patrol to try to find some of our men who had been missing since the battle of June 11. We had no idea what had happened to them, or why this patrol should be an unforgettable one. I soon found out. The Nazi heroes of the 12th Panzer Division (Hitler Jugend) had lined them up in a wheatfield and machine-gunned them in cold blood. They lay now where they had fallen, among the crushed and bloodied wheat stalks. My men and I had the dubious privilege of being the first Canadians in our division to discover just how the Germans planned to fight this war.

I know that some outrage has been caused among the Canadian public by the publication of books such as *Six War Years* in which Canadian soldiers state that, on occasion, they killed German prisoners. Some readers seem to have been unable to believe such a thing could possibly be done by "our boys". Perhaps I can make a useful contribution to the debate by noting that after that day in the wheatfield surprisingly few prisoners from the Hitler Youth or other SS divisions were taken.

But that was in the future. On the scene of the massacre there was nothing I could do but take off our men's dog tags—a task I shall never forget as long as I live, since every one of the murdered men was a personal friend, and their bodies had lain in the July sun for three days—and report to battalion headquarters. After I told my grim story to Colonel Spragge, he was called away, and he left me sitting in his dug-out. I was in pretty bad shape, after a week of constant action, with scarcely any time to rest. On top of that, I was still shocked and heart-sickened by the atrocity I had just discovered. The reeking dog tags of my murdered friends were in my pocket as a reminder—if I needed one.

While I was sitting there, dazed and exhausted, I was joined by the Colonel of the 1st Hussars, who with D Company had taken such a beating on June 11. He, too, was in a foul mood. As we sat there, commiserating with one another, we happened to notice my colonel's bottle of Scotch. Like everyone else, he had been allowed to bring in one solitary bottle on D-day, so it was a prized possession. Trying to overcome our depression, we began to take swigs of the Scotch. The liquor combined with my state of total exhaustion to put me right out, so that when Colonel Spragge got back, he found me under the table, dead to the world. He got Francis, my batman, to lug me to a safe trench, which happened to be inside a shed. When I woke up the next morning, I found myself in pitch darkness, without the faintest idea of where I was or how I'd got there. It was a frightening experience.

As for Jock Spragge, he bore me no grudge for my ruthless treatment of his Scotch. He was a great commanding officer, He looked after us well in England, and then, after D-day, he did his best to bring us through alive.

CHAPTER ELEVEN

Friendly Fire

When we were ordered to take over from the Regina Rifles in Brettville, I found it hard to believe that it was only June 17, since we seemed to have been fighting for months. The reason, I suppose, was that as mortar officer I was involved in every action and plan as well as all necessary reconnaissance. These extra-curricular duties kept our group busy at times when other members of the battalion had an opportunity to rest.

I have never seen anything like Brettville, before or since. The town had been totally deserted, quite suddenly, leaving us feeling as if we were walking through a ghost town, or a fairy tale. As we made our way down the main street, the doors of the shops were wide open and their windows and shelves looked just as they would on any busy shopping day — except that there were no people. Unfortunately, among the fully stocked shops with open doors were some that contained a tempting display of beverages. The open-door invitation was hard to resist, and when the officers' backs were turned a lot of the men just stepped in and made themselves at home.

The regimental history laconically states: "The next week was full of incident. It became apparent that large quantities of the local Calvados had been discovered. Calvados is a fiery brandy distilled from cider. Drastic measures were introduced to clean up these extra-curricular supplies."

One of my dispatch riders, a good young kid, got into the bottles, or vice versa, just as the owner of the store miraculously reappeared and caught him in the act. I do not know exactly what happened, but a hell of a brawl ensued; this speaks well for the sturdy merchant, because my dispatch rider was a very tall and powerful Indian lad, and not many people would have chosen to tangle with him. The next thing I knew, I had been ordered to put my dispatch rider under close arrest.

I had set up headquarters in a backroom of a house protected from the enemy side, and the prisoner was duly brought before me there, very drunk indeed. It was getting dark and I decided to keep him with us overnight. We all lay down on the floor to sleep, the prisoner between my driver and my signaller. Francis, my batman, lay beside me. It was pitch dark, so that you literally could not see your hand in front of your face.

Suddenly I heard a sharp click, and then the prisoner's voice boomed out: "I've got one round in the chamber, and you all know who it's for." I knew that he was holding one of our 303 Lee-Enfields and that it was now cocked and ready. I felt Francis's arm on my shoulder and we rolled together silently through the pitch blackness to the other end of the room.

Our prisoner had resented the fact that I had arrested him, and had been mumbling and threatening me since his arrest, but I had not thought it would go so far. Now here we were, in a stand off. I could have provoked a showdown by throwing something into the corner to induce him to shoot, giving away his position, so that I could shoot him. But that was the last thing (well, the second last) that I wanted to happen. He was a good lad when he was sober, and I didn't want him hurt if it could be avoided. There were the others to think of, too; I could not be sure where everyone was.

I decided to take a chance and give away my position. Pulling back the hammer of my pistol, I ordered him to throw down his rifle. I warned him that I would have to kill him if he opened fire, and ordered the others to back me up. "You won't stand a chance," I warned him; "on the first shot you'll go down full of lead."

The tense silence remained unbroken. Then there came a sob, and he started to mumble, "You're supposed to be my friends and now you're going to put me in jail."

"I will do everything in my power. Just trust me."

More silence. Then, "It's all right, sir" and the sound of the rifle being laid down on the floor. My driver scrambled for it and we all sighed with relief, noticing that the room now seemed to be unusually hot.

A field court-martial was ordered, which was held in a château not far from the forward positions. It was an unusually dramatic trial, because heavy shelling forced the court to adjourn to the basement three times. I was called upon to give character evidence for the accused, and at my request he was ordered to serve his sentence in my custody in the field. The mayor of Brettville and the complainant were satisfied. The mayor, indeed, kissed the prosecutor on both cheeks and produced a round of champagne.

This would have been a happy ending if the enemy had not taken a hand in the proceedings. They began to sweep our positions and the town from end to end with barrages of unbelievable intensity. During this period I was serving as duty officer at our headquarters in the château, which meant that during the heaviest barrages, when everyone else had retired to the cellar, I had to remain on the main floor. My job was to man the phone on the duty officer's desk, which was out in front beside the grand château windows, fully exposed to enemy fire. In the midst of one terrifyingly thorough barrage, when I had prudently retired a few steps to shelter behind the nearby stone staircase, the phone started to ring.

It was like an insane Charlie Chaplin comedy. The château was being hit repeatedly, yet the phone kept on ringing.

Whenever I would think about making a dart to answer the damned thing, another shell would fall. One shell actually came in through one of the windows, and the phone continued to ring. I prayed that a shell would sever the wire, but no such luck—it just kept on ringing. Finally, almost as unnerved by the ringing as by the continuing shelling, I made a wild dash for the telephone. I picked it up and gasped anti-climactically, "Duty officer." Obviously irritated by the long delay in getting an answer, there was a harsh response: "Who is speaking?" Now I was irritated, too. "Who the hell wants to know?" I snarled. "This is Brigadier Blackader. What's happening?" The barrage was again increasing in intensity, and must have spoken for itself, but I informed him, "We are being heavily shelled, sir. Nothing else." He asked me to keep him advised. Good communications play a vital role in modern warfare.

When the shelling died down, I asked for permission to rejoin my men, for I was deeply concerned about their safety, although I knew that our slit-trenches were safe havens in almost any artillery barrage. It was eerie walking back through the town. Just a few days before, when we had first entered it, it had been nearly intact. Now it was almost unrecognizable, since so many sections had been reduced to heaps of rubble, including, regrettably, the grog shops.

As I turned into my platoon area, I was stopped by one of my biggest and toughest sergeants. Although he was smiling and trying to hide his feelings, he was shaking like a leaf in a storm. He assured me that everything was all right, but insisted on bringing me to his slit-trench to show me something. His greatcoat lay stretched out in the bottom of the trench, where he would normally have been. He bent down and held up his coat at arm's length for me to examine it; it was riddled with shrapnel. Nearly every other trench had been hit; I have never before or since seen narrow slit-trenches penetrated to such an extent. Miraculously, we suffered no casualties. By happy chance, when there was a long lull in the shelling, the men had moved to their old familiar rooms in the house adjacent to our positions to relax and get some food. That fortuitous shift of position was the only thing that saved us. The sergeant with the riddled coat never did get over his experience, and I had to send him out for a rest.

Shortly after my return, I was recalled to battalion headquarters. The colonel pointed out a wood about fifteen hundred yards in front of us, informing me that he believed that large concentrations of the enemy were forming up there. "Can you reach that target? The artillery doesn't seem to be able to get on it and we want it neutralized in a hurry."

A three-inch-mortar bomb weighs ten pounds, and it breaks up into tiny fragments that can spread a swath of destruction a hundred yards in all directions. Within five minutes from the time we received the order, we had eighty bombs in the air on the way to the target. They appeared to solve the colonel's problem. But although we were not bothered by many further attempts to assault us on the ground, we were constantly harassed by mortar and shell fire. It was astonishing that we only suffered seventeen wounded and one killed from the shelling.

Eleven days after our arrival on the twenty-seventh of June, one day after my thirty-first birthday, we were not sorry to leave Brettville.

By now it was obvious that the Allied foothold in France had to be enlarged. The first step was to capture Caen. So at the beginning of July I was sent ahead to help prepare the fire plan for our attack on the administration buildings at Carpiquet airport, just outside Caen. When I set up the OP — an exposed position, well ahead of our lines and overlooking the airfield — I discovered that its administration buildings were surrounded by huge German Tiger tanks like those whose 88s had wrought such havoc on our Shermans on June 11. They were hull down and had a perfect field of fire over the ground that had to be crossed.

I hurriedly notified battalion headquarters that the airfield was heavily defended by tanks, begging Colonel Spragge to call off the forthcoming assault. He demurred at altering an operation order which came from divisional headquarters, but I warned him that if our men attacked the administration building without heavy support, the Tigers would annihilate them. He consulted brigade and divisional headquarters, and the attack was postponed.

But although the attack had been postponed, I still found the tanks an enticing target. Unable to resist the temptation of trying to get a Tiger with mortar fire, I phoned back to the platoon, ordering them to drop a few HE and phosphorus bombs on the tanks. As the bombs started to fall around them, the tank commanders swiftly closed their turrets. Whatever else can be said about them, the Germans were proficient soldiers: they knew that such an accurate barrage must be directed from some OP, without which the mortars would fire blind. We could see them start to hunt for us. The building we occupied was perilously close to the enemy position and only a few hundred yards from the Tigers, but we were well out of sight. Nevertheless, one tank commander made an accurate guess at our position. We saw his turret swivel round until the barrel was pointing towards us. In the nick of time, we hurled ourselves out of the building; we just got clear as the shell struck it.

Going out to exposed observation positions like that was a dangerous undertaking—and not all the dangers came from the enemy, as I was to learn very soon, before we took the administration building at Carpiquet airport. Once again, I was in my forward observation post, with Sergeant Styles, when our preliminary artillery barrage opened up. The shelling was very intensive, being backed on this occasion by the navy with heavy sixteen-inch guns. Through some miscalculation, the start line for the shelling had been placed too far back, and the shells began to land *behind* our OP. I knew that the guns would gradually increase their range and the shells would soon be landing on top of us. As we stood desperately trying to work out what to do, the Germans opened up, and their shells also began to rain down. We were trapped! Styles decided to jump out of the back and make a run for it. As he hurled himself from the window, one of our shells got him.

I was alone now, and had to think fast if I was to have a chance of surviving the next few minutes. Our op was in what appeared to be an old barn. We had been using the loft, which was a flimsy slate-covered wood structure covering the massively built stone barn below. There were steps going down from the loft, but they seemed to be completely blocked by a mass of rubble and old wire. In desperation I jumped into the stairwell, struggling to push my way down, kicking madly with all the force I could muster. All of a sudden the rubble gave way and I started to slide through it and down the stairwell. But almost at once I halted with a jerk, hung up on the wire, which had wrapped itself all around my webbing and ammunition pouches. And the shells were getting closer with every passing moment.

By now, I was completely exhausted from the struggle and from the sheer terror of my predicament. Slowly regaining control of myself, I started to unwind the wire from around my pouches, and managed to untangle myself. I then worked my way down to the bottom.

The building was now under a full-scale barrage and the din was ear-splitting as the shells hit the building. The ground was shaking beneath my feet as I ran into a cattle stall in the back, which contained a heavily built dogcart. I turned it over and pulled it on top of me. But despite the dogcart and the heavy stone walls, my situation seemed hopeless; with that weight of high explosive raining down, something was bound to hit me — and there was nothing I could do.

I do not know how long I lay there, helpless and utterly terrified. But after what seemed like an eternity, the ground stopped shaking and the deafening inferno passed overhead and moved forward. Many minutes passed before I stopped quaking enough to make my way back to our lines. There I was greeted by Francis, my batman. He was very pleased to see me after my ordeal, although he pooh-poohed the danger of the situation, reassuring me: "Don't worry, sir. If you are killed, I will bring back your body."

At battalion headquarters, our adjutant, Bill Weir, was a little more sympathetic. He took one look at me and, without a word, handed me a bottle of Scotch.

CHAPTER TWELVE

The Killing Ground

The road from Caen to Falaise runs due south for twenty miles. Today you can drive along it in less than half an hour, admiring the woods and gentle ridges of the Normandy landscape. For a month in the summer of 1944 that twenty miles was the setting for one of the great battles of history, a foot-by-foot battle that blooded the Allied units involved — English, Poles, and Canadians — and crushed the flower of the German Army.

"Ten feet gained on the Caen sector," said Eisenhower, "was equivalent to a mile elsewhere." That was doubly true, first because the fighting against a desperate and entrenched enemy was hard, with every inch of ground bitterly contested. It was also true because, although the territorial gains were slight, the strategic gains were great. The British and Canadian offensives in the north were successful in confusing the Germans into concentrating their strength there, allowing the Americans, under Patton, to break out to the south.

It was a good strategy and it worked well. It could have worked even better if the inevitable nonsense of politics and national rivalry had not interfered, as we shall see. But perhaps my complaints about Patton's showboating cross-country jaunts when he should have been closing the trap on the Germans, bottling them up in the "killing ground" around Falaise, should be taken with a pinch of salt. For I, and the rest of the Canadian divisions in Northwest Europe, have bitter memories of always being landed with the tough, unglamorous, dirty jobs—like the Caen-Falaise road.

Significantly (in what was to become standard practice) the Germans paid our Canadian 3rd Infantry Division the compliment of concentrating large numbers of their élite troops — especially the 12th SS Division—opposite us, in a vain attempt to halt our advance. They launched costly and fruitless counter-attacks against all of the units in the 21st Army group, transferring troops from other sectors to do so — which was precisely what the Allied command hoped for.

When we attacked at seven in the morning on the eighteenth of July, our first objective was Colombelles, a strongly held industrial suburb on the east side of Caen. The industrial nature of the town may seem unimportant to the modern reader, but where there are factories, there are chimneys, and where there are chimneys, there are observation posts and snipers — as we learned to our cost. It was tough sledding, but we finally took the town.

At this point, field-grey uniforms started to pop out every-where, as great numbers of Germans surrendered. This was a welcome sign, but prisoners were so numerous that they were an embarrassment; our resources were strained to escort them back behind the lines and at the same time keep up the fighting in front. I can remember talking with Jimmy Auld, then a lieuten-ant, now a minister in the Ontario cabinet, as he led several hundred prisoners back with the help of only a few men. We were horrified to see one of the two escorts in the rear hand over his Bren gun to one of the Germans to carry. But a Bren gun, after all, is pretty heavy and I suppose it seemed a pity not to put the strength of the Master Race to use.

The file of prisoners had just shuffled by and Jimmy had said hasty farewells and run to rejoin the column when all hell broke loose, and prisoners started toppling over in the road. Amid the screams and curses, it took me some time to work out what was happening, and to realize that the fire was coming from the enemy side. It was the SS at work. They disapproved of Germans who were reluctant to fight to the death and allowed themselves to be captured; when this group of their former comrades came into their sights, they opened up, killing several and wounding many more.

Giberville was next on our shopping list. On our approach we found ourselves up against entrenched machine guns and mortars, and when we gained a foothold in the town, the house-clearing with grenade, rifle, and sub-machine gun was confusing and hair-raising, like a series of Wild West shoot-outs, as men kicked open doors and dashed into houses, guns at the ready. The fighting was so fierce that at one point the men of C Company ran out of ammunition and had to use freshly captured German Schmeisser pistols against their former owners. But we came out on top, and at the end of the day we had taken about six hundred prisoners, while two hundred enemy dead littered the area. We spent a wet, miserable night huddled in what shelter from the rain we could find.

Looking back, that was one of the most astonishing things about the war; we lived like animals. Often we were soaked through for days on end, constantly wet, cold, tired, and hungry. Frequently the only sustenance we had was the rum in our canteens, and the only sleep we got was snatched in moments crouched at the bottom of a narrow, puddled trench. It was just as well my mother—and every other mother I've ever known—had no idea of the conditions in which we were surviving; she would have marvelled that we didn't "catch our death of cold", and she would have been right to marvel. I can hardly understand it now. But I became so hardened and, yes, animal-like that eventually I came to dislike going inside a house.

At Giberville I had other things than the misery of the wet and cold to occupy my mind. In the fierce fighting we lost all three

platoon commanders of A Company, including my dear friend
Ken MacLeod. To prevent myself from dwelling on his loss, I
took temporary command of his platoon at the invitation of
Sergeant Taylor, Ken's sergeant. I had had several run-ins with
Sergeant Taylor in England and up until this time we had not
been too friendly, but with so many casualties among the officers
and NCOs he was glad to have me.

My first job as officer in command of the platoon was to
persuade the men to give up a fortune. We were advancing
along a road, under fire, when suddenly all of the men jumped
into the ditch on the left. They surfaced on the road whooping
with delight and clutching bundles of money in their hands; a
few even had satchels bulging with money, all of it evidently
thrown there by a German divisional paymaster making his
hasty withdrawal. The men seemed completely oblivious to the
danger around them and I had to order them to take cover and
throw the money away. For a few moments it was nip and tuck
whether they were going to obey my orders or not. Finally, with
deep regret, they dropped the satchels and piles of banknotes
back in the ditch, picked up their equipment, and set off down
the road towards the enemy. God knows how much money we
left behind that day.

As his commander, I found that my relationship with
Sergeant Taylor improved. A couple of days later, he invited me
to join him in a drink, which sounded like a good idea. He
brought out a bottle of Calvados and poured me a tumblerful,
the finest I've ever tasted, and I polished it off. I remember very
little of what happened after that, except that a "Desert Rats"
tank squadron passed by, without their officer. I seem to remember them inviting me to take over command, and I have
hazy recollections of clinging on to a tank, shouting battle-
cries. . . .

The next thing I remember is waking up on a stretcher, near a
crossroads. (The whole battalion had passed by in the meantime;

seeing me stretched out cold, surrounded by woeful-looking men, they circulated the rumour that Dunkelman had been killed, at last!) On top of a monumental headache, I had to contend with another form of discomfort: the men of my mortar platoon, resenting the way I had driven off with the tanks, "neglecting them", refused to speak to me. They were now holed up in a château, whose cellar seemed pretty secure, and when I joined them down there, hung-over but friendly, I found myself cold-shouldered. This angered me so much that I stalked off to find myself another billet. Climbing the château's wide staircase, I found a bedroom, complete with an enormous four-poster bed, with white linen sheets. After what we had been through, it seemed to be too good to be true, a mirage produced by the Calvados. But I reached out with a very grubby hand, touched and found that it was real, and irresistible. Oblivious to the large double window which offered little protection from stray bullets or shells, I stretched out on it.

I had a wonderful few hours' sleep in those luxurious surroundings, and when I awoke, I went downstairs. I was strolling about the grounds in front of the house when I noticed four planes approaching. At first I took them for Typhoons and paid little attention, but as they roared towards me, I realized that they were German Focke-Wulf dive-bombers. As I stood there, horror-struck and hopelessly caught out in the open, the planes let go with cannon and rocket. I flung myself down, flinching as the shells tore up the turf around me. Somehow I wasn't hit.

When I got back to the château I found that my men hadn't been so lucky. One of the rockets had scored a direct hit on the "safe" cellar, where, but for that trivial tiff with my men, I would still have been sleeping. Several of my men were killed.

A few days later Fate also stepped in to provide another narrow escape. We were driving along the road when the roar of planes made us look up. Six German planes were poised to swoop down on our column. We were quite exposed, on an open road; there was nothing to stop them making mincemeat out of us.

Just before they began their dive to attack, British Spitfires appeared out of nowhere to intercept them. All six German planes burst into flames simultaneously, an unforgettable sight. It was a pointed reminder of what it would be like to fight without good air cover.

On July 31, after fifty-seven days under incessant fire, we were sent back for our first real rest, at Fontaine Henry. We had a so-called "rest period" earlier at Gaimanche; but that was within shell-range of the front, and the place was a charnel house after the recent fighting, so that we spent most of our time in burial details. After that, action was almost a pleasant change.

But now we really are resting at Fontaine Henry, lush and green, where I can let my mind wander and soak up what is going on around me. I watch a herd of cows graze placidly in the pasture. Suddenly, one of them tumbles soundlessly into the tall grass. Soon the grass in the area moves again, and a short time later a self-appointed foraging party stealthily emerges, bearing the neatly quartered carcass past the "Shooting for Looting" sign, and sneaking it away under the very noses of the brigade's provost corps. Later, we hold an illicit barbecue — and are punished for our transgressions. The fresh meat gives us all upset stomachs.

It's wonderfully peaceful here. There are real showers, and it's a great luxury to feel clean, and to be able to go down to the nearby beach for a swim without fear of snipers. A few days ago, I got my hands on an open Volkswagen, left behind by the retreating Germans, and visited the D-day cemetery, where I found the grave of a Jewish friend, Sergeant Harris — with a cross over it!

The officers' mess: what a wonderful feeling to sit there, without the constant fear of an unexpected shell dropping out of nowhere. How peaceful ... and how terrible to sit there and notice how many familiar faces are absent. MacLeod is dead. So is McNeily. Ellie Dalton is still in hospital with his D-day injuries, along with his brother, Charley. Many others have gone, friends from officers' school or combat courses, men who spent months with me in the battalion. Their places have been taken by new and unfamiliar men — replacement officers, the first of a long procession. There'll be many I won't even get to know. So often, they are killed within days of arriving.

At this time, we also get rifle replacements. I'm asked to address them, to tell them about the battalion's history and prepare them for battle. I find them somewhat uncertain and apprehensive, which is not surprising. We've been suffering such terrible casualties that by August 16 our division will have suffered losses to seventy-six per cent of our total strength. Naturally, too, the new men wonder if they will do "all right" in action, or will panic and let their comrades down. One of them need not have worried: Rifleman Aubrey Cosens would do all right in action, when his time came.

The eight days at the rest camp came to an end and we headed back to the front. In the meantime, rumours had spread that I had developed a way of pinpointing enemy artillery and mortars, by using the inclination of the craters to work out the direction and distance of the shells. Making these calculations while the bombardment is in progress is nerve-wracking, but it pays off, since the guns can be silenced before they do much harm.

I was summoned to brigade command to explain the technique. The headquarters was housed in a large château, right in the front line, and under sporadic shell-fire. To my amazement, I saw sentries standing in the doorway, and cooks working in the open, totally exposed to shells. Finding the brigade major, I told him in no uncertain terms that these men were being placed in danger unnecessarily, and suggested he move them to the back of the château, where they'd have better protection.

I should have known better than to give advice to headquarters staff. A few moments later I met the brigade commander, who had obviously been alerted to my "presumption". Walking up to me, he looked down his nose and proclaimed, loudly and distinctly: "Dunkelman, we've done very well without you up until now!"

There was nothing much I could do — although I expressed my feelings by shunning the comparative safety of the château, spending as much time as possible with the men in front. Later, when shells landed outside the château killing the cooks and sentries, I got no satisfaction from being proved correct.

Meanwhile, the Americans had been mounting their attack to the south with such success that the Führer personally ordered a counter-attack to be launched against them, withdrawing two divisions opposing us for this purpose. This allowed us to speed up Operation Totalize, the plan to push on to Falaise and encircle the enemy. Bottled up in this way in a killing ground, the Germans would be at the mercy of our planes and artillery who could keep pouring in concentrated fire until the trapped Germans surrendered—or until there was nobody left to surrender.

The German Army now was fighting with its back to the wall, and fighting damned well, contesting every foot of ground. But our assault was going well, and our breakthrough on August 7 was held only by General Meyer's personal appearance to halt a retreat that was becoming a rout. Then disaster struck the second phase of the attack. I saw it happen.

A major daylight bombing assault by American Flying Fortresses — 492 bombers altogether — had been planned to assist the advance. As we moved up to the assembly area, all of our forces seemed to congregate at a crossroads, and a minor traffic jam naturally resulted. I rode to the crossroads on my motorbike and waited there for half an hour in the hope of receiving instructions. I saw the divisional headquarters set up near the corner, but although this was clearly the centre of command, the press of urgent business as thousands of men and vehicles of all sorts formed up around the crossroads made it clear to me that no instructions were going to be immediately forthcoming. I lost patience and rode back to my men, whom I had halted about a thousand yards away. I was in the act of getting off my bike when I looked up to see a wave of Flying Fortresses appear. The men had started to cheer them on when the cheers died in their throats—the bomb-bay doors were open and from them bombs were falling...falling on the crossroads I had just left.

"My God," I said to my men, "there goes the General!" Sure enough, among the many casualties was Major-General Keller, General Officer Commanding 3rd Canadian Division since D-day. It was a tragic error — at a stroke, much of our attack force was wiped out. If the Luftwaffe had been responsible for the raid they could rightly have counted it one of the most destructive raids of the war.

But in time we recovered and pressed on, encountering fierce German resistance as they were pushed back on Falaise, back into the killing ground. The plan seemed to be working perfectly. Then Allied co-operation broke down, and instead of closing the other half of Montgomery's pincer movement, Patton was allowed to hare off north towards the Seine, encountering very little resistance as he went. It looked terrific on a map and in the headlines—just as his pearl-handled revolvers looked good in photographs—but he was moving away from where the action really was, from where he was needed. If he had been kept in position and had swung around in the planned right hook to join our armies and to close the Falaise Gap, we might have ended the war there and then. As it was, on the twentieth of August, the remnants of the German armies were able to break out of the Falaise pocket in considerable numbers, to live to fight another day.

Nevertheless, in that pocket we crushed a whole damned army. Between the seventeenth and the twenty-third of August our air forces and artillery made a shambles of eight German divisions and mangled sixteen other enemy formations. In *Remember Me* Edward Meads has described the scene: "From dawn until nightfall the air forces bombed, machine-gunned and shot up enemy transport, tanks and guns. Roads were blocked with wrecked equipment. The dead lay everywhere, among burned tanks and in the tangled wreckage of guns, lorries and wagons, next to the grotesque swollen carcasses of horses.

"The Allied noose tightened. Trapped amid their own countless dead, driven to panic, Germans surrendered in thousands. But many fought on. With the fury of caged animals, clawing over masses of their own dead, they attacked the walls of the ring that pressed in on them."

From Eisenhower's report, the German losses by August 25 were 400,000 killed, wounded, or captured, of which 200,000 were prisoners of war. German records put their total casualties at that date at a higher figure, 460,000. The 12th SS, a unit of special interest to me, were 20,000 strong on June 7. They got out of the gap with 300 men.

It was clear that we had won a great victory. Now it was just a matter of time until the war was won. But for some it was already too late. On the sixteenth I had a narrow escape when a sniper in Damblainville shot at me from a great distance and the bullet hit the road in front of me and whined between my legs. I told the story to David Owen that evening. He was my best friend and we'd been together ever since Brockville, sharing every posting. He dropped over to visit me at my headquarters in a farmhouse after our meal. We laughed about my escape from an unfortunate wound and talked about what we were going to do after the war, and wondered if we'd ever get used to peacetime life again.

The next day David Owen was killed.

CHAPTER THIRTEEN

On to the Scheldt

Now the enemy were in full retreat and our orders were to overtake and destroy them. I took my turn as officer in command of the special assault group that forged ahead of the battalion. Our group had four machine-gun carriers, four mortar carriers, and two anti-tank guns, and a 50-calibre heavy machine gun was mounted in front of me in my carrier. We were very mobile and packed a considerable wallop, and racing ahead victoriously in open country with the wind in your face is a headily romantic feeling. But never knowing when you would run into a rearguard ambush or a minefield was a little nerve-wracking, and I was not sorry that the honour was shared on a rotated basis with the other officers of the support company.

We passed through a veritable graveyard of men, horses, and vehicles of all types. The devastation was stunning — tanks, supply trucks, troop carriers — even mobile field kitchens with the porridge still warm.

The horses were a surprise, and an unpleasant one. For whatever reason, the super-efficient mechanized German Army had obviously relied on horses as transport animals. Our planes and artillery had killed them in the hundreds and they lay there with their former masters in the August heat, bloating and stinking to high heaven. The stench of the bodies, human and equine, was unforgettable and unavoidable, and left some of us retching.

Even pilots flying over the line of retreat were assailed by the stench and commented on it.

Our forces had complete control of the air, which was just as well. The grim evidence around us reminded us of the importance of air power; jammed on the road, bumper to bumper, with both lanes heading in the same direction, we would have been like fish in a barrel for the Luftwaffe.

In these conditions I was horrified to find a first-aid jeep pull up alongside me with one of my men squirming in agony on the top stretcher. It was my dispatch rider, the lad who had given us some interesting moments in the dark when he was being held under arrest. The first-aid man reported that he had crashed at speed into the side of a tank, but that there was no way of telling how badly he was injured. He was obviously in great pain and needed a doctor as quickly as possible, but trapped in that great river of vehicles there was no way that we could turn against the flow and get him back to our field hospitals.

All the long hours of that day we treated him as best we could, on the move. All the while he writhed and moaned, shouting occasionally at the top of his voice. Everyone within earshot suffered with him, hour after hour. We did not feel like conquering liberators.

That incident had a happy ending when he pulled through and returned to us as good as new. And there were many other happy incidents, notably on the occasions when we were the first Allied troops to pass through a French village, where we would be given a tumultuous welcome, with kisses, flowers, and—even more important—cheeses and wines pressed upon us.

We became more used to this sort of attention when we were detached from the pursuit to head west to clear out the Channel ports. By now the Allied lines of communication, still based on the original D-day beachhead, were much too long. Foreseeing this, the Germans had left the Channel ports garrisoned, to prevent our using them, and (in time) to stage attacks from them on our extended lines of supply. This obviously posed a great danger to our army's very existence (the task of supplying it with food, ammunition, and other necessities was difficult enough, without Germans running around ambushing the wagon train), and we were given the task of clearing them out, starting with Boulogne.

It was obvious from the outset that a full-scale assault was going to be necessary, for Boulogne, ringed with massive concrete fortifications, was almost impregnable. The Germans had spent years perfecting the town's defences and had done a regrettably good job of it, basing their defences on the hills to the east of the city. The ground around each strongpoint was wired, mined, and booby-trapped, and deeply burrowed with a maze of concrete emplacements and interconnecting underground passages. It was a fine example of military engineering skill, and it was defended by ten thousand Germans armed to the teeth with the most sophisticated weapons of the day, lavishly supplied with ammunition, and under orders to fight "zum letzten Mann".

The job of taking this fortress had been given to two under-strength brigades of the Canadian 3rd Infantry Division. We deliberately took our time, planning a careful set-piece assault.

During the planning stages, our unit was stationed at La Capelle, a tiny hamlet five miles east of the city. Because I was in command of the unit that first entered the town, to the usual rousing welcome, I seemed to be adopted as their liberator, a minor deity. It was pleasant to be showered with gifts; every day I received fresh eggs (very welcome, indeed, after the months of rationed food in England) and the host of my billet was very free with his brandy, at a nominal price. Unfortunately, the local people's affection also showed up in their insistence that I act as the battalion interpreter and link with the Resistance. The only problem there was that I was a typical Torontonian; I had spent many years in school studying Canada's other official language, and yet the brand of French that I spoke was understandable only to other English-speakers. But on a tide of goodwill and brandy, we managed to overcome the language barrier and life in La Capelle was very pleasant.

This idyllic interlude came to an end abruptly when the German garrison of Boulogne started to shell us heavily. Orders came through to evacuate the civilian population (the Germans had already done this in Boulogne) and my host had to leave. In a gesture that must have broken his Norman heart, he gave me the key to his wine cellar and told me to help myself to whatever I wanted.

The Resistance remained to help us. The enemy shelling continued, taking its toll. My company commander, the popular Captain Jack Price, was killed, and my old D-day friend, Major Nickson, was wounded by the same shell. But gradually, with meticulous care, our assault plans were being completed, and the air and artillery barrage prepared.

Because of the tremendous weight of fire that the enemy could bring to bear and the dominant positions they controlled, it was essential that heavy supporting fire be poured in on them to force them to keep their heads down while our infantry got as close as possible to their lines. Up until this time, it had been our policy not to bring the attacking troops closer than six thousand yards to the bomb line of the heavy bombers. But now, because of the impregnability of the Germans' position, we were ordered to move to within four thousand yards of the heavy bombers' targets. As we had already been bombed in error on several occasions and had suffered very heavily, we had grave misgivings regarding the order to approach so close. This was, however, a direct order from Field Marshal Montgomery, whom we respected, and we realized that our chances of getting on to our objectives were zero without this heavy support, and that we had to be prepared to take the risk of the bombers screwing up again.

At 6.15 a.m. on September 17, the Queen's Own mounted their vehicles and moved to their assembly area, with the objective of capturing the northern half of the city. From 8.55 to 9.55 a.m. precisely, the heavy bombing attack went in, with hundreds of heavy and medium bombers participating. All the while, our own artillery blasted the enemy positions, which were soon covered with a pall of smoke. We saw the bombs landing on the objectives as we moved forward. As we got close to the four-thousand-yard line, we looked up and saw a squadron of bombers approaching us, with their bomb-bay doors open. There was no place to take cover, and we all felt that this was the end. At the last moment, two great Pathfinder Lancasters swooped in under the very noses of the bombers and guided them away from us towards more appropriate targets.

The artillery bombardment now took over to allow us to move in even closer on the enemy positions. No fewer than three regiments of heavy artillery, eight regiments of medium artillery, and two heavy anti-aircraft regiments took part, and the rocket-firing Typhoons were also used in close support. The rifle companies succeeded in getting into their initial objectives practically unscathed under this magnificent blanket of support.

The many strongpoints had to be overrun one by one. We inched our way forward from strongpoint to strongpoint, shrewdly bringing all the supporting arms to bear on each enemy position in succession. The enemy held on tenaciously, and only great courage kept our rifle companies moving forward into their defences. The battle lasted five full days, and all the while our mortars were pouring in concentrated fire wherever it was needed.

A wonderful demonstration of the superiority of the mortar and the virtuosity of its crews was provided by Sergeant Corrigan, who managed to drop a bomb down the ventilation shaft of the main German arsenal, which blew up with a very satisfying roar. Sergeant Corrigan, naturally enough, was called "One-Shot" thereafter. I can also remember seeing my old brawling partner, Don Hogarth, limping and half-crazed with rage, standing in the middle of the street in full view of the Germans, directing the fire of his anti-tank guns straight at their firing slits, and George Bean, wounded for the second time, painfully leading his men into the attack.

After the garrison had surrendered, a last hilarious touch was supplied by an NCO who brought out a group of prisoners in style. For reasons best known to himself, the corporal was wearing a silk hat and playing a violin he had "liberated". To the tune of "The Skater's Waltz", the prisoners solemnly jigged along behind him. Perhaps we were all temporarily crazy.

By the twenty-second of September, 185 officers and 8,500 enemy of other ranks had been taken prisoner by the two brigades, and Boulogne was completely in our hands after five days of continuous fighting. This was really an amazing feat of arms; I'm a prejudiced observer, of course, but I doubt that any other infantrymen in the world could have accomplished it.

The Queen's Own was not to be given any rest. By six o'clock in the evening on the twenty-second of September, A Company and the Pioneer Platoon had already been dispatched towards Calais.

On September 29 we moved in to the final attack on Calais. The morale of the German garrison had been destroyed by the fall of Boulogne as well as the surrender of Cape Gris Nez, and after the heavy bombers had softened up the enemy, our attack was met with white flags. The German commander formally surrendered on the thirtieth. Honour, apparently, had been satisfied. We took seven thousand prisoners at Calais, but more important than anything else, the Pas de Calais had been completely cleared, and all the V-1 bomb sites and cross-Channel heavy-gun positions had been captured. The English coast and London would no longer be subjected to the terror and destruction created by these buzz bombs.

Now, after clearing the Channel ports, we had another dirty job to do. We were moved into Belgium to clear the banks of the

Scheldt, opening up the great port of Antwerp. General Dempsey's British 2nd Army had captured the port intact early in September, but there were still fifty grim miles on both sides of the Scheldt River firmly in enemy hands. The Germans had always recognized the crucial necessity of holding the Scheldt and denying the use of the port to the Allies, causing their advance to peter out through a lack of supplies. They knew that Antwerp was useless to the Allies as long as they continued to control the sea approaches and the long winding estuary. Yet while all the Allies agreed on the importance of clearing the Scheldt, not a hell of a lot was done to give us the support needed to do the job. The Americans were busy invading the south of France and Dempsey's British Army was actually ordered *away* from Antwerp, to the northeast. Once again the Canadians had been stuck with a tough, dirty, dangerous campaign, a "Cinderella" campaign. Once again we had been left with badly extended forces, facing the tremendous task of clearing out an enemy who was firmly entrenched and well prepared in ground that was eminently suited for defence.

Nobody who was there will ever forget that countryside. Montgomery called the terrain "appalling". The Canadians who were living and fighting in it, often waist-deep in water, would have been less restrained. The ground had all been reclaimed from the sea and consisted of dead flat fields ("polders") crisscrossed with a maze of dikes. The dikes, with roads on top, provided the defenders with marvellous fifteen-foot defensive positions, while if we were ever unfortunate enough to find ourselves advancing along the top of one, we soon discovered that the Germans had previously ranged in their guns and mortars with great precision. So we would usually take the hard route, waist-deep through the flooded polders. We were under fire from the massive fortifications and gun positions on Walcheren Island to the north, until other formations captured it. By contrast we rarely were faced with fortifications of the

Boulogne type. Our task was to slog through the polders, dikes, and villages. Everywhere the enemy had prepared defensive tricks — felled trees, wire, minefields. Even the floating corpses of their comrades were booby-trapped. In the mud and the rain and the cold and the wet, we lived and fought in a bleak, featureless wilderness, an apparently endless expanse of grey hell.

Our 3rd Division had the task of clearing out the south bank of the river, the area that became known as the Breskens pocket, just north of the Belgian-Dutch border. Facing us were fourteen thousand men of the German 64th Infantry Division, tough veterans of the Russian front, well supplied and, above all, protected by the ubiquitous water that bogs down any attack.

The 7th Brigade soon gave them a shock, however, attacking across the Leopold Canal with a special force of flame-throwers. A few days later another of General Simond's inventions, a group of new amphibious vehicles called Buffaloes, allowed us to surprise the enemy by outflanking him in a waterborne assault. We pressed on slowly, constantly under fire. The historian of our 3rd Division neighbours, the North Shore Regiment, has accurately described the campaign as "a misery they had not known before. It was like Indian warfare, small sections taking desperate chances, probing, feeling, trying to outguess the enemy, and advancing day after day, night after night, with nothing but courage and the hope of luck." In conditions like these, the old 3rd Division nickname was revived. We were, indeed, "Water Rats".

Polder after polder. Strongpoint after strongpoint. Mud and more mud. A few incidents stand out in my memory. I vividly remember racing across the top of a dike on a motorcycle as an enemy tank on the next dike a thousand yards away fired everything it had at me. I went like hell as the shells and bullets whipped over me. And I can't forget the devastation inflicted on the enemy by our flame-throwers or by the rocket-firing Typhoons.

Finally, on November 7 the operations in this sector officially ended. We looked forward to some leave, perhaps even a return to England to rest and reorganize, since we had been in action at this point for four months with virtually no leave, and were all dazed with battle-weariness.

Of course, we knew why leaves were so scarce. Thanks to Prime Minister Mackenzie King's handling of the Conscription Issue at home, the Canadians in Europe were desperately short of reinforcements, with every unit far below strength and repeatedly requesting reserves who never came. The reserves were there, all right, thousands of them, all fit and well — and living in comfort in barracks in Canada. "Wily Willie" Mackenzie King, mindful of the unpopularity of conscription in Quebec (and even more mindful of the support that province regularly gave to his Liberal Party), had promised not to send men outside Canada against their will. I had disagreed with my French-Canadian colonel about this policy in Cornwall; now, seeing the condition of our fighting units in Europe, I was even more certain that King's political pussy-footing was wrong, and was causing Canadian deaths in the field. I was not alone in this opinion. Early in the war our soldiers on parade at Aldershot had booed King when he made an inspection, so it is hardly surprising that he never visited us in the field in Europe. If he had showed up in the Breskens pocket to visit us, an unfortunate and unaccountable accident might have befallen his plump person.

My own experiences with leaves were not encouraging. In the first one, after four months in action, I was given forty-eight hours. I hastily found a Belgian nurse I'd encountered when she came to complain that our artillery fire had caused unnecessary casualties among the civilian population (a complaint that was not initially well received) and we arranged a rendezvous in Antwerp. Aboard the leave bus, I found that it was heading for Brussels; so much for skilful logistical planning, and maintaining good local relations.

Worse was to come. In Brussels I settled in for a riotous

forty-eight hours so successfully that three V-2 rockets landed close by without my noticing. But after only a few delightfully alcoholic hours, I heard a voice in the hotel lobby bellowing: "Where's Ben Dunkelman?" Unsuspectingly, I weaved my way out and answered "Here!" It was Don Hogarth. "Ben, get the hell back to the battalion!" And then, without pausing to draw breath, he shouted across the crowded lobby, *"Where are the girls?"* Clearly, my leave had ended before it had properly begun. My fellow officers rolled me onto a truck and I was carted back to my watery home on the Scheldt, bitterly wondering why my old buddy Don was so damned quick in finding me.

Later on, I did get one real leave—a week in London, a leave to end all leaves. Before I set off, the battalion commanding officer asked me to visit our Colonel-in-Chief, Queen Mary, during my stay in London. I was the only senior combat officer in the regiment who had never met the Queen Mother, and with her keen interest in the Queen's Own, she always inquired after me. I looked forward to meeting her, but I didn't have the opportunity and I've always regretted it. I was in poor condition, physically and mentally — and morally, too — since I spent the week in a manner that rendered me quite unfit for a courtesy visit over a cup of tea.

During that week, tea was about the only beverage I didn't touch. I woke up on the Channel steamer which was taking me back to find a group of Canadian officers standing guard over me: every time I fell asleep, I'd find myself creeping through a steaming swamp, where giant alligators opened enormous jaws to swallow me. . . .

With that background, it's hardly surprising that after clearing the Scheldt, we took with a very large grain of salt the news that we were to proceed to Ghent for a week's rest. But it proved to be true, and to be one of the best weeks in our war. As a heart-warming start, when I formed my men up on the City Square we were mobbed by housewives and children, all demanding a Canadian soldier. After my men had been billeted, a shy elderly couple approached me and invited me to accept the hospitality of their home. It was much appreciated.

Less appreciated were the formal mess dinners (with the exception of a visit from Field Marshal Montgomery), since I had other ideas about how I should spend my time on my first real rest since D-day. But the mess dinners were a command performance and I would stagger in and try to pay our honoured guests the proper respect. I was often excused early after dinner by the commanding officer, as in those days my actions were a little unpredictable. After six months of action, the clean sheets and hot water in a comfortable, affectionate home were too much for me. Perhaps it was something I never expected to experience again; in those days you just kept going until you were killed or wounded, and I suppose I had come to terms with that. Now the sudden change of scene burst some private dam inside me. I visited every pub in town, and would wake up in strange houses wondering where I was, while search parties combed the town looking for me.

On the ninth of November we moved out of Ghent to a training area, then on the eleventh we started our long haul to Nijmegen. Like us, our vehicles were pretty tired by now and it was a tough job to keep them moving, as carriers started to throw tracks, and trucks gave up. We finally reached Berenn Dal, just south of Nijmegen where we relieved troops of the 82nd U.S. Airborne Division. We were now to play a new role; during the next three winter months we were to be in a static role of defence.

At this time I left the mortar platoon and was given D Company to command, with the rank of acting major. By now I was one of the very few combat officers who had been in action from the beginning of the campaign and were still in one piece.

It was a long, cold winter. We were responsible for nearly a mile of front in the hills and forests overlooking the polders that stretched forward to the Rhine. We saw our first jets here, as the Germans tried to strafe and bomb the Nijmegen Bridge crossing over to Arnhem on our left. The flak would go up like a screen, covering the sky with white puffs of smoke, while the jets screamed by so fast that you could hardly get a look at them; even their pilots seemed unused to them, since their bombs would drop miles from the bridge — sometimes close to us. We also watched with awe as zigzag chains of lightning took off from the other side of the Rhine and headed straight up into the air. It was only after the war that we learned that they were V-2 rockets heading for London.

Our position was a crucial one on our front, situated on a forward slope and in open ground, which meant that we were constantly under enemy fire. It was weird and eerie at night, when we could hear flapping sounds from high in a row of trees on our left; it came from the parachutes that had been left by the 82nd Paratroop Division in that fateful airborne assault on Nijmegen and Arnhem. We couldn't move out of our trenches during the day, but during the night we would wander about quite freely.

Everyone has heard stories of friendly incidents between the opposing armies in the trenches at Christmas during the First World War. I can add a postscript. On Christmas Eve, 1944, we could hear quite a commotion in the enemy lines. Girls were singing, their carols ringing out strangely in the bleak military atmosphere. As the evening progressed, the celebrations and singing intensified. My men started to join in the spirit of the thing, and I could see them relax, leaving their trenches and lounging about. The Germans then started to fire bursts of tracer up in the air, which was very pretty, as good as any display of fireworks. My men by now seemed utterly relaxed, imbued with the Christmas spirit of comradeship, and when I ordered them back in to the trenches, I think that only those in my immediate area obeyed me. At this point, without warning, the enemy let loose a tremendous barrage of fire at our positions.

CHAPTER FOURTEEN

The Rhineland

We had hoped that in January we would make our attack on the Rhineland into Germany itself. The successful German counter-attack on the Americans in the Ardennes caused that assault to be postponed; it seemed that our forces were going to continue to pay dearly for the lack of a united and co-ordinated command of the sort that Montgomery was still recommending repeatedly to Eisenhower.

We were now in another long period of waiting, and I was given a free hand to take the men on some training exercises. Out on patrol with Doug Hamilton we found a wonderful, isolated training area. Suddenly, bullets started to fly around us. Because this was meant to be a friendly training exercise, the only weapon we had with us was my tiny 9 mm Beretta short automatic. We jumped into a ditch, I emptied a few magazines rapidly in the direction of the enemy, and we beat a hasty retreat. I guess it must have been some small patrol who were running just as fast in the other direction, but it gave all of us a bad moment as we thought of being shot down, unarmed, on a training exercise after surviving so many real battles. It would have been doubly ironic, since our company hadn't lost a man in the three months of my command.

One day at headquarters, Steve Lett, our commanding officer, informed me, "You have just been nominated as Liberal candidate for the Spadina constituency in the forthcoming elections." This was a bolt from the blue, since I had never shown much interest in Liberal Party politics. He advised me to accept: if I were to stand for election I'd be unopposed.

There was a certain logic here that began to dawn on me: Spadina was a heavily Jewish constituency; the Liberals reckoned that a Jewish "war hero", campaigning in khaki, would be unbeatable. Prospects of a political career — a very tempting thought. Another tempting factor was that accepting would mean being withdrawn from the front line and getting sent back to Canada to conduct my election campaign. Out of this inferno, in one piece; it was another enticing thought.

A little consideration made it clear, however, that I could not, in good conscience, join the party headed by Mackenzie King, because of his stand on conscription. As I came to this decision, I got back to D Company. The news of my nomination had preceded me and I was met by a delegation of my men. One of them, a young lad, said tearfully: "Don't leave us, sir. If you go, we'll all be dead before long."

That sort of superstitious faith in an officer is totally illogical, of course; but when you have it, nothing is impossible and your men will follow you anywhere. I prayed that our luck would hold, and advised the colonel that I must decline the nomination.

Up to this time, my health had been good, but recently I had been suffering from intermittent attacks of high fever. I told the medical officer that I thought it was malaria, but he wouldn't give me quinine unless I went into hospital for tests, and I felt that my place was with my men as we prepared for the attack on the Rhineland. As part of the preparation, we had all been kitted up in white suits to camouflage us as we attacked through the snow. The white suits were to be useless to us: the Germans blew the dikes on the Rhine, and we had to attack through the flooded polders stretched out below us.

The attack was to be one of the crucial offensives of the war. Under General Crerar, the first Canadian to lead a full army in the field, we were to roll the Germans back across the Rhine. Our own division's role was to move from Nijmegen north to Millingen, then southeast through the heavily defended Reichwald and Hochwald to the Rhine, near Wesel.

In accordance with sound tradition, our attack on the morning of the ninth was preceded by hours of heavy air and artillery bombardment of the enemy positions. I don't know what effect they had on the enemy, but, by God, they frightened me. The noise of the guns around us was so infernal that it left us numbed and dazed with shock. Then the signal came and we started to advance across the rain-soaked and flooded Waal flats which we knew so well by sight. The North Shore Regiment preceded us on the left and the Régiment de la Chaudière on the right; meeting little opposition, the two battalions soon reached their objective and we passed on through them. We had little opposition as we moved forward on the roads that were only a few inches under water: if anything, the enemy had done more harm than good by blowing up the dikes, since his defensive positions were inundated, and we simply plastered any pieces of high ground in our path with heavy mortar fire, often setting buildings ablaze. We were able to move forward without any casualties, soon entering our objective, the town of Millingen.

As I cautiously entered Millingen with our advance troops I saw what appeared to be an enemy paratrooper advancing casually towards us down the centre of the road. In a flash we were all concealed behind a fence and every gun in the unit was trained on him. When he was about six feet away, I stood up with my Sten gun pointing at his stomach, and ordered him to halt. He turned surprised and hurt eyes on me and said, "Don't you know me, Ben?" I didn't recognize him at first, which insulted him greatly, since he was an old friend from Canada, Leo Heaps. His father was a Member of Parliament and Leo would occasionally spend part of his summer holidays in our home on Lake Simcoe. Leo had a very distinguished war and did some very mysterious things in odd places, but what he was doing strolling about beside the Rhine in a uniform deceptively like a German paratrooper's has continued to elude me.

Recovered from our surprise, we pushed on and took up positions on the reverse slope of the dike on the Rhine. As far as I know, we were the first Allied troops in the Second World War to take up and hold positions on the Rhine. The position was directly opposite the convergence of the Rhine with the Neder-Rhine and to our west it flowed into the Maas. It had all been incredibly easy so far. In fact, the enemy was less of a nuisance than the icy flood waters; at one spot in the advance where the road was low, I had to assist two of the shorter men over the deep spot, holding their collars so that their chins would be above water.

Our troops spread out along the side of the dike on the higher ground, each platoon using a farmhouse as its headquarters. The farm cellars were full of preserves, the barnyards with chicken and cattle; they would only have drowned, anyway, and our cooks, humanitarians to a man, were only too pleased to save them from a slow death. Although the capture of Millingen had been amazingly easy, three hundred enemy shells were dropped on the village and among those killed was a good friend, Captain George Bean, MC.

On the twentieth of February we were relieved by a detachment of the 43rd British Division, which had taken a terrible beating in the attacks in the Reichwald area. Their commanding officer warned me that if we were to be involved in the fighting in that area, if we wanted to survive we should get off the objectives immediately, as the enemy brought down massive artillery and mortar fire on all positions that were overrun. By now, the water had risen several feet, and we were evacuated from our positions by Buffaloes. As we disembarked from the vehicles and I formed my men up, it struck me that they really were a bunch of scarecrows. Our filthy uniforms could have been any colour, and so could our unshaven faces; the crowning bandit touch was that each man had two chickens hanging from his belt. As luck would have it, Brigadier Roberts and Colonel Lett were there to greet us, but were too polite—or too aware of the importance of a secure food supply on the battlefield — to pass any comment.

The second phase of the operation was called "Blockbuster", and its aim was to drive the enemy back from their Hochwald positions, known to them as the Schlieffen Line. Once again, our support was as impressive and deafening as that given to the first phase of the operation. On the twenty-sixth we were to go in at 0430 hours, the Régiment de la Chaudière on the right flank at 0845 hours, and the North Shore Regiment down the centre at 0830 hours.

We were roused at 0330 hours, a dreadful time to waken and realize that your chances of never wakening again are pretty high. As usual, we were all fed hot coffee, rum, and sandwiches, and the men's equipment and weapons were checked. The artillery reached a crescendo as we moved off towards the start line at 0400. Our first objective was a little village named Mooshof; previous attacks on Mooshof and Steeg and Wimmershof had been thrown back with very heavy losses by crack German paratroopers, who had succeeded in halting the whole Allied advance on this front. We knew we were in for a real scrap.

Every incident of the attack on Mooshof is clear in my mind. . . . As we advance we keep as close as possible to the creeping barrage. Shells explode as little as ten yards ahead. Although it is four o'clock on a February morning, it's bright as day because Monty, as usual, is supplying us with artificial moonlight, produced by searchlights playing on the clouds above.

I advance in the centre of the company: 16 Platoon to my left,

17 to my right, and 18, under John Hancock, following behind. We move as cautiously as we can, keeping close to the creeping barrage. Overcoming enemy resistance, we reach our objective — the farm buildings of Mooshof.

So far, so good. Not a single casualty! But I know what's coming, and I roar out instructions to the platoon commanders to spread out ahead, and get dug in well away from the captured German positions.

The enemy's defensive tactics are brilliantly conceived, and carried out with great tenacity by some of the best soldiers in Europe. No rigid defence: under attack, they hold on as long as possible in their excellently concealed slit-trenches, then withdraw to prepared positions a little farther back. Instantly, previously ranged mortar and artillery fire is poured on the positions they've just vacated — even if a few of their own men are still there. The shelling is co-ordinated with infantry assaults to retake the ground they've lost. Superb tactics.

That's precisely what they're doing now. No sooner have they pulled back from the farmhouses than they begin their counter-attack. They pour heavy and accurate fire on our men; a runner comes over to tell me that 16 Platoon, which hasn't moved off the objective, is caught in a fire-storm as the bombs rain down, and is taking a battering. I run over there to find that all hell has broken loose. Every minute, more men are hit. Men from 17 Platoon come over to help get the wounded out of there, and are caught in the same deadly fire. The whole area is turning into a shambles; the bodies of wounded, dead, and dying lie everywhere you look. It's a nightmare.

These are the men I've lived with for over three months. I've led them and trained them; I've looked after them and, like a good officer, I've tried to shield them from precisely this. They followed me into this assault with their usual complete faith, believing I'd get them through safely. And there's nothing I can do for them now but help carry their bodies to cover, while trying frantically to patch them up enough to save them from bleeding to death.

The onslaught continues, murderously effective. We try to hang on, but an enemy counter-attack secures the buildings once occupied by 16 Platoon. The fight sways back and forth, attack and counter-attack, with heavy losses on both sides. The struggle for Mooshof—and a lot more—hangs in the balance. But one of the few survivors of 16 Platoon is Sergeant Aubrey Cosens, and Sergeant Cosens does not give up easily. What follows is an official description:

"In Holland on the night of 25th–26th February, 1945, the 1st Battalion, the Queen's Own Rifles of Canada, launched an attack on the hamlet of Mooshof, to capture ground which was considered essential for the development of future operations.

"Sergeant Cosens' platoon, with two tanks in support, attacked enemy strong-points in three farm buildings, but were twice beaten back by fanatical enemy resistance and then fiercely counter-attacked, during which time the platoon suffered heavy casualties and the platoon commander was killed.

"Sergeant Cosens at once assumed command of the only other four survivors of his platoon, whom he placed in a position to give him covering fire, while he himself ran across open ground under heavy mortar and shell fire to the one remaining tank, where, regardless of danger, he took up an exposed place in front of the turret and directed his fire.

"After a further enemy counter-attack had been repulsed, Sergeant Cosens ordered the tank to attack the farm buildings, while the four survivors of his platoon followed in close support. After the tank had rammed the first building he entered it alone, killing several of the defenders and taking the rest prisoner.

"Single-handed he then entered the second and third buildings, and personally killed or captured all the occupants, although under intense machine-gun and small-arms fire.

"Just after the reduction of these important enemy strong-points, Sergeant Cosens was shot through the head by an enemy sniper and died almost instantly.

"The outstanding gallantry, initiative and determined leadership of this brave NCO, who himself killed at least twenty of the enemy and took an equal number of prisoners, resulted in the capture of a position which was vital to the success of the future operations of the Brigade."

The London Gazette, May 22, 1945.

Sergeant Aubrey Cosens was posthumously awarded the Victoria Cross.

There were now dozens of dead and wounded in 16 and 17 Platoons, which, to all intents and purposes, had ceased to exist as fighting formations. With enemy fire still raining down, there wasn't much we could do, except hang on, aided by John Hancock's 18 Platoon and a few supporting tanks, and hope that the enemy counter-attacks would stop.

That was exactly what happened. First the shelling stopped, and then a couple of my men brought in six prisoners. Our ordeal was over, and we were in control of the objective. After Cosens's heroism had broken the enemy counter-attacks, we had won the position by the simple expedient of just sweating it out.

But the price was dreadful. At the end of that gruesome day, there were only 36 fighting men left in my company, out of the 115 who had crossed the start line. I was the only officer to come through unwounded, along with only one NCO.

Now B Company arrived and moved up ahead of us, taking their objective, Wimmershof, without encountering opposition. We, too, now moved forward to Wimmershof, where, deadly tired, we took over a farmhouse, occupying the cellar. It's not difficult to fit an entire company into one cellar when the "company" consists of no more than thirty-six combat troops. My men dragged down a bed for me, and I collapsed on it. The others lay down on the floor all around.

I was exhausted: sick in body, and even sicker in spirit. Never in my life, either before or since, have I found a body of men who were closer or dearer to me than the young soldiers of D Company. They had put their trust in me, and I had always done my best to justify that trust. For all my exhaustion, I did not sleep well that night.

We were in a sorry state after Mooshof. I was the only officer and I had almost no NCOs. We'd taken terrible punishment, the men were in urgent need of rest, and the company urgently needed to be reinforced and reorganized. It seemed unthinkable that we'd be sent into action in our present state. But at orders the following day, the commanding officer announced that the battalion, including D Company, was to move forward to clear the Hochwald. I was astounded. I told him that I had thirty-six combat soldiers, with one NCO and no officers, and that the company was unfit for action. He nodded sympathetically, but there was no change in the orders; he told me to follow behind the other companies, and help in any way we could.

I can scarcely remember what happened during the next couple of days. I was scarcely lucid: my fever was raging, and I was exhausted, physically and mentally. But I can piece together the day's events to give a fairly accurate account. As the battalion moved off through the Balberger Wald and on into the Hochwald, my company was following B Company, which in turn was following some tanks. Suddenly, there were explosions ahead, followed by shouts and screams. One of the tanks had hit a Teller mine, which blew off a track, leaving it immobilized. At the same time, B Company's scouts entered the minefield. Several of them stepped on shoe-mines, which blew their feet off. One of the crew of the disabled tank jumped out, and he, too, trod on a mine. The wounded men were lying on the ground, rolling about in uncontrollable agony, biting at the dirt in an attempt to muffle their screams. But of course the screams welled up and rang out again and again as their buddies desperately tried to get morphine into them to dull the pain.

I went ahead to see what was happening, and why the advance had halted. Unnerved by the mines, neither the tanks nor B Company were prepared to move on. I ordered the tank commander to advance and blaze a trail for us; he had little to lose — at the very worst, a mine might blow a tank's tracks. He refused to take orders from me, claiming that his tanks were not under the command of our battalion, but merely "in support", which left him under no obligation to obey the orders of our officers. I contacted my battalion commander, who backed my view, but the tank officer still refused to budge. Our commanding officer contacted the tank officer's superior — to no avail. The dispute was long and bitter; at one point, I drew my pistol and threatened to shoot the tank commander unless he went ahead, but he had his own brand of courage and refused to be swayed by the threat. I consulted with our colonel again. It was getting late, our advance was being held up, throwing the timing of the whole assault out; the situation was critical. Almost inevitably, the colonel's answer was: "I leave it up to you to find a way out."

As the tanks still refused to advance and B Company was too unnerved to make the move, that left me with only one option: I would have to take the lead, with my mauled remnant of a company. It seemed very unjust, but there was nothing else to be done. I would have been within my rights if I had insisted on calling for engineers to clear the mines, but that would waste precious time, and we couldn't afford the delay.

I got the men of D Company together, and told them we would be going into the lead. My men had followed the lengthy dispute, and they completely understood the situation. They probably resented it as much as I did, but they accepted the responsibility without a murmur. And the constant screams of the men who had blundered into the minefield and been crippled for life were grim reminders of just how rotten the responsibility was. We were going to approach this as carefully as possible — we knew how much was at stake.

We put our heads together. Who had an idea? I always asked my men for their suggestions; it may not be standard procedure for other officers, but it surely is effective. I threw out the questions: if you were planting a minefield in a wood, how would you do it? It must be quite difficult, they said, with the tree roots getting in the way. I seized on this eagerly. Quite right! No one would go to the trouble of planting a mine underneath a root. And where were a lot of roots? Of course — *near the tree trunks!*

That was it. We moved off under the eyes of the column. We began to advance through the forest, leaping from tree to tree, taking care to land right beside the tree and cling to its trunk. It wasn't as difficult as it sounds, for the trees were close together. It must have looked damned odd, like a strange version of a ballet, but the stratagem worked. After a tense and fearful hour, we were through the minefield, without any further mishap.

There were two sequels.

For my part in the Hochwald action, I was awarded the Distinguished Service Order.

Then, years later, I went for a hearing before the deputy head of the Ontario Department of Highways, a man named Allen. I was having planning difficulties over a Toronto shopping centre. My experts presented our case; the department's engineers put forward the opposing viewpoint. Then Allen spoke, dismissing the views of his own engineers. "D'you see that man— Dunkelman? Well, he can have anything he asks for!" There was a startled silence. "You see," he explained, "I followed him through the Hochwald. We engineers lost half our men—I don't know how he got through."

As far as I can recall, that was the only occasion when I received any tangible benefit from my wartime adventures.

I had a headquarters runner — a man from the West, by the name of Paradis. He was one of the company's veterans; intelligent, brave, and reliable. As we advanced through the forest, I called him over. "You're a sergeant now," I told him. He looked unhappy at the idea, because he never wanted promotion. But I insisted. It wasn't only that I was short of sergeants: I thought this promotion, and the resulting course at NCO school, would be a way of protecting him. After all the slaughter we had endured, it seemed to me to be the least I could do, to try to save the remnants.

We moved forward behind a knoll, making maximum use of cover, until some of my scouts came under fire. I had a replacement officer with me; I asked him to take some men around the other side to see if he could get whoever was firing at us. Paradis volunteered to go along as his sergeant to help out. They set off round the flank, as I told them. But the officer, inexperienced and excited, led them around the wrong side of the knoll — straight into the enemy's line of fire. Paradis was killed.

Needless to say, we wouldn't have got very far in any of our advances without the hot meals and ammunition brought up to us by the devoted group led by Company Sergeant-Major Billy Ives and Company Quartermaster-Sergeant Saltstone. How well I remember Billy Ives arriving with a hot meal towards evening on the day of our encounter with the minefield. How he got there through the mines, I'll never know. But however hard our cooks laboured, there was nothing like home cooking. After clearing out the Hochwald, we rested in the Reichwald and there I received a wonderful surprise: one of Mother's magnificent parcels, with all kinds of delicacies, including some fine salami. After savouring a few slices, I hung the rest of the salami from a branch above my dug-out. Some time later, I went to cut off some more — and found the salami gone!

I must have been quite delirious. There's no other way of

explaining my behaviour. I ordered the sergeant-major to put the company on parade. I was quite convinced that one of them — my best friends and loyal comrades-in-arms — had stolen my salami! I proceeded to march up and down in front of them for God knows how long, haranguing them on their ingratitude for treating me like this, after I had proved myself to be their friend, looking after them, etc., etc., etc. When I exhausted all I had to say on the subject, I dismissed them all in disgust and returned to my dug-out. I was just about to jump in when my foot encountered something lying on the ground. Kicking away the leaves, I bent over and found — my missing salami. It had simply fallen off the branch.

My shame and mortification were boundless, and I didn't have the courage to confess my mistake. Instead, I hid the salami and never referred to the subject again. If these lines are read by any of the men who received that undeserved dressing down, I hope they will accept my belated apologies....

On the twenty-eighth of March the battalion crossed the Rhine on the Bridge at Rees, which had been taken a few days earlier by the 51st British Division supported by a commando unit. The battalion was in pursuit of the enemy again, and he was very disorganized, although every once in a while he would stop and give you a good bump. Soon, however, we were pulled off the pursuit and sent back into Holland to complete the liberation of the North of that country.

This was a pleasant part of the war, the sort of war that the movies portray. My company was detached from the main body of the battalion for many days at a time, and accompanied by a troop of tanks and twenty-five-pounders, some three-inch mortars, and light machine guns, we would go chasing about the countryside, accepting the surrenders of German garrisons and having a ball. The Dutch treated us royally, baking us cakes with big maple leaves on them and throwing big banquets. There was nothing too good for their liberators, the Canadians.

It was not all fun and games, however. You never knew when you were going to run into some Nazi fanatic who was prepared to hold out to the bitter end, which is just what happened to us in our last action. When we got to the Zuider Zee near the causeway, I was ordered north with my company with supporting tanks, artillery, carriers, and mortars to clear out the town of Pingum, which was reputed to be held by a garrison of three hundred Nazis led by a notorious Green Shirt SS commander (a Green Shirt was an SS instructor, so one degree crazier than the rest of the SS). The country was as flat as it could be, and we moved forward high and exposed on the main road towards the town. About a mile out we stopped to reconnoitre. There was a house at the crossroads, and a Dutchman there advised me that the Germans were ready to surrender, and that I could in fact speak to the commander on the telephone if I wished. When I spoke to him, he agreed that he would surrender and that he would consult with his staff and call me back as to the timing. After waiting for about six hours, he still hadn't called me and the leader of the Dutch underground volunteered to contact him on my behalf. He reported back that the German commander wanted more time. We waited there all day and in the evening the story repeated itself. Our Nazi friend was playing games with us.

The town was full of Dutch civilians and I was in a great quandary about attacking it. The situation was also difficult tactically, as the enemy were entrenched around the town and in buildings which were on a slightly higher piece of ground overlooking all the countryside. Our advance, unfortunately, seemed to be restricted to the main road, which ran high and exposed towards the town and had no doubt been ranged in long ago. I sat there all night studying the map and wondering what to do. Finally, I saw that there was a road leading in from the north; it must have been about fifteen miles around. I contacted the German commander again and gave him an ultimatum.

While he hemmed and hawed some more, I put the troops of tanks, machine guns, and mortars under John Hancock's command, and ordered him to come around from the right and be ready to attack from the rear. I figured that it would take John about three hours to get around the fifteen miles and into position, and gave the German a two-hour ultimatum. Sure enough, the ultimatum expired and the Germans made no move to surrender; we promptly put in a feint attack from the south, drawing heavy fire, and just at that time John appeared, as if out of nowhere, from the north. As he got close to the buildings, I ordered him to move in. There were some enemy in the rear and they opened fire, but Big John, all six feet four of him, raced ahead of his men down the road calling in German to the enemy to surrender, telling them that there was no point in fighting on. His brave action no doubt saved many lives, and he was awarded the Military Cross for his deeds that day.

The battalion was now scattered all over the countryside of Northern Holland, having a wonderful time. But from the twentieth to the twenty-second of April we were relieved in the North of Holland and ordered to return to Germany. The battle was just about over for me; after we reached Germany I turned my company over to Captain C. W. Fullerton and collapsed with battle exhaustion. I was suffering from continual attacks of malaria with constant high fevers. The strain was not only physical; the tension of constant combat and danger, the heavy responsibility of command, the shock of the Mooshof bloodbath—all these combined with my illness to put me in hospital at Ghent. I was there when the official ceasefire came at 0800 hours of May 5, 1945.

I don't know how our campaign can be described to anyone who never endured such an experience. For 330 days, Canadian soldiers, under-manned and under-supplied, fought from the Normandy beaches to the shores of the Baltic, playing their part in a series of battles as hard-fought as any in history. In his final report, Eisenhower spoke of three "episodes" as being the most decisive in ensuring victory: the battle of the Normandy beaches, the battle of the Falaise Gap, and the battles of the Rhine during February and March. In all three of these battles the Canadians played a vital part. As for the clearing of the Channel ports and of the Scheldt Estuary, the Cinderella campaigns, let Montgomery have the last word on that:

"The Canadians have proved themselves magnificent fighters, truly magnificent. Their job along the Channel coast and clearing the Scheldt was a great military achievement for which they deserve the fullest credit. It was a job that could have been done only by first-rate troops. Second-rate troops would have failed."

CHAPTER FIFTEEN

Leaving the War

When the war ended I had two immediate ambitions: to get well again, and to get out of the army and back home. I made good progress on the first after the doctors in Ghent found the bug that had been plaguing me, and even better progress after Major "Butch" Morgan of the Queen's Own thoughtfully commandeered a case of whisky and, in defiance of every hospital rule under the sun, smuggled it into my room. It lurked inspirationally under my bed, until I regained my full health at about the time the last bottle was empty.

Getting out of the army took a little longer.

I was posted back to the battalion, which was now stationed at Amersford and Doorn, in Holland, guarding twenty thousand German prisoners of war. Our duties were far from irksome, and our main concern was to initiate rehabilitation schemes for our men, and keep their morale high. The officers' morale was excellent, reflecting our living conditions. B and D Companies had their own officers' mess in a château in Doorn, where eight officers were served by two Dutch chefs, in addition to the regular Company cooks! We had organized a leave centre in a sailing club on the beautiful Loostrech Lakes near by. The Dutch civilians were grateful and friendly, there were many attractive young ladies around who showed great interest in us Canadians, and our parties—making up for lost time—were truly memorable events.

To complete my feeling of well-being, I now found myself the recipient of a great honour. My commanding officer, Steve Lett, called me to inform me that I was being offered command of the 1st Battalion of the Queen's Own. I couldn't imagine a greater compliment, or a more tempting proposal. After five years with the regiment, I was deeply attached to the Queen's Own, a feeling which has not changed in the intervening years. To command one of its battalions was a very enticing prospect and I was greatly honoured by the offer.

But I had many reasons for deciding to decline the honour: I didn't intend to make the army my career, so that the post and the lieutenant-colonel's rank that came with it were not of long-term importance to me. Above all, I wanted to get back to Toronto, where I knew my services were badly needed in the family business.

When I told Steve Lett that I was regretfully declining the honour, giving him my reasons, I mentioned an additional factor in my decision. I explained how incensed I was to hear of British Navy vessels hunting immigrant boats carrying concentration camp survivors to Palestine. When I learned of such actions by the British government, I told him, I was often inclined to resign my commission as a gesture of protest. The commanding officer listened to me very sympathetically, but advised me not to resign: I could do a lot more to help the Jewish cause by remaining a respected Canadian officer. He was sure, he said, that the average Canadian sympathized with the Zionist cause — and, indeed, events bore him out.

I had a further reason for declining the command: the 1st Battalion was on garrison duty in Germany, and the thought of serving in that country was repulsive to me. During the short period I spent on German soil as a combat soldier, I did not find myself hating the cowering and frightened civilians I encountered. Nor did I feel any great malice towards the German POWs we were guarding, who came from some garrison division and looked like a bunch of ordinary soldiers to me. I felt that the Germans, in general, were very little worse than most other people the Jews had to contend with. If there is any particular feeling I harbour towards the Germans, it's pity for their gullibility, which has cost the world — and them — so dear.

It goes without saying, however, that I hated the Nazis. I hated the élite Nazi units—the Hitler Jugend, the Hermann Goering divisions, the SS, the Green Shirts, and their like. Such creatures deserved no mercy. As our armies drove across Europe, the advance units encountered examples of Nazi handiwork, sights which surpassed in horror anything these hardened soldiers had ever witnessed on the battlefield. One by one, they liberated the Nazi death camps, where some tens of thousands of emaciated skeleton-like beings were the only survivors of the millions of men, women, and children who had been herded into these hells on earth. Like the rest of the world, I gazed in stupefaction and loathing at the pictures which came out of there, telling of a bestiality which defies all human reason. For me, there was the additional outrage that came from the knowledge that most of those tortured victims were Jews like myself. I could feel nothing but abomination for the Nazi beasts who perpetrated these "scientific" atrocities—and I didn't want to serve in a country where so many of these men walked free and unpunished.

It may seem strange, but despite their proximity I never went to visit a concentration camp. Steve Lett offered me transportation, to enable me to see for myself. He knew of my deep Jewish commitment, and must have been deeply perplexed when I declined his offer. I simply didn't have the heart and stomach for horror on such a scale, and although I didn't explain this to Steve, he was too wise to press the point. And although he himself went, he never told me what he saw there.

Somehow, the very proximity of the camps had the effect of

12. D-day 1944. The view from the landing craft.

13. On the beach at Bernières after the defenders' strongpoints have been taken.

14. Within hours the beach at Bernières was full of German prisoners.

15. Wounded lie on the Bernières beach, waiting to be shipped back to Britain.

16. A corporal from the Régiment de la Chaudière (moving in behind the Queen's Own) fraternizes with the enemy.

17. "Iron rations" and liquid refreshments.

18. Pushing on and digging in.

19. A prisoner — from the Hitler Jugend.

20. Mortar men of the Regina Rifles. The Queen's Own worked with them in Normandy, at Brettville, and at Le Mesnil-Patry.

21. Caen, July 10, 1944.

22. Entering Falaise, August 17, 1944. Bayonets fixed, these Canadians advance cautiously, searching for snipers.

23. Falaise, August 26, 1944. The killing ground.

24. Finis.

jolting me into awareness of the plight of my fellow-Jews. If there was ever a time when Jews needed all the help available, this was it. Whether they had somehow survived the death camps, or spent the war years in hiding, now, as the pitiful remnants of Europe's Jews emerged once more into the light of day, it was only natural that most of them wanted to get away from the continent which had hounded millions of Jews to their deaths. It was only natural that they wanted to live among their own people in a place where they felt safe. Tens of thousands of Jewish refugees set off for Palestine.

This was easier said than done. With the 1939 White Paper the Conservative government had finally reneged on British promises to the Jewish people concerning Palestine. Closing the last door open to Jews fleeing Hitler, Britain adopted a policy whereby Jewish immigration was to be limited and then, after five years, halted altogether. Restrictions were imposed on Jewish land purchases in Palestine, making it impossible to extend existing settlements, or establish new ones.

At the time the Labour Opposition sharply criticized the White Paper policies, vowing to abolish them when it came to power. In the first post-war election, in June 1945, Labour gained a sweeping majority, and Jews everywhere were overjoyed. They hoped that the new Labour cabinet, true to its pre-election promises, would revert to the pro-Zionist policies of the 1917 Balfour Declaration, by virtue of which the League of Nations had awarded Great Britain the mandate to administer Palestine.

It did not take long to discover that the Labour government had no intention of changing the policies of its Conservative predecessors—as far as Palestine was concerned. Again Jewish hopes were dashed. Legally, Jewish immigrants were not allowed to exceed the White Paper quota of fifteen thousand per year. But the Jewish refugees ("DPs"—"displaced persons"—as they were called then) had endured too much to halt before legal obstacles. Many of those who failed to gain the precious immigration certificates began to seek "illegal" ways to Palestine. From ports all around Southern Europe, rickety little fishing vessels and river steamers with doused lights set sail across the Mediterranean, packed with hundreds of refugees.

The British authorities did not feel able to ignore this challenge to their laws. Warships of the Royal Navy were sent out to intercept the boats, and the heartbroken would-be immigrants were forcibly deported to detention camps in Cyprus. The Jewish community in Palestine, the Yishuv, was up in arms against the British policies; the Hagana, the Jewish underground, helped organize a stream of "illegal immigrants". On occasion, when Hagana units were covering the landing of the immigrant vessels, there were armed clashes with the British Army and police.

The British hit back. The 1945 Defence Regulations gave the authorities almost unlimited powers, and these were put to full use. There were widespread searches for Hagana arms caches. Suspected members of Hagana, and of other clandestine Jewish groups — the Etzel and Lehi — were thrown into prison, along with many leaders of the Yishuv. Despite all of this, British repression failed to break Jewish opposition; on the contrary, resistance became more vigorous and violent.

The news from Palestine was occupying a steadily more prominent place on the front pages of the newspapers. I continued my round of post-war amusements in Holland, but there was an underlying feeling of unease. I had begun to feel that I would soon be needed elsewhere, and I was becoming more impatient for my discharge. I was very glad to board the troopship which carried us back—in rather greater comfort this time—across the Atlantic.

Fresh off the train from Halifax, the battalion is on parade in front of Union Station in Toronto. It's December 17, 1945—a bitterly cold winter's day. The men can move about a little, but I, standing at the head of my company, have to maintain decorum and stay rooted to the spot, absolutely motionless. I can feel my fingers freezing up, and the discomfort is intense.

Without any warning, one of the men steps out of line and walks up to me. He hands me his gloves, and marches back to the ranks. No words are spoken, but it is a last eloquent demonstration of that simple camaraderie which is my most cherished memory of the Queen's Own.

From Union Station, we march the short distance up University Avenue, to our Armouries. A brief ceremony, and then, for the last time:

"Dis-*miss*!"

CHAPTER SIXTEEN

Bad News from Palestine

It was wonderful to be out of uniform, a normal citizen again. Like all of my old comrades, of course, I did my share of basking in the role of "returned war hero" amid the admiring attentions of family and friends. Like them, too, I found that the role was good only for a few days; after that, nobody waited on you hand and foot, and you were expected to get to work.

As it turned out, I had plenty of work on my plate. During the war, Tip Top Tailors had gone badly downhill and salvaging the business was going to require my full attention. I threw myself into the job with such dedication that eventually I sold my beloved *Dinny* to friends who pointed out that I never had the time to sail her.

At first all my work in the business meant that I had no time for Zionist activity of any kind. I scarcely had time to glance at the newspapers, but what I saw displeased me greatly. The situation in Palestine was worsening, with growing clashes between the British government and the Jewish Yishuv, while Royal Navy ships continued to hunt down "illegal" immigrant ships. There was a body of opinion in Canada which sided with the senior member of the Commonwealth, Britain, and some Toronto papers displayed a distinctly anti-Zionist bias in their reporting. Finally, Jewish organizations in Toronto formed a delegation to meet the press and request changes. The group included several rabbis and Jewish lay leaders, and I, presumably because of my wartime record, was invited to join the delegation.

On the appointed day, we were ushered into the formidable presence of George McCullagh, the publisher of the *Telegram* and the *Globe and Mail* — two of Toronto's most influential papers at that time. Various members of the delegation presented their views, adopting a very tactful and timid approach, which made no impression whatsoever on McCullagh.

It came to my turn to speak.

"Mr. McCullagh," I said, "your brand of anti-Semitism is no better than Hitler's."

His Irish temper flared. He jumped to his feet, stuck his reddening face close to mine, and bellowed: "What the hell do you mean by that?"

It looked as if we were going to come to blows, and out of the corner of my eye I could see my fellow delegates rolling their eyes to the ceiling in dismay. But I stood my ground and bellowed right back at him, telling him that his papers gave off an anti-Semitic whiff in their editorials, and that on the Palestine question their statistics and historical facts were just plain wrong, which meant that the Jewish case never received a fair hearing.

We had a very hot session with no punches pulled on either side, and my fellow delegates seemed to be studying the walls in the hope of finding escape hatches. But all the shouting seemed to produce results: following the meeting, the papers began to take a much more favourable view of the Zionist position.

This episode, insignificant in itself, was what prompted the Zionist Organization of Canada to ask me to take over as its public relations officer in Ontario. Busy as I was in my work, I devoted as much time as I could to this task, which wasn't as difficult as it may seem. There was a strong body of opinion in Canada that supported the Zionist cause. A few years earlier, a group of non-Jews had formed a body called the Canadian

Palestine Committee to back the Jewish case, and in 1944 it had sent a delegation, headed by the Honourable Arthur Roebuck, to meet the prime minister, Mackenzie King. The delegation was backed by Zionist representatives, my mother among them. They outlined the history of Zionism, and presented the case for opening the gates of Palestine to the Jewish refugees from Europe. The delegation then urged the premier to use his influence with the British government to further its demands.

Mackenzie King's reaction was unfavourable at that time. Later, however, he took up a more noncommittal attitude, while some of his appointees went much further in support of the Zionist position. Justice Rand, Canada's representative on the Anglo-American Committee of Inquiry, and Lester Pearson, the United Nations delegate, were of great help in passing the partition plan. This change in attitude was, at least in part, due to the efforts of the Canadian Palestine Committee, under the late Herb Mowat. Despite their powerful links of loyalty to Britain, its members did not waver in their support for the Jewish people, nor did they tone down their criticism of British policy in Palestine.

With such helpful backing, I was able to do useful work in Zionist public relations. But as the days passed and the news from Palestine grew more ominous, it became clear that the struggle was entering a decisive stage, where the Jewish people would need more than good public relations.

Nonetheless, I was minding my own business in Toronto when Lady Lorna Wingate challenged me directly. Like her late husband, the legendary Major-General Orde Wingate, who had been killed in a plane crash while commanding the British forces in Burma, she was a dedicated Zionist. In the course of her world-wide travels to recruit support for the cause, she came to make a speech in Ottawa; from there she made a special journey to meet me at my home.

Her message was simple: she wanted me to leave the peace of

Toronto and go back to Palestine as a soldier. She was very direct: "Were my husband alive, he would not take no for an answer. He would demand that you go to Palestine and volunteer your services!"

I was embarrassed, and tried to explain my situation: I had responsibilities, there was a business to run, I had to consider my family. . . . I had done enough fighting to last me a lifetime and I liked being a civilian, with nobody trying to kill me. Anyway, I was thirty-four, too old to be going to war again. There must be other, younger men.

She heard me out. Then she told me of her late husband's concern over the Hagana's lack of trained combat officers. Disconcertingly, she seemed to know all about my military background, and her conclusion was clear: with my training and experience, I was needed in Palestine.

Soon after her thought-provoking visit, I was chairing the first Negev dinner, held to raise funds for settlement in Israel, when I met George Fielding Eliot, the military writer, who was our guest speaker. He impressed me with his warnings that the Yishuv had to prepare for war, and that the support of the Jewish people all over the world was essential for victory. That made me think even harder. But what caused me to make up my mind was a speech by an American clergyman — an Arab sympathizer — who described in lurid detail what the Arabs would do to the Jews in the inevitable military showdown. My mind was now made up; when the time came, I would volunteer my services to the Jewish forces in Palestine.

It seemed that the time was not far distant. The horrifying symbolism of British soldiers forcibly deporting Jewish refugees had aroused world public opinion against Britain's anti-Zionist repression, and both the United States and the Soviet Union had expressed public support for a solution guaranteeing rights of self-determination for both Jews and Arabs in Palestine. The British government, then leaning heavily towards the Arabs, announced that it was giving up the mandate, leaving it to the United Nations to find a way out. On November 29, 1947, after months of discussion, the United Nations General Assembly decided, by thirty-three votes to thirteen, to partition Palestine into two states: Jewish and Arab.

The Jewish leaders were not totally satisfied with this solution, but saw it as the best attainable in current conditions, and immediately proclaimed their support for partition. The Arabs, however, were violently opposed to the resolution. Having failed to muster enough United Nations votes to defeat a plan which enjoyed joint U.S.-Soviet support, the Arab leaders in Palestine promptly announced that they rejected the partition plan and would use force to oppose it. With Britain about to relinquish the mandate on May 14, 1948, the decisive confrontation was at hand.

Jewish prospects looked bleak. When the British withdrew, the Yishuv would have to face the armed opposition of Palestine's Arab population, who outnumbered the Jews by two to one. That was bad enough. But what completely unbalanced the equation was the fact that the Arabs could count on support from the regular armies of the neighbouring states. The Arab armies lacked combat experience, but they were trained as regular formations, and supplied with heavy modern arms. Syria and Lebanon had French equipment, while Britain had armed Egypt, Iraq, and Transjordan, whose Arab Legion was commanded by British officers.

Jewish forces consisted only of the Hagana and other clandestine organizations. They had limited formal military training, and some combat experience from clashes with the Arabs and the British Army; in addition, many Jews had served in regular armies during the Second World War, either in the British Army's Jewish Brigade or with the 8th Army in the desert against Rommel. However, harassed by British arms searches, the Jews had only a limited amount of light weapons, with no artillery, armour, or planes. The odds against the Jews seemed heavy — almost hopelessly heavy.

My decision had been reached; the time for its implementation had not yet arrived. In the meantime, I was given an opportunity to make an immediate contribution to Jewish military preparations. I was at work in my office when I received a distinguished but unexpected visitor, Mrs. Ayala Zacks, who had attained renown for her exploits as an Allied agent in Occupied France and was now the wife of Samuel Zacks, the president of the Zionist Organization of Canada. With the secrecy appropriate to her wartime background and to the occasion, Mrs. Zacks introduced me to her companion, a Palestinian Jew by the name of Gutman. It turned out that Gutman was the Hagana representative in North America, and had an enticing proposition: he invited me to become chairman of Hagana in Canada. I was very glad to accept his offer, and set to work in conditions of the greatest secrecy.

At that time, we were told to refrain from recruiting, since the Jews possessed more men than guns; the Yishuv would have enough to do looking after itself, without having to arm, feed, and maintain a body of foreign volunteers. Arms, we were told, were the top priority. Getting them was only part of the problem, for the British Navy still maintained a tight blockade of the Palestine coast, and gun-running was a complex and hazardous activity. Our Canadian Hagana committee could do nothing about that part of it, but what we could do was raise the funds necessary for the purchase of weapons. With the help of dedicated workers like Justice Harry Batshaw, Moe Myerson, and Moe Shulemson and many more, we had considerable success in collecting money from Canadian sympathizers.

The actual buying of arms was not my province, and given the need for secrecy, I was glad to know nothing about it. But I knew enough to be aware of the enormous problems. At the best of times, you don't simply walk into a friendly neighbourhood arms store and buy a hundred anti-tank guns, or a thousand grenades, or fifty machine guns. Add to that the fact that British Intelligence was on the watch and you have a major problem, how to find the arms you need and buy them secretly—and then get them to Palestine. Yet somehow Yosef Eitan (Joe Eisen) — whom I had met in Israel—managed to supervise this operation in Canada with great success. He was assisted by many individuals, including my brother Joe, who helped to buy machine-gun parts and even assisted in the delicate operation of smuggling them into Palestine. Throughout this whole process, great assistance was given by Jewish businessmen dealing in surplus army equipment, who used their connections to get hold of some very important items, and generally donated them free of charge.

I once became directly involved with the arms purchase issue when I travelled to New York with Samuel Zacks to consult Eliezer Kaplan, the Jewish Agency treasurer. I needed his permission to spend the enormous sum of one thousand dollars on some portable anti-tank guns. He refused to give his permission, explaining that his funds were so short that the first priority was the purchase of wheat to feed the eight hundred thousand Jews who would be left when the British withdrew. Anti-tank guns, he insisted, did not have top priority. I was astounded, and expressed the opinion that if certain vital arms were not bought, there would be very few Jewish mouths left to feed. He remained immovable. The money, he said, could not be spared. With that, the meeting ended: since the money was not forthcoming, the deal was cancelled.

While such purchases normally went fairly smoothly in Canada, it was far harder in the United States, where severe restrictions were imposed on the export of military equipment to the Middle East. The State Department did such a thorough job of applying the ban that they even classified barbed wire as an offensive weapon. By contrast, in Canada there was no great difficulty in purchasing important auxiliary equipment, including surplus jeeps, trucks, and signals sets, whose sale was unrestricted. I myself got hold of some Canadian "19" signals sets, which had been produced late in the war for the Red Army, but never shipped. Later, these sets were the only signals equipment we had available during the siege of Jerusalem. There could be no mistaking them—two-way radios labelled "Made in Canada", with Russian markings, are fairly distinctive.

The work of the Hagana committee was going well, everything seemed to be functioning smoothly, and I was looking forward to going to Palestine, where I had already been accepted for active service with Hagana, when I received two visitors who dashed my hopes. Colonel David Marcus, a Jewish graduate of West Point who had served in an administrative post with the U.S. Army during the war, was accompanied by Shlomo Shamir, whom I was to meet later in Palestine. They had come to tell me that the Hagana command had decided to recruit experienced combat soldiers to serve in the Jewish forces. They wanted me to get to work on recruiting an infantry brigade of English-speaking volunteers, which I would lead in action.

This was a major project, of great importance, and it excited me a great deal. But it obviously took precedence over my planned departure for Palestine, which had to be postponed.

Recruiting those volunteers was, in many ways, a heartwarming experience. It was wonderful to see how hundreds of Canadian veterans, Jews and Gentiles, came forward to offer their services. Inevitably, some of these men must have been adventurers, though ordinary "soldiers of fortune" would certainly have lost interest when we told them that they would get no more than their keep. Most of the men came with a clear sense of purpose, perhaps best expressed by the famous Canadian fighter ace George "Buzz" Beurling: "I believe," he declared simply, "that the Jews deserve a state of their own after wandering around homeless for thousands of years. I just want to offer my help."

He was an unusual man — lean, blond, and handsome, a "loner", with a poise and serenity which made him stand out in a crowd. He was a much-decorated hero of the bitter air battles over Malta in 1942, a pilot of legendary skill with twenty-nine "kills" to his credit. There was nothing that he wasn't prepared to do for us. He helped recruit other pilots, and came up with a plan to take a group of pilots on a visit to Cyprus, where they would help him steal a squadron of RAF Spitfires from the British airfield there! Another scheme of his was to volunteer to fly for the Arabs, and then take their planes over to the Jewish lines.

Cynics believe that Beurling only joined us for the money (being a specialist, he got a modest salary), but I believe that he couldn't have cared less about that aspect. As it happened, he never got to Palestine: on his way to serve with the Israeli forces, he was killed in an air crash in Italy.

There were many surprises involved in the recruiting campaign. For example, there was the pleasant surprise of finding that the Jewish volunteers were outnumbered by non-Jews, who offered their services without having any personal stake in the Middle East conflict. (Unfortunately, my orders were to recruit Jews only for the proposed infantry brigade.)

We encountered no legal difficulties in our recruiting work in Canada. When we embarked on the campaign, I consulted Senator Arthur Roebuck of the Canadian Palestine Committee, who was a distinguished lawyer. He explained that Canadian law banned recruiting by an accredited foreign government. Since there was as yet no Jewish government, the ban did not apply, and my actions were perfectly legitimate. Nevertheless, to forestall any possible misunderstanding, I decided at this time to withdraw from the Queen's Own militia — a step I undertook with great regret.

A great deal has been written about the gallant volunteers who went to Spain in the 1930s to fight in the International Brigade against Franco's Fascists. By contrast, almost nothing is known about the men—especially the Canadians—who volunteered to fight for Israel when it seemed that their quixotic mission was bound to end in death. A whole book could—and should—be written about the Canadians, about one thousand in all, who fought to establish Israel in 1948. To give just one example of their contribution, Canadian pilots accounted for one-third of all Arab planes shot down in that war.

Of course, our recruiting was legal. In the United States our counterparts had a much tougher job, since, by law, Americans who volunteered for foreign armies could forfeit their citizenship. To make matters worse, the American Legion backed this ban, putting many Jewish veterans in an anguished position. In the end, faced by these problems, the United States recruiters only managed to raise a total of five hundred volunteers.

I was very disappointed by this, of course, but I understood the dilemma of American Jewish veterans, even if I didn't share it. Being a Canadian citizen had never stood in the way of my duties to the Jewish people. I had clearly demonstrated my loyalty to Canada — now, I knew my duties to the Jews.

Naturally, I encountered a number of Canadian Jews who did experience a conflict of allegiances, and who hesitated to support Zionism because of Britain's stand. On one occasion, when I was head of recruitment, I attended a Zionist convention in Ottawa. During the debate a Toronto Jewish leader stood up and said that if it came to the point of the British fighting the Jews, he would put on his uniform and fight on the British side! As though that were not sufficient, he added that my work in recruiting volunteers should be outlawed.

I was hurt and astounded by his attitude. But perhaps I shouldn't have taken his words so seriously: when the time came for me to leave Canada to fight in Palestine, I handed over my job in the Hagana committee to — that very same gentleman.

Although there was nothing illegal about our recruiting efforts, for various obvious reasons we did not conduct our activities publicly. On the contrary, it was all very cloak and dagger. In private homes all over the country, men would arrive in ones and twos to meet in small groups of ten or fifteen. I had to go and speak to many of these groups myself, and with thousands of men involved, in many different places, I had to do a great deal of travelling and speaking. At the same time, the responsibility for Tip Top Tailors was on my shoulders; with the business still in difficulties, I had my hands full there also.

No one could say that I was idle. My recruiting and fund-raising work was definitely an important contribution to Hagana preparations — and yet, I felt that I should be doing more important things than interviewing and screening volunteers. After all, I was a trained officer with considerable combat experience, and the Hagana was desperately short of that sort of man. And every day the news from Palestine reported increasing clashes between Arabs and Jews, with attacks and counter-attacks, roads blocked, and settlements under siege.

I was chafing at the bit. I wanted to get to Palestine before the British left, when the fighting was certain to start in earnest. I felt that the last few weeks of British rule had to be put to good use in large-scale preparations and training, so that the few forces we had could be organized and deployed to give the best possible account of themselves when the decisive moment came, and I knew that my knowledge and training could be as useful there as in actual combat. In addition, I wanted to prepare the ground for the arrival in Palestine of our Canadian volunteers. My impatience was growing.

At long last, the good news: I was given permission to go! Travelling very light, I boarded the plane to France on March 12, 1948.

CHAPTER SEVENTEEN

Off to War Again

Paris! It was only three years after war's end, and the French metropolis was returning to its gay pre-war self. But I wasn't in Paris to amuse myself: instead, I met at once with Hagana representatives to discuss arrangements for the transportation and housing of the volunteers who were to follow me along the secret pipeline we were establishing. We also worked out a training program to be followed in the transit camps, until the men set off on the last leg of their journey to Palestine.

The Hagana men in France were damned impressive, and they had a first-class organization set up all over the country, with reception centres to house volunteers on their way through. It was like the Resistance all over again. But I found myself worrying about the attitude of the French government, which, according to my contacts, was keeping an eye on our doings. At that time, Hagana's principal enemy was Britain. The French, having their own scores to settle with the British (who had dislodged them from Syria and Lebanon), were not unfavourably disposed towards any group engaged in twisting the lion's tail. At the same time, French interests in the Middle East were complex and ramified. France was the Hagana's principal staging ground in Europe—and French Intelligence was fully aware of the large camps around Marseilles, and of the clandestine military training going on there. If, for reasons of high politics, the French authorities decided to crack down on us, our entire volunteer program would be destroyed. I determined to be as careful and discreet as possible inside France, and to keep my fingers crossed.

In Marseilles I visited the transit camp, hidden away in the hills to the north of the city, and inspected the training facilities. Training would not be intensive: the volunteers were all supposedly combat veterans, and they would need little more than some exercise to get back in shape, and some practice to familiarize themselves with the weapons they would be using. The main thing would be for them to get to know one another, and get used to functioning as a unit.

In Marseilles, I underwent a personal metamorphosis: I became an "illegal". With Britain controlling access to Palestine, immigration restrictions were still in force — at least, as far as Jews were concerned. To enter the country, I would have to adopt a false identify, with a "borrowed" passport.

It was a strange experience. I had never lived an illegal existence before, and here I was, giving up my own name and personality, and taking over the identity of some total stranger. On receiving my new passport, I was intrigued to learn that I was now an Englishman by the name of Fox, who hailed from Twickenham, was five feet eight, weighed 160 pounds, and had brown eyes and dark hair. My difficulty in assuming this identity will be understood if I mention that I was six feet two, weighed close on 240 pounds, had blue eyes and light brown hair. Apart from that, we might have been twins.

To make matters worse, I found it impossible to disguise my Canadian accent, and never could learn to pronounce "Twickenem" in the English way. Later, on the boat, I spent hours with my travelling companion, Maxie Brown, practising what to do if British immigration officials put me through a searching interrogation. It was laughable, but it was no laughing matter: if I was caught, I'd end up in prison, perhaps to be handed over to the Arabs when the British withdrew.

When the first group of volunteers, under the command of Lionel Drucker, arrived in Marseilles, I saw that they were safely settled in the training camp, and then set off.

While the rest of the volunteers would have to join the European illegal immigrants in their antiquated vessels and take their chance at running the British blockade, my presence in Palestine was considered urgent enough to make me eligible for the relatively luxurious "VIP route". Together with Maxie Brown, I boarded a regular Mediterranean passenger liner en route for Haifa. Although there were some other Jewish passengers, some of them no doubt also "illegals", only Maxie knew my true identity. Nevertheless, we were both very careful, watching our words to avoid giving ourselves away.

We had heard that the Jewish passengers on a previous boat had been attacked by Arabs in Alexandria and after disembarking at Haifa. In case of a recurrence of such an incident, Maxie and I began very discreetly to befriend the other Jewish passengers. I became particularly friendly with two young Jewish war orphans. They were accompanied by an old Ukrainian peasant woman, who idolized and pampered them, and it was through her that I got to know their story, a true story that is literally stranger than fiction.

Their father had been a famous doctor in the Ukraine. When the Germans came, they killed the parents, but the old woman rescued the children, keeping them hidden throughout the long, harsh years of the German occupation. After the liberation, she decided that the orphans had to be delivered back to their own people, making it her life's ambition to bring them to Palestine. She was a primitive woman, poor, ignorant, and backward. Somehow, with two small children in tow, she managed to overcome all the seemingly insurmountable obstacles involved in travelling from the Ukraine across a dozen countries of war-torn Europe to Marseilles; and now, here she was, on the ship to Haifa, about to complete the task she had taken upon herself.

I grew very fond of her, and her charges—two young children whose brief and tragic stories personified for me all the suffering of Jewish children in Europe during the Nazi nightmare. When we walked down the gangplank at Haifa, I took their little hands in mine, to give them what reassurance I could.

Our arrival at Haifa passed without any great incident. I walked past the Arab immigration official, airily waving the passport of Mr. Fox of Twickenham. The official gave me a knowing glance, and I don't think for a moment that he was fooled. But I presume that he had been adequately bribed, and if he detected any discrepancies between this "Mr. Fox" and the description in the passport, he kept his observations to himself. After this "passport control", we were all carefully searched for arms or ammunition. Apparently, this was not yet enough, because we were subjected to a second search by British troops, who behaved very roughly as they herded us off the bus at the port exit.

When we got back to the bus, we found the driver very upset over the delay. The port lay in an Arab neighbourhood, and he was afraid that the bus would come under sniper fire as we drove through. There was little we could do to prepare for such an eventuality except to place the women and children in the centre of the bus, where they would gain some slight protection from the men who sat near the windows. Fortunately, these precautions proved unnecessary. The short drive was very tense, but it passed without any incident whatsoever, and we soon reached Hadar Hacarmel, which was then the principal Jewish quarter of Haifa. Maxie and I were directed to a small hotel where we were to be met. Maxie was a military technician: he was an expert on small arms, and his expertise was obviously highly valued, for no sooner did we arrive than he was whisked away. In my case, things did not work out so smoothly.

I had the privilege of being the very first foreign volunteer ("Machal") to arrive. I had reached Palestine, not as an immigrant who came to settle in, but as a soldier who had come to fight. As such, I presented something of a problem. After years of immigration, the Jewish Yishuv had well-organized facilities for the reception of immigrants, who found themselves handled with well-oiled precision. If I had been an immigrant, I would have been looked after. But I wasn't immigrating, I was enlisting as a soldier. Or rather, I *wanted* to enlist, but the Hagana hadn't yet established the facilities or procedures for receiving foreign volunteers.

After Maxie Brown was led away, I remained in the hotel, waiting impatiently. My only consolation was the beautiful panorama of Haifa and its surroundings. I couldn't have chosen a better spot to while away the time: from the hotel, halfway up Mount Carmel, I had a wonderful view, with the deep blue of the Mediterranean below, and the snow-capped peak of Mount Hermon gleaming in the distance, beyond the Syrian border. But as I surveyed this picturesque scene, my eye was caught by a grim reminder of Palestinian realities. Down in the harbour I could see a row of ramshackle little ships. These were captured immigrant boats, trophies of one of the Royal Navy's less glorious victories, over helpless refugees. I was filled with indignation at the heartlessness of the British authorities, who were now compounding that sin by actually helping the Arabs in their fight against the Jewish community in Palestine. If I was to join in that fight, I would have to confront the British, my old comrades in arms in many a fight in Europe. My anger at seeing what they had done to those pathetic little immigrant ships was a good mental preparation for that encounter.

But in the meantime, I was in the hotel, wondering whether I had been forgotten. I began to have visions of sitting out the war in that hotel lounge. Then, after a full day when I was on the verge of despair, I was approached by a Palmach courier who introduced himself and told me he had instructions to escort me to Tel Aviv, to Palmach headquarters. This was one small example of the quality of the Palmach, which always seemed ready to take on each and every task. Since no one else seemed ready to receive the foreign volunteers, the Palmach — the élite unit of Hagana—stepped in. I picked up my belongings, and we set off for Tel Aviv.

Getting from Haifa to Tel Aviv was a major undertaking. The main road between the two cities was cut, so we took a detour by way of the Yezre'el Valley. This route wasn't entirely safe, either, since one of its sections was under the control of the Arab Legion. The Legion was commanded by British officers, and officially it was part of the British garrison in Palestine, charged with maintaining law and order. But the soldiers were Arabs from Transjordan, and its units adopted a hostile attitude towards Jews, specializing in sniping at Jewish traffic on the highways. As we sped along, my guide kept clutching at the concealed pistol he was carrying. Without the pistol, he was helpless to defend himself from attack by the British-commanded Legionnaires. Carrying the pistol, he was in danger of arrest by those selfsame Legionnaires for carrying "illegal arms". A neat dilemma.

We were lucky enough to get to Tel Aviv without incident, where we went straight to Palmach headquarters. The "Palmachniks" gave me a warm and friendly welcome, and I soon felt at home among them. The Palmach was Hagana's assault group, consisting of young men and women fully mobilized and organized in full-time military formations, unlike the bulk of Hagana, which was a part-time militia. The Palmachniks were young, Palestine-born "Sabras", and were an interesting type of Jew: clean-limbed and clear-eyed, strong, proud, brave, and down-to-earth. For all the differences in our backgrounds, I instantly felt a great affinity with them. In the coming months, I would spend much time with the Palmach units, and I always felt completely at ease with them; even when language problems impeded conversation, we could usually communicate without any real difficulty.

On arrival, I was taken to meet the Palmach's commander, Yigal Alon. Yigal — a handsome young man in his late twenties, who sped around the countryside in an open roadster with his hair flying in the breeze — had caught the imagination of the Yishuv, and was extremely popular. He and the other Palmach officers greeted me very cordially, and we got on well. It wasn't long, however, before we found ourselves in serious disagreement.

I had always assumed that the Canadian volunteers would constitute an independent unit, under my command: so I was given to understand when I commenced recruiting in Canada, and so I informed the men who enlisted. By staying together, we would avoid most of the communications problems affecting English-speaking soldiers in a Hebrew-speaking army, and I was sure we'd give a good account of ourselves, and make the best possible contribution to the Jewish forces as a unit.

The Palmach commanders thought otherwise. At that time, the Palmach was working desperately to expand its ranks; at the end of 1947, when the conflict began to pick up momentum, it numbered no more than twenty-one hundred men and women with an active reserve of another one thousand. Accordingly, the Palmach took an active interest in all newcomers, making great efforts to fit them into its ranks. Our combat experience made the Canadian volunteers especially desirable; the Palmach officers were looking for seasoned soldiers to stiffen the flow of raw recruits, and they hoped that I, like the other volunteers, would put my experience at their disposal. They made it clear that they were firmly opposed to any idea of a separate Canadian unit.

I was not going to give up without a fight, so for the next few days I banged on doors to try to arrange for the Canadians to fight as a unit. I learned that in the circumstances this would be almost impossible — everyone was opposed to the idea. I could live with that; what I found much more distressing was my discovery of just how chaotic conditions were. There was no real army headquarters; the various military organizations operated separately, often competing against each other like sports teams for star players, and even at the best of times co-ordination was rough-and-ready.

Things were, if anything, even worse among the civilian authorities; for all its considerable prestige, the Jewish Agency Executive still fell far short of functioning as an effective government. At the same time, conditions in the country were chaotic. The British were withdrawing from Palestine in an ill-humour and sometimes seemed to be trying to leave behind as much disorder as possible. The escalating conflict with the Arabs had already led to a partial breakdown of communications, and Jewish settlements in many parts of the country were cut off from supplies. There was a severe shortage of money for the most elementary needs. With so many enormous problems to face, the question of how to employ the Canadian volunteers was, not surprisingly, given less than top priority....

I decided to give my plan for a Canadian unit one last try, taking my problem straight to the top. At that time, David Ben-Gurion's official post was chairman of the Jewish Agency Executive, and he was soon to head Israel's first cabinet. But his attention was focussed on military matters; he had taken over-all control of defence affairs, directing all his energies to the task of turning the Hagana into an army capable of facing and defeating the regular Arab formations. Clearly, Ben-Gurion was the man to see: I asked for an interview.

When I arrived for our meeting, his office was a flurry of activity, with messengers rushing off in all directions. In the inner office I found myself warmly greeted by a stocky man with white hair. He expressed a keen personal interest in me, firing many questions about my background at me while the piercing eyes never left my face. At the end, he promised to give me and the other Canadian volunteers all the help he could in finding our feet in the country; he promised to look into the possibility of creating a Canadian unit.

From that first meeting, I took an immediate liking to Ben-Gurion, and he seemed to feel the same way towards me. I came to know him well, and he made me feel almost like a member of his family; his death late in 1973 was a personal blow to me.

That meeting with Ben-Gurion brought me his attention, and, in time, his confidence, which he demonstrated later by appointing me to take on some important tasks. Thereafter, his door was always open to me; a sure way of getting things done was to enlist his support, because he was prepared to cut red tape, and expedite any matter within his competence.

By this time, I felt that I'd spent enough time in offices and conferences. I wanted to find out what was happening on the battlefields and, if possible, offer my assistance. At Ben-Gurion's suggestion, I went to Yigal Yadin, acting chief of operations, for a briefing on the situation.

Yadin gave me a long and detailed briefing of the military situation. The picture he revealed was appalling. Road communications had been disrupted throughout the country, with the Arabs controlling important sections of all the main highways. Many Jewish settlements had been encircled for weeks, and the hundred thousand Jews of Jerusalem were in a particularly perilous plight, having been cut off from supplies ever since the Arabs blocked the road up from the coast. He told me of the strength of the enemy forces already engaged, and those likely to join battle in the coming weeks, laying special stress on the well-armed regular armies of the neighbouring Arab states. The Jewish forces, by comparison, were weak in numbers, and desperately short of arms and ammunition, with hardly any heavy weapons. Even light arms were in short supply, and there were many soldiers who lacked a weapon of any kind. The odds seemed insurmountable.

The crucial point was Jerusalem. Unless the Arab blockade could be broken, and the civilian population resupplied, the city would be starved into surrender. The Palmach had just launched Operation "Nachshon", whose objective was to open up the Jerusalem road to supply convoys. Eager to make myself useful as quickly as possible and to get acquainted with local conditions, I asked to join the forces fighting there. At my request, Ben-Gurion arranged for me to join the Palmach's "Harel" Brigade, which was then engaged in the final phases of Operation Nachshon.

Once again, I set out for the battlefield.

CHAPTER EIGHTEEN

Running the Gauntlet

Hulda, where the convoy for Jerusalem was forming up, was a prosperous little Jewish settlement to the south of the main Tel-Aviv–Jerusalem road. As we approached it in the jeep I had time to admire the orange groves and the cultivated fields, a picture of plenty and peace.

Dropped off at the brigade headquarters, however, I find myself in the middle of a hubbub of frantic activity. Hulda has been turned into one big transit depot, and the place is jammed with battered trucks, civilian ten-tonners mostly, all being loaded with piles of produce, sacks of provisions, and crates of ammunition. Every minute seems to bring another vehicle to add to the noise and the bustle. As men hurry to and fro intent on various tasks, my rusty Hebrew is not enough to persuade them to stop and tell me where I can report.

After being shunted around a good deal, I finally succeed in presenting my accreditation. The letters I carry explain that I'm being attached temporarily to the Harel Brigade as a supernumerary staff officer, to assist in planning. As an old soldier, I know just how the men on the spot feel about that: "Who the hell is he?" they must be thinking. "And who needs a supernumerary planning officer anyway?" But they're friendly enough to me. Unfortunately, though, everything at headquarters is being conducted in Hebrew, and my knowledge of the language is not nearly good enough to follow the rapid exchanges. One thing is absolutely essential—I must learn military terms in Hebrew; otherwise, I can't even express the most basic notions. I fetch out a notebook and begin to jot down the important words, in English letters, and try to memorize them.

The brigade commander of Harel is a tall, handsome lad with the fair complexion and blue eyes which seem to be so common among the Sabras. He seems a little shy, but his manner is pleasant. The overriding impression is his youth: he's twenty-six and he looks even younger. Yet here he is, in command of the Yishuv's first brigade, which is, in fact, its only effective assault formation. He has to forge his newly assembled brigade into an organized combat unit and take it into action immediately. He looks capable, and he'd better be—the fate of Jerusalem and its hundred thousand Jews is in his hands. His name is Yitzhak Rabin.

The brigade's planning officer and second-in-command is named Itty. He doesn't like me and he makes no effort to conceal his hostility. He speaks no English, and he's impatient with my halting Hebrew. On my second day with the brigade, Itty calls me. He manages to convey to me that he's going out in an armoured car for a reconnaissance along the Jerusalem road; if I'm not too scared, he implies, I might want to come along, too.

"Armoured car" may be rather a grand title for the home-made contraption we're about to mount. It's a Dodge "Power-wagon", completely enclosed in a box-like casing of steel plate, with firing slits. This — and others like it — is a product of Hagana workshops, which have done quite an impressive job with very modest means; it's not pretty, but it looks as though it will be quite effective against ordinary small-arms fire. But we're in trouble if the Arabs have armour-piercing bullets.

Anyway, it's the best thing available. It would be suicide to set out in any soft-skinned vehicle on this trip. Not only will we be driving in full view of Arab sharpshooters; we're supposed to draw their fire and make them reveal their positions.

It's hot and uncomfortable inside the gloom of the car, but all's quiet as we speed along the main road. So far, we're still down in the coastal plain, and the flat countryside doesn't afford good conditions for ambushes. The trouble lies up ahead, when we start to climb into the hills.

We approach the police fortress of Latrun just off the road to the left. Occupied by the Arab Legion, Latrun is a good example of British double-dealing. The Legion's British officers know perfectly well that only a few hundred yards away from their positions, thousands of Arab irregulars are lying in wait, ready to pounce on any Jewish convoy which tries to make its way to Jerusalem. Not only don't the British make any move to flush them out — they sit there and protect the Arabs' flank.

We pass Latrun unmolested, though we catch the flash of binoculars on the fortress walls; we are being watched. Immediately after Latrun comes the crossroads of Bab-el-Wad; there the road begins to climb into the hills, into ambush country.

I grasp my rifle, a British Lee-Enfield, and keep a sharp look-out through the firing slit.

How, in heaven's name, can we ever get a heavily loaded supply convoy up this route? The road itself is like an obstacle course, twisting and turning steeply uphill, edging its way around rocky outcrops that force our driver to nose around them in low gear. To make matters worse, it is overlooked all the way by steep and heavily wooded hillsides, dotted with boulders which make perfect firing positions. As we drive along, there is a deathly hush all around. We are not fired upon, but there is no room for illusion: previous experience shows that the Arabs are massed in force up there on the hilltops, waiting to pour fire on anything that looks like an easy and profitable target. Until then they obviously have been ordered to hold their fire and not give away their position.

We speed along without incident. All is peaceful and quiet. Deadly quiet.

We reach Kiryat Anavim, a large Jewish settlement outside

Jerusalem, where we are to pick up some Palmach soldiers who have been involved in an engagement near by, and escort their buses back through the hills. Our driver swings the armoured car around on the narrow road, intending to turn. With the front wheels near a sheer drop, he tries to back up, but the rear wheels spin helplessly on the tarmac. He tries again. The car is stuck. When we clamber out and push, the car still won't budge. There's no question of moving any further forward—the wheels are perilously close to the edge.

I've had enough experience of this kind of situation to know what to do, but when I try to tell Itty, he ignores me. He shouts to the driver: the wheels spin again. Loud argument, with much waving of hands and emphatic gestures. The car still doesn't move. I try to offer my help, but again Itty brushes me off. This is no joke: it's now late afternoon, and if we waste much more time, we'll be caught on the Bab-el-Wad road in the dark, which is not an enticing prospect.

The arguments continue periodically, the wheels spin again, and the engine whines its protests against this mistreatment. Itty is obviously not getting anywhere. Finally, turning to me with a scowl, he asks: "Well, what do *you* suggest?"

I go to work, patiently. First, I jack up the front wheels, and we push the vehicle a few inches away from the edge. Then I jack it up again, a few more inches. Several times more, and the wheels are well away from the edge. The armoured car moves off without any difficulty.

We get back in, and move off down the road, followed by the buses. The drive is uneventful on the way back, except that now, of course, Itty is even more unfriendly to me. I see him as a blustering fool, nothing more.

With the Palmach soldiers safely escorted past Bab-el-Wad and on their way to their base at Hulda, Itty orders the armoured car's driver to turn again, and to my surprise we head back towards the Bab-el-Wad road junction. Near by, there is a gas station which is often used by the Arabs as a firing position against our convoys. Itty stops the car some way from the station. Carrying something in his hand, he climbs out of the car, and saunters along, in full view of the Arabs concealed on the hillsides. He strolls casually over to the station, and lays down his burden, a bundle wrapped in rags. At that point, his movements lose their leisurely quality, and he races back to the car, jumps in, and snaps at the driver to move off.

At that precise moment, there is a tremendous explosion that rocks our car, tilting it over onto two wheels. When we settle down on an even keel, I glance back. The gas station is in ruins. For a moment, there is a kind of shocked silence. Then, as they overcome their astonishment at the sheer impudence of his deed, the Arab riflemen open up with everything they have, their orders to hold their fire blotted out by this unpardonable effrontery by the Jews. Like hail on a tin roof their bullets beat a tattoo against the side of the armoured car, but bounce off harmlessly.

On the road back to Hulda, there's a lot to think about. That fusillade from the hillsides was just a foretaste of what lies in store for the convoy we're going to take through. There are a lot of guns up there, and they're all waiting for us. . . .

And there's Itty: too arrogant to heed the advice of some newly arrived "foreigner". And one of the bravest men I've ever seen. I wonder what it will be like to work with him?

April 20. Today the convoy goes through. Last night, Ben-Gurion turned up at Hulda with some of his assistants. It was supposed to be a secret, but I caught a glimpse of him, and there's no mistaking that white mane of his. He greeted me with great friendliness, but I didn't get much of a chance to speak to him. He hurried off for a consultation with some of the senior Harel staff.

I'm pretty hazy about what went on — but apparently there

was some argument. Some of the participants at the meeting were opposed to taking the supply convoy up the road, arguing that it's suicidal, that the Arabs will make mincemeat of the slow armourless trucks — and their drivers. But Ben-Gurion was quite adamant: the fate of Jerusalem is at stake, and unless these supplies get through, the city may be starved into surrender, with disastrous consequences. The convoy must go through, whatever the cost!

Now the trucks are forming up; a motley collection, some quite new and powerful, others old and decrepit. Many of the vehicles belong to kibbutzim; all of them were requisitioned for this purpose, their drivers drafted along with them. The drivers, too, are a mixed lot, of all ages and types. Some of them are old hands, men who've spent years pounding the narrow, badly paved highways of Palestine, driving into town to deliver their settlements' produce, and then bring back essential supplies. They know about the Jerusalem road, they know what awaits them. Most of the trucks are quite unprotected, though Arab sniping along the highways during recent months has caused some truckers to protect their engines and gas tanks with steel plating. A few lucky ones will be sitting in armoured drivers' cabins. But most of them will be quite exposed to enemy fire, and as their heavily laden trucks labour slowly up the steep incline, they'll be sitting targets. A few show their apprehensions, their faces reflecting their fears: others try to look unperturbed.

The Palmach escort soldiers are quite well armed. After all the stories about the lack of weapons, it's a pleasant surprise to see them relatively well fitted out with small arms, including quite a number of automatics and machine guns. When I remark on how new the weapons are, I encounter knowing smiles. I've stumbled on another secret: apparently, a whole planeload of MG 42 machine guns was brought in a few days ago, on a deserted airfield. The story goes that they came from Czechoslovakia.

Harry Jaffe, one of my friends and partners a dozen years

previously in the abortive settlement attempt, is in charge of the convoy. It's good to see him again: a dozen years or so have passed since last we met, and we've both been through a lot. I know that he served as a major in the British Service Corps and was decorated for rescuing soldiers from a torpedoed troopship. But there's no time to talk now. He's bustling about with a thousand and one administrative problems to solve. Harry is responsible for having assembled these hundreds of trucks, and he's determined to do his best to see that every single one gets through to Jerusalem.

There's an air of anticipation. Last-minute preparations, shouts, men running back and forth. The truck drivers get into their seats, and from all along the line comes the noise of engines starting.

I'm travelling with some of the Harel staff officers in the back seat of a passenger car. There are three of us in the back seat, and my girth makes that something of an accomplishment. I hope we get there fast — this is very uncomfortable.

Word comes that Ben-Gurion is travelling with us in one of the leading armoured cars! This is what I had understood he intended to do, lead the way. It's as though, by his presence in that lead vehicle, he is trying to express his conviction that the convoy *must* get through, and his faith that it *can* get through. His gesture is a perfect demonstration of what Ben-Gurion's leadership means in Israel's greatest hour of peril.

Up ahead, there's some movement. Yes, this is it. We're moving. I remember the steep hillsides overlooking the road, and the hail of fire which came down when Itty blew up the gas station yesterday. That's what we're going into. . . .

We're moving at a good pace, raising a cloud of dust, which hangs above the road, marking the convoy's progress. So far, we're staying in line, with the rest of the vehicles, trying to keep a steady thirty-five miles an hour. My eyes scan the roadside, but there's no sign of anything suspicious, because we're still down in the plain. After Bab-el-Wad, when the road goes up into the hills. . . .

There's a man at the roadside, waving us down. It turns out that the brigade's administrative officer, Maccabi Mosseri, is an inexperienced driver, and he can't handle the car he's supposed to be driving. He wants someone to take over from him. I volunteer to trade places with him, glad of the chance to get out of that cramped back seat. Maccabi settles into my old place. I take the wheel of his car and the convoy rolls on again. My new car is carrying the brigade doctor, and a tough-looking young Palmachnik is seated in the back. My instructions are to take the doctor through as quickly as possible; it's assumed that he'll be needed. I promise to do my best.

We pass the police fortress at Latrun, then come to the crossroads. I fling a quick glance to my left at the ruins of the gas station. Itty did a good job—there's nothing much left of it. Now the leading vehicles are climbing the incline. The first shots break out from both sides of the road.

It's a storm, a veritable storm of bullets. Rifles crackle and clatter, accompanied by the snarl of machine guns. As soon as they got the signal to fire, the Arabs must have let go with everything they've got, and they're firing as fast as their fingers can squeeze the triggers. They can't be suffering from any shortage of ammunition, which is more than we can say.

The Palmachniks fire back. From every truck window, from behind piles of sacks, from every armoured car, the escort soldiers shoot at the hillsides. It must be well-nigh impossible to aim, perched on those swaying trucks, and trying to get a glimpse of the well-concealed Arabs. But hit or miss, the convoy is striking back, and even if it doesn't cause the Arabs many casualties, at least it encourages them to keep their heads down.

Where are they? I hardly dare take my eyes off the road for a second, but it's clear that the Arabs are well under cover. The hillsides are steep and heavily wooded with young pines. They're in there, hidden behind rocks. And we're out in the open.

I keep my foot on the accelerator, swerving as much as I can to throw them off their aim. Bullets are flying in all directions. It's like a tropical rainstorm. I can see bursts of fire splatter and splash on the tarmac in front of the car.

The Palmachnik in the back seat has stretched himself out and is now lying full-length, taking careful aim as he fires out of the window. Every now and then, he changes his position and fires out the other side. The noise around us is so deafening that I scarcely notice when he fires.

The fire is getting more intensive—and it's making itself felt. Suddenly, at the roadside, there's a truck standing immobile, its tires riddled and flat. I snatch a quick glance; no, the driver's cabin is empty—the occupants must have transferred to another vehicle. They were luckier than the driver of the next truck we come on; he was killed by the same burst of fire that set his vehicle ablaze.

Following instructions, on the slower sections of the climb I move over to the left side of the road and race through as quickly as I can. It's faster and also safer to present a moving target. To my right, the ten-tonners are crawling along in low gear, weighed down by their heavy loads. They make perfect targets.

Sometimes, the fusillade slackens for a few moments and I start to think that we've passed through the worst; but then it opens up again, heavier than ever. The Arabs have been up there for days, waiting for this opportunity, and now they're making the most of it, firing as fast as they can reload. It's a miracle that more trucks haven't been hit. Or maybe it's not such a miracle; the convoy's fire has forced the enemy to move away from the roadside. Up on those wooded slopes, their view is partly obscured. And it doesn't matter how many bullets go through the side of a truck — it'll keep going unless they hit something vital, like the engine, or the radiator, or the fuel tank. Or the driver.

To add a little excitement to the scene inside my car, the doctor has a Sten gun, and he's using it for all he's worth. Not only does he fire out of his side; every now and then, when he spots a target to the left, he leans over and lets fly right behind my ear! Once or twice, in the heat of the moment, he has sent his bullets whizzing past my face.

Another truck is hit. I swerve violently over to the left to avoid it, without slackening speed, narrowly skirting a sheer drop of thirty or forty feet on the other side. The doctor murmurs a compliment about my co-ordination; imminent death seems to sharpen my reactions—perhaps it's a by-product of sheer terror.

But now there's a hold-up, and the whole column has halted. What's happened? With the vehicles stalled, the Arabs redouble their fire, trying to make the most of the opportunity. I inch up ahead to find that several trucks have been hit and have blocked the road. One of the armoured cars comes along and tries to shove the blazing vehicles to the side of the road, but the wreckage is entangled, and the task is difficult. Some of the Palmach soldiers jump off their trucks to help, while others take up positions at the roadside, firing back at the gun posts above.

A way is cleared. The remaining trucks are revved up, the gears crash, and they squeeze past.

Up ahead, there are several sharp and fierce actions. Where the enemy gun positions above us are particularly troublesome, sections of Palmachniks, both men and women, leave the convoy and try to storm the hillsides. The attempt to storm those bullet-swept slopes is almost hopeless — a few brave youngsters trying to charge a well-entrenched enemy. Most of them die.

Another halt. The road is blocked again. Blazing trucks, bodies in the roadway. The armoured car noses the wreckage aside, assisted by Palmachniks. As the column squeezes by, I recognize a familiar figure. Harry Jaffe is directing the efforts to clear the road, and at the same time urging the truck drivers to keep moving, go on, go on! It doesn't seem to bother him in the slightest that he's standing in the centre of the road, a perfect target for the enemy. Bullets are flying in all directions as the Arabs concentrate their fire around the blockage, trying to get the convoy completely stalled. But Harry stands there calmly, helping to clear the wreckage off, until the way is completely cleared.

There's a wounded man at the roadside—I don't know if it's a Palmachnik or a driver. I slam on the brakes and we rush out and haul him inside. The fire increases all around as the Arabs try to get us while we're stationary. A few shots hit the car but there is no serious damage. I let in the clutch and race away.

Will this ever end? It seems to have been going on for hours, and the strain of just sitting there, knowing that your survival depends on the enemy's bad aim, is even worse than battle—I'd almost trade Mooshof for this. Surely this is just mass suicide.

Suddenly, I notice that the firing is only coming from behind. Around us, the firing is slackening off, apart from a few last bursts of machine-gun fire. I put on an extra spurt of speed.

We're through! We've made it!

I've had my first taste of action, in my second war. It might have been my last. Occupying my old seat in the back of the passenger car, Maccabi Mosseri was hit by a bullet and fatally wounded.

CHAPTER NINETEEN

The Bloody Route to Mount Scopus

As we drove into the beleaguered city, we were greeted by cheering crowds of Jerusalemites who flocked into the streets, overjoyed to see us. Their joy, however, was tempered by sorrow. The numerous dead and wounded in the trucks were a vivid reminder of the bitter price paid for the badly needed truckloads of food and supplies. We had broken the iron ring that was choking the city, but only at great cost.

I was only too aware of that cost since I had a wounded man lying unconscious in the back of my car, and I didn't know what to do with him. Halting near a crowd of citizens, I asked the way to a hospital. Naturally, I asked in English. "Who are you?" came a voice from the crowd. The question seemed irrelevant, but I automatically said my name. "From Canada?" the man asked. It was Dov Joseph, one of the first Canadian Jews to settle in Palestine, and at the time governor of Jerusalem. I was amazed to see him, but there was no time to stop and renew our acquaintance — I had to get to a hospital.

I shall never forget the scene which met my eyes when I got to the hospital. The place was full of young Palmachniks, boys and girls, lying on stretchers, their bodies fearfully wounded. Some of them were clearly dying. The nurses, many of them civilian volunteers, bent over them, trying to do what they could, their faces full of grief as they watched those young lives ebb away.

We had triumphed—but the price was bitter, and the success

only partial. Immediately after the convoy fought its way through, the Arabs strengthened their grip on the Bab-el-Wad road, and six weeks were to pass before it was reopened.

But we did achieve the immediate aim: the supplies we brought had saved Jerusalem from starvation. And we brought ourselves; the Harel Brigade's presence greatly strengthened the city's garrison, and gave everyone renewed hope. Reinforced and resupplied, the city would be able to hold out, until the blockade could be broken, once and for all.

In military terms, we had done the impossible. Enjoying such superior positions, and able to pour down such a weight of fire, the Arabs should have been able to halt our convoy and annihilate it completely. But we had got through, thanks to the Palmachniks and the drivers who took on the apparently hopeless task, with the guidance of the service corps men under Harry Jaffe. Many of them paid with their lives for their daring and determination. To this day, those who travel up and down the Sha'ar Hagay (Bab-el-Wad) road can see, at the roadside, the twisted metal remains of the trucks which didn't get through: a lasting reminder of the men and women who fought and died in them.

Not everyone in Jerusalem was glad to see us. In addition to the hundred thousand Jews who lived there in 1948, no fewer than sixty thousand Arabs inhabited various sectors of the city. As a result, Jerusalem was a confused checkerboard of interlocking Arab and Jewish neighbourhoods. The Old City, within the walls, was largely inhabited by Moslem and Christian Arabs, but it also contained a Jewish quarter with about two thousand inhabitants, mostly rabbinical students and elderly people, who had no direct link with any of the other Jewish neighbourhoods. Another Jewish area — Mount Scopus, the site of the Hebrew University and the Hadassah Hospital — was similarly cut off from the rest of Jewish Jerusalem by the new Arab suburb of Sheikh Jerrah.

It wasn't the Jews alone who had to contend with such problems. The Arabs, too, were in a difficult situation: although they enjoyed the backing of their brethren from the surrounding villages (and the support and protection of the British garrison), they were a minority within the city, and their neighbourhoods were isolated. This situation increased tensions: each side sat astride the other's lines of communication.

To make matters even more complicated, the British were still in Jerusalem and would only leave on May 14. They had given up almost all pretence of policing the city, withdrawing into the safety of their so-called "security zones" (the Jews called them "Bevingrads" after Britain's notoriously anti-Jewish Foreign Secretary, Ernest Bevin). The British would not allow anyone through their zones, thus further isolating and dividing the different sections of the city.

Despite their declarations of neutrality, there was no doubt of British hostility towards the Jews. Right up to the end of their presence in the city, British troops continued to hamper the operations of the Hagana, staging "police actions" in which they arrested Hagana members and confiscated their weapons. These deeds (and other darker, less official ones) provoked anti-British reprisals by the smaller Jewish underground organizations, the Etzel and Lehi groups, who fuelled animosities with their attacks on individual British soldiers and officials: furthermore, these groups also carried out attacks on Arab centres, the most notorious being their assault on the village of Dir Yassin, where many Arab civilians were killed.

The bloodshed was spreading, and it was soon to engulf the whole city. With Mount Scopus surrounded by Arab-held areas, the doctors and nurses of the Hadassah Hospital travelled in convoys between their homes and the medical centre, together with their out-patients and Hebrew University staff. On April 13, 1948—a week before our arrival in Jerusalem—one of these convoys was ambushed while passing through the Arab suburb of Sheikh Jerrah. For seven hours, merciless fire pinned them down in their cars while the Arabs set the vehicles on fire with Molotov cocktails. Seventy-five people were killed in the attack, and the victims included well-known doctors and medical specialists. The massacre occurred within a stone's-throw of a British police post; while the attack was going on, British armoured cars cruised past, turning a blind eye to the carnage.

I blamed the British for what had happened, no less than the Arabs. On the pretence of maintaining law and order, the British Army was harassing the Hagana as an "illegal armed organization". But British troops had sat idly by while helpless civilians were killed within a few paces of their positions. This example of British hypocrisy and double-dealing destroyed any remnants of fellow-feeling I felt towards them. I was a citizen of the British Commonwealth, and an officer of the Canadian Army owing allegiance to the British Crown—but I now felt no hesitation about confronting the British Army.

On April 25, just five days after we arrived in Jerusalem, Harel troops attacked Sheikh Jerrah, the Arab area where the Hadassah convoy was ambushed. The Mount Scopus supply route passed through there, and we had to make sure it was kept open. Unless the isolated Mount Scopus garrison was kept supplied and reinforced, the future Jewish state was in danger of losing the hospital and university, with their enormous practical value and symbolical importance.

Unlike other attacks in those days when weapons and ammunition were scarce, the Sheikh Jerrah operation enjoyed the unusual luxury of armoured support, in the form of an armoured car "borrowed" from the British police. At a time when standard weapons were primitive (often home-made) Sten guns, and a two-inch mortar ranked as heavy artillery, the car was a priceless acquisition. It had a two-pounder anti-tank gun, and a Beza machine gun; even though we were permitted to use no more than five hundred rounds for the Beza, and the two-pounder was allowed precisely two shells, these support weapons could be damned useful if we employed them properly.

Our objective was the Nashashibi house—a strategic position dominating the Mount Scopus route. I was given the task of arranging the fire-support plan, so I went out on reconnaissance with the armoured car's commander and found a good position from which to give supporting fire. Then, the infantry went in according to plan, we laid on the fire support as arranged, and the company occupied its objective without any casualties. A message went to Jerusalem headquarters: "The road to Mount Scopus is open!"

We were all starting to relax, feeling very pleased with ourselves, when from my look-out post in the nearby Mea Shearim quarter, I noticed a group of British officers on a nearby hill. From the gestures of the colonel who headed them, I had no difficulty in guessing what they were doing. Knowing that he was quite safe from enemy fire, the colonel was going through an observation-and-orders group. His formal, almost ritualistic movements left no room for doubt in my mind; the British were about to attack our newly captured positions in Sheikh Jerrah!

I hastily called up the battalion commander to warn him what was afoot and to make a suggestion. My inspection of the area had given me a clear idea of what ought to be done: I begged for permission to forestall the attack by storming the British police post controlling the entrance to the quarter. The post was held by one platoon, with two six-pounder anti-tank guns, two three-inch mortars, and a machine-gun section. I didn't anticipate any difficulty in taking the position; it was commanded by a British officer who was sympathetic towards us, and he probably wouldn't put up much resistance. Taking the post would give us the tactical position—and the arms—to nip the British attack in the bud.

An all-out attack on a British post, however, would have major political repercussions, so we had to contact the Jewish Agency leaders for permission. As the moments ticked away and the

British assault became more and more certain, I waited impatiently for the Agency's answer. When it came it was No — the Agency leaders strictly forbade us to do anything which the British could construe as aggression against them. This caution was understandable since, for all their covert partiality to the Arabs, the British usually refrained from large-scale, open attacks on regular Hagana units; until they showed a change in that policy, it was risky to provoke them. At least, that's the way it must have seemed at the Jewish Agency offices. But from where I was, I could see a major British attack in the offing. But now our orders were clear, and there was nothing to be done but wait for the inevitable. It came soon enough.

Against our forces, less than a full company, the British sent in a whole battalion of infantry, with tank and artillery support. Even with such odds, they didn't take the risk of a direct assault. Instead, their tanks stood off at a good distance, outside the effective range of our light weapons, and their flat-trajectory, high-velocity guns proceeded to pound the Nashashibi house where our men lay. Standing in my look-out post, I watched helplessly as their positions were smashed to bits. The onslaught was terrible, and within a short time, the Palmach company had practically ceased to exist as a combat formation.

At this precise moment, while we were wondering when the British would launch their final assault to come in and mop up, we received a message from Eliezer Kaplan, the Jewish Agency representative in Jerusalem, telling us that the British had just delivered an ultimatum, demanding that we leave Sheikh Jerrah immediately. The British justified their demand — and the violent assault which preceded it — by claiming that Sheikh Jerrah was on their evacuation route, and our occupation of the quarter endangered their forces which were soon to withdraw from Jerusalem. Their contention was ridiculous — as far as we were concerned, they couldn't leave too soon, and we weren't going to do anything to impede their departure.

By now the British could have moved right in on our force,

unresisted, since the sixty men of the force were all dead or wounded. But the British obviously had no idea of the terrible losses they'd inflicted on our men; to our surprise, they were prepared to negotiate. They feared that the Palmach troops were still capable of putting up a fight, and, rather than risk casualties to their troops, they were prepared to "talk us out" of the Nashashibi mansion.

It was a time for bluff. Three of us set off for the British camp to talk to the commander: Yitzhak Rabin; Shnurman, our liaison officer with the British forces; and myself. I was to keep silent, to conceal my identity; Shnurman would do the talking, and then consult with us in Hebrew. We would graciously declare ourselves ready to withdraw from Sheikh Jerrah — but only on condition that the British guaranteed not to turn it over to the Arabs, but to hold it as a neutral zone until their departure. (If this were done, we would gain our main objective of opening the route to Mount Scopus.) But if the British called our bluff and rejected our conditions, we'd have no alternative but to withdraw without any guarantee.

A jeep driver took the three of us through the British lines to the headquarters of the unit which had just attacked our men. We went with considerable feelings of apprehension: this battalion, an especially fierce and volatile one, had suffered recently from Jewish terrorist attacks, so that their mood was bitter, and their actions could not be predicted. Their sentries gave us very hard looks as they waved us through, and we were uncomfortably aware that we might find ourselves arrested at any moment. A pretext wasn't hard to find — we were all "illegally" armed, with pistols in the waistbands of our battledress trousers.

While I stayed outside by the jeep, trying to look unconcerned, Shnurman and Yitzhak entered the headquarters building. They soon returned, their faces white and tense. Furtively, they handed me their pistols. The two of them, with a British escort, were to drive to Sheikh Jerrah, in the jeep — unarmed. I'd have to stay behind. How was I to return to our lines? They could offer no advice. I was on my own—with three "illegal" pistols— in the very heart of a British security zone, surrounded by hostile British troops in battle gear.

I slipped their pistols into my belt, under my loose-fitting paratrooper's jacket. For once, I blessed my overweight — my ample girth made the bulges look less suspicious. That done, I looked around to see what was to be done. Now that the jeep had roared off, leaving me standing alone in the British parade ground, the soldiers passing in and out of the headquarters had been eyeing me with increasing suspicion. I knew that it wouldn't take much for them to shoot me out of hand.

As I stood there trying to look relaxed and casual, while my heart pounded in my throat, a Jewish civilian came along. I didn't know what he was doing inside the British camp, but as he glanced at me, I greeted him quietly with a Hebrew "Shalom!" I was dressed like a British soldier, with beret, battledress, and a British paratrooper's jacket; not surprisingly, he gave me rather a suspicious look. "Atta yehudi?" ("Are you a Jew?") he demanded. "Yes," I said. He still looked uncertain, but after another searching look at me, he seemed reassured. In an urgent undertone, I asked him to get me out of this predicament, and he whispered back that he would help me.

I felt as if my back had a large target painted on it as we started to stroll away from the headquarters, towards a house adjoining the security zone. For a second, I wondered if I had been betrayed; the house obviously contained large numbers of British soldiers, and I could hear the noise of a party with girls' voices, singing, and laughter. But my guide slipped me inside, smuggling me from room to room, to keep me from being detected by the British soldiers who were lurching tipsily around the house. After what seemed like an eternity—long enough to leave me in no doubt about the house's function—I was smuggled out of a side door. In the meantime, night had fallen, but fortunately the moon was up. The pale light threw an eerie glow over the rubble of no-man's-land, lighting our path. For hours, we crept through deserted houses and along alleys, flattening ourselves against doorways when we heard the clump of sentries' boots, hardly daring to breathe until the steps moved off out of earshot. Somehow, through luck and my guide's skill, we got back to our own lines without incident.

The next day, when I showed up at our brigade headquarters, I was greeted with such pleased surprise that it was clear that they had given me up for lost, or supposed me to have been arrested by the British.

I, of course, was eager to learn the outcome of the negotiations with the British. It seemed that our bluff had worked: Yitzhak and Shnurman adopted an aggressive posture, refusing to withdraw our troops without a British promise not to hand Sheikh Jerrah over to the Arabs. The British officer gave the necessary guarantee, and Yitzhak and Shnurman were escorted back to our lines, to supervise the withdrawal of our troops. They seemed quite pleased with the way the talks had gone.

Their pleasure was premature.[1] Usually, a British officer's pledge is binding. This was an exception; after giving his word of honour, that colonel proceeded to hand the quarter to the Iraqi forces, who promptly reimposed the blockade on Mount Scopus.

This action had a bitterly ironic sequel. After our battered troops left Sheikh Jerrah, Yitzhak and I went to the Jewish Agency offices to report on the action. We described the British attack, and the grievous losses the Palmach soldiers had suffered. Feeling it was necessary for the civilian leaders to understand precisely why we took such a beating, I explained in detail how the British tanks had pounded our positions, safe from any reply from us. "We didn't have any anti-tank weapons!" I concluded bitterly. "We just didn't have any damn anti-tank weapons to stop them with!" At that moment, I turned my head and found myself staring into the face of Eliezer Kaplan — the

[1]See Appendix, paragraph II.

man who, six months earlier in New York, had decided that it was more important to buy wheat than to spend one thousand dollars on PIAT anti-tank guns.

British duplicity had deprived us of our costly victory. Once again, Mount Scopus was cut off, and once again its small garrison was appealing for supplies and reinforcements. There was no question of a renewed attempt to seize Sheikh Jerrah and open the road by force; clearly, the British would drive us out again. How were we to get through to Mount Scopus? Since force had failed, it was decided to make a renewed attempt—by stealth this time. I helped to plan the operation, which was carried out just four days after our tragic Sheikh Jerrah attack; it was to be one of the riskiest undertakings I have ever experienced.

A British police camp lay a short way north of Sheikh Jerrah, which was now occupied by a force of Iraqis. The plan we adopted required one of Harel's battalions to slip through, under cover of darkness, between the camp and Sheikh Jerrah. Our only chance of success was to remain undetected; if our presence were suspected, we'd be caught between the British and the Iraqis — where our light arms and exposed position would put us in danger of total annihilation. Unless we could move a whole battalion in complete silence, we'd face disaster.

The force chosen for this operation was Menahem Rossak's battalion, which included a large number of new recruits. These troops were young and untrained; there could be no doubt about their fighting spirit, but they lacked discipline, and it proved almost impossible to keep them quiet; in fact, before leaving, we had great difficulty in silencing their high-spirited singing — which did not seem a good omen to me.

But I underestimated them. As soon as we neared the critical area, all talking ceased. Even so, as the long column marched along, it made quite a considerable amount of noise. We were traversing steep hillsides, devoid of grass or vegetation; the rock surface was hard and covered with loose stones and shale. In addition to their personal equipment, the soldiers were weighted down with supplies for Mount Scopus. Although they were wearing crepe-soled shoes to muffle their footsteps, it was almost impossible for heavy-laden men to avoid stumbling in the dark, or accidentally kicking a stone. In the cool night air, the slightest sound carried a long way; to our nervous ears, every clattering pebble sounded like an avalanche.

Both the British and the Iraqis were clearly restless and suspicious. Star shells and searchlights began to probe the darkness, and it seemed almost inevitable that they'd detect us. If that happened, the positions on both sides of us would open fire, and I knew that we'd be cut to ribbons. It seemed I wasn't the only one with that thought in his mind. Every time a star shell lit the sky, the whole column froze into immobility, with every single soldier standing stock still, motionless as a statue. It was an impressive display of natural discipline and understanding. Then, as the flare faded, we marched on.

After heart-stopping hours of this, we reached the safety of the Imperial War Cemetery, just north of the Hadassah Hospital. The tension relaxed. We had made it!

This was only one of the many amazing feats performed by Menahem's battalion, who could always be relied upon to do the impossible. By successfully taking their battalion through the enemy lines, and bringing it safely to Mount Scopus, Menahem and his second-in-command, Iska, had performed a military feat of the highest order, without firing a single shot!

The Mount Scopus garrison was immensely relieved to see us, and overjoyed to get the food and ammunition we had brought. But, of course, such a major operation was mounted with more in mind than just bringing them flour and bullets. Mount Scopus is one of a line of hills to the east of the Old City, and the rest of these strategic heights were in Arab hands. Menahem's battalion had been sent to Mount Scopus with the aim of thrusting southwards, to seize control of the rest of the ridge. The first objective was Augusta Victoria Hospital, which borders on the Hebrew University campus. Here the Arabs had a powerful vantage point which overlooked the Old City, and which also provided an ideal site for artillery attack on the Jewish New City. In addition to denying the enemy this strategic point, taking it would give us control of the road from Jericho, the Arabs' only secure route for supplies and reinforcements.

As soon as we reached Mount Scopus, we began preparing for the attack. We had completed all the necessary preparations, and our men were beginning to take up assault positions, when an unexpected development threatened the whole operation. Somehow or other, the commander of the British forces in Jerusalem had got wind of what was up. Two hours before the time scheduled for the assault he phoned through to the university and warned us that if we attacked from Mount Scopus, he would throw in the full weight of his troops, backed by their heavy armament, with the aim of annihilating our forces.

The threat was not to be taken lightly, and caused great consternation to Menahem, whose experience of the British attack on Sheikh Jerrah was still horrifyingly fresh. In view of the standing order to avoid clashing with the British, he felt that we should postpone our attack, and ask the Jewish Agency for new instructions. There was no doubt in my mind that if we consulted the Agency, we'd be ordered to cancel the assault.

My own dilemma was no less severe than Menahem's, since I was the senior brigade officer present, and shared responsibility for the operation. After witnessing the shelling of our positions at Sheikh Jerrah, I knew the risks involved in disregarding the British warning. But I also knew how enormously important it would be for the defence of Jerusalem if we could take the Augusta Victoria area now, before Arab regular armies were committed to the battle. Furthermore, I doubted the determination of the British commander, and questioned whether he would be prepared to risk heavy casualties among his men only a few days before their planned withdrawal.

This time, our defensive disposition was incomparably better —and the British problem in attacking us far harder—than in Sheikh Jerrah. Mount Scopus is a long ridge, several thousand yards in length, and our positions were spread out, offering much less of a target than the single house our men occupied in Sheikh Jerrah. Even more important, there was only one road leading up from Jerusalem, and it traversed a boulder-strewn slope which was impassable for tanks or other vehicles. With the British forced to keep to that roadway, it would not be too hard to block their way.

I persuaded Menahem to go ahead with the attack, as planned.

"What about the British?" he asked, still uncertain.

"The British?" I said grandly, with an air of complete certainty. "Leave them to me!" I undertook to take command of the troops protecting our rear, defending the assault against any possible British intervention. At the same time, I also accepted full responsibility towards the Jewish Agency.

Menahem and his men went on with their preparations. Just before zero hour, I left the crew that was manning our Davidka mortar and headed for the university library, where I phoned to the neighbouring British headquarters. When an officer replied, I informed him briefly that we were opening fire in precisely one minute. "If you want to," I added, "you can come up here. But I promise you that none of your men or vehicles will get back!" Without waiting for his reply, I hung up. The attack could go ahead.

The Augusta Victoria building was on the other side of a deep ravine. As the sun set, our troops had slipped down silently into their assault positions at the foot of the ravine; from here, they would have to run up and storm the enemy defences. Hampered as we were by a chronic shortage of ammunition, the fire plan prepared for our support weapons was highly economical and far from complex. The "softening-up" (beloved of Field Marshal Montgomery) would consist of a single round from our Davidka mortar, which would also serve as the signal for the infantry to attack. We were depending on surprise, darkness, and the terrifying blast of the Davidka bomb.

The Davidka was one of the wonders of the 1948 war. It was a very heavy mortar, turned out in Hagana workshops, which fired an exceptionally heavy shell. Although its range was short and it did not always cause any real damage, it made an enormously loud explosion, and the psychological effect on the Arabs was incalculable. Unfortunately, the Davidka was made clandestinely, in primitive workshops, and its reliability left a lot to be desired.

At zero hour, the order was given: "Fire!" There was a deafening roar from the Davidka's position. After a few seconds, the smoke cleared, revealing the full extent of the disaster: the contraption had blown up on firing, killing or wounding a large number of our troops. The surviving soldiers were too few to carry on the attack, and it had to be abandoned.

The Mount Scopus operation had already attained its main objective: strengthening the garrison and bringing much needed supplies. But we were disappointed by our failure to take Augusta Victoria, which would have enabled us to cut the vital Jericho supply route. To console ourselves, we sent a raiding party to attack the road. The raid was commanded by Uri (formerly of the Palmach's highly secret "German Platoon", which consisted of German-born Jews who trained in German uniforms with German weapons until they could successfully masquerade as Wehrmacht soldiers for operations behind the German lines). The raid did not require Uri to display his command of German, but it did give him a chance to display his skills as demolition expert: by blowing up a series of culverts, he was able to make the Jericho road temporarily unusable.

The abortive Augusta Victoria attack deserves two further comments. First, until two minutes before the assault, I was with the Davidka crew. Shortly after I left them to telephone the British, the mortar blew up, wiping out the entire mortar crew. If I had not been commanding the covering force, I would have been beside the mortar. My phone call also proved to be fateful in a less personal way; the British troops never showed up.

Two weeks later, the British left Palestine. I wasn't sorry to see them go.

CHAPTER TWENTY

New Problems, Old Solutions

After successfully clearing the route to Mount Scopus, we moved back to our old lines in the city. Instead of staying there, however, we soon moved our base back to Ma'aleh Hahamisha, a suburban area on the western side of the city, high on the hills overlooking the kibbutz of Kiryat Anavim and the Tel Aviv road.

I was glad to be near that road again. Ever since we had fought our way along it to get into the city, I had been convinced that the key to our holding Jerusalem—and apart from the one hundred thousand Jews whose lives were on the block, the symbolic value of holding Jerusalem was incalculable—lay in somehow breaking the stranglehold that was cutting us off from Tel Aviv, and breaking it permanently. From our arrival in Jerusalem, I had started to argue that we should be clearing the Tel Aviv road, but it seemed a crazy idea to almost all of my colleagues, who argued that the business of defending the city required every single man and woman we had. I couldn't argue against the fact that we were thinly stretched, but I continued to press for a break-out.

That was for the future. In the meantime, we were faced with more immediate problems. Ma'aleh Hahamisha was in many ways an excellent base for our Harel Brigade and the hospitality of the local people was astoundingly generous; many of them cut down on their already meagre daily rations to ensure that we were well fed. But its major drawback as a base was the fact that it was overlooked by a radar station on a nearby hilltop. It was bad enough when the British occupied it; when, however, a few days before pulling out, they handed the station over to the Legion, the situation called for immediate action. That same day, soldiers of Yosefele Tabenkin's battalion stormed the station, driving the Legionnaires out of what seemed a very strong position. It was a considerable feat of arms, and a damned important capture.

I was so convinced of the radar station's strategic importance that I strongly recommended that the hilltop be held in force, with a Palmach platoon on the site to stiffen the defence. But we were so short of assault troops that there could be no question of drawing off any Palmach units for defensive work, and arrangements were made for the defence to be taken over by militia men from Jerusalem. The city's command was, perhaps understandably, reluctant to spare anyone and the detachment it finally sent, under protest, consisted of inexperienced troops.

Since I was convinced that the Legion would try to recapture this key post, the assignment of raw troops for its defence displeased me and I said so, rather loudly, to everyone who would listen. Yitzhak Rabin, remembering the woeful accuracy of my predictions about how the Jewish Etzion settlements to the east would be overrun unless they changed their defensive tactics, asked me to lay out a new defensive plan for the hilltop and instruct the garrison on how to defend their positions.

The German High Command would have approved of my plan, which is hardly surprising, since it was plagiarized directly from the masterly German defensive tactics I had encountered, often painfully, in Europe. The plan required our defenders to leave the apparent safety of the neat trenches in the defensive posts around the station (which were, in fact, highly vulnerable because they were both visible and known intimately to the enemy, who had occupied them) and dig in secretly in concealed positions in the surrounding hills, leaving their old posts as dummy defences. I knew that these tactics would neutralize the Legion's advantage in heavy long-range weapons. After the enemy's flat-trajectory shells had knocked hell out of our dummy defences, our men could pop up, unexpected and unharmed, to fight off the armoured and infantry attacks that would follow. My plan also called for a unit of Harel to be held ready to counter-attack.

It was a nice plan, but it didn't work. First, our shortage of troops meant that we could not spare any Harel men to come to the defenders' assistance when they were attacked. Secondly, only confident, well-trained men have the courage to leave neatly prepared, solid trenches to go out in small lonely units into possibly hostile countryside. So the militia men happily disregarded my instructions, stayed in the trenches, and were wiped out by the accurate bombardment which preceded the Legion's successful attack. Within minutes, the Arabs were in full control of the radar-station hilltop once again.

With the Legion's guns looking down our throats, the situation was uncomfortable, to say the least, and the enemy soon tried to exploit their advantage. While their twenty-five-pounders and other weapons gave covering fire from the hilltops, their armoured cars now advanced on Ma'aleh Hahamisha, firing at our positions as they came. I remember the feeling of helplessness that gripped me as we fired everything we had at them — I knew that we had no armour-piercing weapons. The cars came on and on, our bullets bouncing off them until it seemed certain that we were going to be overrun. At this point, heroism intervened. In full view of the enemy, some of the troops of Yosefele's battalion ran across open ground to clamber up a steep hillside. Under heavy fire every second, they crossed the exposed hillside until they were able to drop Molotov cocktails on the armoured cars. Two of the cars blew up, the rest retired behind the radar station, and we lived to fight again.

Although there were no further attacks on our positions, the

Legion remained in possession of the radar station, a constant threat to our position—and a constant reminder to me of one of our major problems, indiscipline. We had lost our chance of holding that station because my orders to the militia men had been totally ignored. We were trying to fight a war against heavily armed professionals using poorly armed recruits, and, as an experienced old infantryman, I knew that such a system would not work, until we ourselves became professional. As a reluctant soldier it went against my grain, but I knew that an army at war needs tight organization and iron discipline.

The trouble was that the make-shift system had worked in the past. All of our fighting experience had been acquired over many years of small-scale clashes with Arab irregulars. Now that we were facing an all-out war against regular military formations, it was clear to me that an entirely new form of organization and a new military doctrine would be necessary.

A case in point was the Palmach itself. From the organization's secret inception under the noses of the British, these young people had been formed into small platoons which were usually quartered in kibbutzim. Deeply influenced by the kibbutzim where they lived and worked, they placed great stress on their egalitarian life-style. Their discipline was based on equality, loyalty, and close friendship between all ranks. The soldiers bore no insignia or badges of rank, both as a matter of principle and also because badges could serve no useful purpose. Officers and NCOs were well-known personally to their small units; they enjoyed considerable personal respect, and their orders were not questioned, even without the backing of formal military discipline.

As a result, they functioned extremely well in actions and operations conducted by small units. I had many occasions to observe the courage and self-sacrifice — and the irrepressible gaiety — which these young and dedicated soldiers brought to their fighting. They went into battle singing, buoyed up by an *esprit de corps* that I have never seen equalled.

So far, so good. But the situation changed almost overnight

with the formation of the Harel Brigade. Strangers were thrown together; reinforcements were attached to existing platoons; platoons were integrated into companies and battalions, with other outfits which were unknown to them. Under such circumstances, it was impossible to retain the Palmach tradition of mutual recognition and informal understanding. When hundreds of total strangers—most of them civilians with only a little, small-scale military training—were hurriedly thrown together and expected to go into battle immediately in cohesive military formations, regular military organization and discipline became essential.

This became obvious in some of the brigade's earliest engagements, when officers found that their commands were not obeyed because the Palmachniks didn't know that the orders were coming from an officer—and there were no rank insignia to aid recognition. The outcome was a costly confusion, intolerable under combat conditions since it cost lives.

A case in point: one of the brigade's first actions, the attack on Nebi Samwil, ended in disaster, with the loss of almost the entire attacking force. The reason was simple — although the assault plan called for an attack under cover of darkness, the officer in command failed to obey orders, and mounted the attack at dawn. In the dawn light his troops were easy pickings for the defenders, and they were rolled back with heavy losses. Nabi Samwil, on one of the highest hills in the Jerusalem area, remained in Arab hands, a constant threat to our communications. This failure highlighted another weakness: the lack of discipline within the chain of command.

I began to press for the needed changes, but it was not an easy task; Harel's officers and soldiers were kept so busy with one engagement after another that attempting any reorganization would have been like trying to shear a running sheep. Every day we were fighting for sheer physical survival.

Naturally, I wasn't the only one aware of the need for changes. Most of the Harel officers knew they were necessary, and my proposals were usually well received. When I proposed the introduction of rank insignia, the idea was quite welcome to some of the senior officers — to Yitzhak Rabin (who smilingly agreed, "If you can talk them into it") and to Menahem Rossak, the commander of one of the battalions. But there was strenuous opposition from Itty, the brigade's chief of operations, who had great influence on Yosefele Tabenkin, the commander of the other battalion. As this was regarded as a matter of principle — opposition to badges of rank was part of the Palmach's holy of holies — it was difficult to get the idea adopted immediately. But in time the idea began to catch on; first, corporals and sergeants started to wear insignia, and then, in a moving gesture of support, Menahem publicly identified himself with my policy by wearing the badges of his rank, the first high-ranking officer to do so.

It was easier to get action on less symbolic, more practical issues. One of the problems bedevilling Harel was organizing its supplies and administration. This, too, was a problem of scale. When the usual formation was a platoon, which was permanently based in some kibbutz, logistics were fairly simple — either the supplies were available, or they weren't. It was an entirely different proposition with the brigade stationed in or around Jerusalem, lacking a proper logistic base, especially when shortages plagued all the inhabitants of the beleaguered city — soldiers as well as civilians. As the Palmach lacked any formal military supply organization, one had to be created from scratch. How was this to be done?

It struck me that we had one resource of great potential value which we had not tapped. Everyone in our convoy was now trapped in Jerusalem, including Jaffe and his helpers, the men who had helped him organize the supplies and requisition the trucks. Like Harry, these Palestinian Jews had served in the British supply corps in the Western Desert, where they had acquired extensive knowledge and experience in organizing logistics. They were now standing idle — why shouldn't we press

them into service? I put the idea to Yitzhak, who presented it to
the other senior officers. The idea was received somewhat dubiously, but the difficulties were so enormous, and the advantages
of the plan so obvious, that it was agreed. I consulted Harry
Jaffe, who agreed with the idea, lending his second-in-
command, Shmorak, to serve as the brigade's deputy adjutant
and quartermaster general. With him came a group of officers
and NCOs, who provided the brigade with the organizational
structure and services it lacked. They did their work with great
vigour and enthusiasm, and it wasn't long before their efforts
had an impact on the whole brigade, which began to function
much more efficiently.

When I first joined the brigade as a newcomer, I was an
unknown, and there was no automatic acceptance of my views.
Nor could I impose my opinions by formal authority, since I had
none. Even Yitzhak, with the formal authority of brigade commander, often encountered difficulty in getting his orders
obeyed by some of his more independent-minded subordinates!

But right from the start, my relationships with most of the
Palmachniks were of the best. Almost everyone offered me a
warm welcome, and was clearly pleased and grateful to find that
I, like other volunteers from abroad, had come from afar, of my
own free will, to help defend the Jewish state. In gaining their
acceptance, and in time their acceptance of my opinions and
proposals, I was undoubtedly helped by my previous experience
of living and working in Palestine, and by my temperamental
affinity with the proud, outspoken Sabras.

When Hagana and Palmach activities were still largely clandestine, my appearance at a staff meeting would be explained
with the words: "Hu mi'shelanu!" ("He's one of ours!"). I could
ask for no greater honour....

But now I meant to use my influence to the full, to persuade
my colleagues that we had to break out of Jerusalem, to establish
once again our link with Tel Aviv. If my job of persuasion was a

tough one, it was not because everybody was comfortably settled and selfishly reluctant to move. Far from it; throughout the siege of Jerusalem we soldiers were living and fighting under terrible conditions. We were all ill-clad in an assortment of hand-me-down uniforms mixed with civilian outfits which were less than ideal for the hot days and cold nights we encountered. Food was always scarce and growing noticeably scarcer, although the city's population, soldier and civilian alike, had been on short rations for months. The same applied to water, which had been strictly rationed by Jerusalem's governor, Dov Joseph, ever since water supplies were cut off by the Legion's occupation of the Latrun pumping station. From that point the city had to rely on rainwater collected in very ancient cisterns, which had played the same part many times before in the other sieges Jerusalem had endured in the course of its long and painful history. As a result, there was barely enough water for drinking, and washing was out of the question.

Weeks passed without my getting a chance to change my underwear. On one occasion, when I heard of a place where there was enough water for a wash, I cheerfully walked several miles through the hills for the luxury of a thorough wash. It was one of the most pleasant moments in my service in Jerusalem; going around, under combat conditions, with the dirt literally caked on us in layers, made our lives even more miserable and gave new meaning to the term "offensive troops". There were times when I would gladly have exchanged those parched, dusty conditions for the grey, gloomy wetness of the Breskens pocket, where water was available in limitless quantities.

Our shortages and hardships were, of course, gallantly shared by the city's civilian population. In addition, they shared our military hazards; the Arab snipers, who seemed to be able to keep up a constant fire into the Jewish areas of the city, did not restrict their attentions to Jews in uniform. Later, when the regular Arab armies entered the battle, this continual sniping was increased and was supplemented by almost unceasing shelling, day and night, which took a regular toll of soldiers and civilians alike.

Despite it all, the people of Jerusalem remained undaunted; their bravery under hardship and danger was undoubtedly one of the chief factors in enabling the city to withstand the siege. But bravery alone, whether of soldiers or civilians, was not enough to gain victory in the battle for Jerusalem. We were short of arms and ammunition and military supplies of all kinds. At a time when Arab artillery fire was growing steadily heavier and more destructive, we were almost powerless to fight back; we were desperately short of artillery and mortars, and our ammunition stocks were tiny. As the Arabs shelled us, unmolested, I became more and more determined to break out to Tel Aviv for fresh supplies, and for mortars with which we could hit back at them.

I knew, of course, that the Jerusalem command had its hands full, enemy pressure was growing, and worse was yet in store: with Iraq and Egypt openly joining the war, we would soon be facing additional regular formations. The battle would be a bitter one, and the Jerusalem command was mainly concerned with seizing control of the city's strongpoints, to strengthen our defences for the impending confrontation; our resources, men and weapons, were fully stretched.

Nevertheless, I formally proposed that the forces in Jerusalem —specifically, the Harel Brigade—take on the task of reopening the supply route from the coast.

As I expected, the Jerusalem command rejected my proposal out of hand. They were convinced that the route would be cleared by forces fighting their way through from Tel Aviv. But I strongly advised them not to put their trust in salvation from the outside: it was Jerusalem which was feeling the pressures of blockade, not Tel Aviv! Whether we liked it or not, it was up to us. There was no point in repelling the Legion's attacks on Jerusalem, only to have the city starved into surrender, or forced to lay down its arms when the bullets ran out, which was a real possibility.

In Harel my idea was given a mixed reception. Yitzak Rabin approved of the whole idea, with the enthusiastic support of Menahem Rossak. But there was fierce opposition from Itty and Yosefele, who felt that clearing the road wasn't "our baby". This was not the first disagreement which divided the Harel command along these lines.

Menahem, with whom I had a close rapport, tended to support my suggestions, as his defiance of hallowed Palmach tradition by wearing badges of rank showed. At the other end of the scale was Itty, who disliked me and all I stood for; on one occasion when I explained how I was planning an operation with the aid of large-scale maps, he remarked acidly: "In the Palmach, we have to see the ground — we don't do our planning from *maps!*" As my early encounter with him at the gas station had shown, he was extremely brave and seemed to distrust the planning and preparation that I advocated as somehow cowardly. And closely allied with Itty came Yosefele Tabenkin, with whom I frequently disagreed but always enjoyed a friendly relationship. Yosefele, too, was a traditional Palmach officer—a very dashing one — and was deeply suspicious of my proposed innovations, which were intended to create the tight organization necessary for large-scale operations. So, with Itty (who planned most of his battalion's operations, as I did for Menahem's), he opposed most of my ideas, including my plan for a break-out.

There were seemingly unending discussions of the plan, and my impatience with the delay was not helped by the fact that every time we travelled to meet with the Jerusalem command we came under sniper fire. Nevertheless, the Jerusalem command remained opposed, as did Itty. The idea gradually gained ground, with the support of Yitzhak, but it was finally adopted as the result of "outside intervention", literally from out of the blue. Jerusalem was cut off from road communications with the outside world, but there was still one way of access: by air. Every day a tiny Auster plane would brave the flight from Tel Aviv to land on a rough air-strip, carrying mail and important visitors, including Ben-Gurion, who made several visits to the beleaguered city. On several of his visits, I was invited to meet him; we had grown fast friends, and he seemed to set great store by my recommendations—particularly as they were backed by Yitzhak Rabin. Ben-Gurion had gone along with my suggestions for reorganizing the brigade on conventional lines, and he now lent his strong support to the idea of Harel clearing the road to Tel Aviv. That settled it. We were going to give it a try.

CHAPTER TWENTY-ONE

Break-Out

I was formally put in charge of planning the break-out. Working at top pace (with the aid of the large-scale maps that Itty so despised), I soon came up with a detailed plan for an assault on all of the Arab strongholds between Jerusalem and Bab-el-Wad, roughly halfway to Tel Aviv. My plan (later called Operation Maccabi in honour of Maccabi Mosseri, who had been fatally wounded after exchanging places with me in the convoy to Jerusalem) called for a phased attack, which would clear first the northern, and then the southern, side of the road, down to the coastal plain.

Since Menahem showed the greatest enthusiasm for the whole operation, his battalion was "rewarded" with the most difficult task. The strongholds on the hills to the north were lightly held by Arab irregulars; these Arabs, however, enjoyed the powerful support of the Arab Legion units stationed in the Latrun area. Menahem's men were ordered to seize these hilltop strongholds, and secure them against the inevitable counter-attack by the Legion.

The Arab force entrenched on the hills was not much of an obstacle. The worst enemy was the terrain, the steep and precipitous boulder-strewn hills which had proved such a formidable obstacle when we brought the convoy up the road from the coast.

On May 10 we began the operation. As darkness fell, the

battalion set off from our advanced headquarters at Abu Ghosh. The force was personally led by Menahem's deputy, Iska, who set a fine example in scrambling nimbly up and down the stony hillsides. It was exhausting terrain, and the darkness did not make movement any easier. But in one night's hard slugging, the battalion cleared out one enemy stronghold after another over an eight-mile stretch, until all the hills overlooking the road from its northern side were in our hands, as far as Bab-el-Wad.

The first part of the operation was a brilliant success, but Menahem's battalion was not given much time to rest on its laurels. The routed Arab irregulars hurried to Latrun, to appeal to the Arab Legion for help, and the Legion obliged. Its artillery soon ranged in on the hillsides, directing a heavy barrage at the Palmach troops, catching them in the open, since the rocky terrain made trench-digging impossible. Under cover of the shelling, the Legion then launched infantry attacks to dislodge our men, who took cover from the shell-fire behind rocks and boulders, at the same time trying to fight off the attackers swarming up the hill towards them. Some of our troops were forced to withdraw, but their company commanders quickly reorganized them for a counter-attack, and they regained their positions. The battle swayed back and forth for hours.

The Legion's units enjoyed the advantage of superior weapons, and unlimited ammunition, as well as the support of a considerable number of local Arab villagers. Our men, however, were now battle-hardened, and they fought with the courage of those who have nothing to lose. They knew that surrender was out of the question — we were all aware of the lingering death that awaited any Jew captured by Arab irregulars—and that the only line of retreat was back to Jerusalem, which was being slowly squeezed to death by the surrounding armies. So for hour after hour they held their positions, beating off attack after attack, until the Arabs withdrew.

This battle was one of Menahem's battalion's finest hours. In taking control of the northern hilltops, they had gained the operation's principal objective. Their contribution fully justified their battalion's official name: The Sha'ar Hagay Battalion, since Sha'ar Hagay is the Hebrew name of Bab-el-Wad.

That battle, like all battles, was won by the guts of the individual infantrymen; but credit for our success should also go to the brigade's intelligence officer, Z'rubavel, who gave us precise information about enemy positions and strength. He was a tower of strength in all the brigade's operations, often going out in person to collect the vital information without which we would have been working in the dark. Much of his work was done from the air, in a tiny Auster reconnaissance plane. I remember one occasion when he was shot down. Miraculously, he survived the crash and came limping back to brigade headquarters, heavily bandaged but undaunted. That very night he was out again on another reconnaissance, on foot in no-man's-land.

We were now in control of the northern side of the road, a vital step towards breaking the blockade. We gained another important advantage when our men took over the pumping station on the southern side of the road. This strong structure, which the British had built along the lines of a fortress, stood just off the main road. It was an important tactical position, which we took the moment we saw the British march off, as part of their general withdrawal to the coast. Three days later on May 15 they left Palestine for ever. We were glad to see them go, but in these vital intervening days we had other things on our mind.

Despite the success of the first phase of our attack, no supply convoy could get through with the Arabs still dominating the hills to the south of the road. To break this hold, we launched the second phase of the operation: the capture of Beit Mahsir, an Arab village with a population of about four thousand, situated in the hills just over two miles southeast of Bab-el-Wad. Although it did not overlook the road itself, Beit Mahsir had served as a base for most of the attacks on our convoys. Until we

25. "Jock" Spragge, commanding officer of the Queen's Own during the Normandy campaign.

26. "Monty" — an inspiring general.

27. Clearing the Scheldt, the Queen's Own faced a bleak, watery terrain that was an infantryman's hell.

28. Amphibious vehicles soon proved to be invaluable.

29. Flame-throwers proved to be terrifyingly effective at close range.

30. On dry land, for once.

31. A cake presented to B.D.'s company, the liberators of the Dutch town of Kuinre.

32. Major Dunkelman (centre) at the head of D Company in the Utrecht Victory Parade.

33. Queen's Own men training for the winter attack on the Rhineland. The white camouflage suits proved to be useless when the Germans flooded the attack area.

34. Searching for mines in the Hochwald — not everyone succeeded in avoiding them.

35. Canadians slogging forward into Germany — and to victory.

36. Another war, another country, another band of comrades-in-arms. These are typical members of the Palmach (the élite of the Israeli Army) en route to reinforce the defenders of Jerusalem in 1948.

37. B.D. in Israel, 1948.

dislodged the enemy from there, the road could not be re-opened.

Our plan called for a surprise night attack by Yosefele's battalion. Yosefele, of course, had always been opposed to the entire operation. Even though that issue should have been resolved by the official decision that Harel was opening the road (at least to Bab-el-Wad) Yosefele, under Itty's influence, remained reserved and critical, even when given direct orders by Yitzhak Rabin, his brigade commander. Yosefele finally shelved his objections to the plan in general and to his particular role in it, but he did so with such bad grace that Yitzhak thought it advisable for someone to keep an eye on him, and I was ordered to join Yosefele's headquarters for the attack on Beit Mahsir.

The attack was planned as a surprise operation, which was to be conducted under cover of darkness. The troops were to proceed by bus to the start line, at Abu Ghosh, in territory under our control. From there they were to advance, as quietly as possible, down the road below Beit Mahsir, and to take the village by surprise.

We set out, as planned. The buses passed Abu Ghosh, and headed for the place chosen as the start line. But when we got there, I was horrified to find that we weren't stopping to allow the troops to de-bus stealthily in safety, as I had planned. Instead, the force blundered noisily down the road, without any attempt at quiet or concealment. Suddenly, I had the feeling of having been through all this before: my mind flashed back to Normandy, four years earlier, when I had watched the tanks of the Hussars charge through the start line, with the hapless soldiers of our D Company clinging on behind. . . .

I was furious — and helpless. There was nothing I could do, since I was riding in the signal truck, behind Yosefele's vehicle, and there was no way I could contact him. The convoy clattered blithely on its way, for all the world as though we were on an outing, and not heading straight towards a powerful enemy defensive position! There could only be one outcome to this kind of foolhardiness. Within a few moments, the buses came under fire. At first, the enemy fire was light, but it soon turned into a heavy fusillade. Clearly, the sound of our approach had warned the Arabs, who were now hurrying out in increasing numbers to take up firing positions. Obviously, we could have taken the village with next to no opposition if we had adhered to the original plan and swooped silently down to take the defenders by surprise. Instead, our plans had been thrown right out of joint, and we had landed in a very sticky position.

While the Arab fire grew progressively stronger, our men jumped out of the buses and took up firing positions at the side of the road. Claiming that it was impossible to reorganize the unit in the darkness, Yosefele ordered a withdrawal, but this proved to be no easy matter. The buses were in a deep valley, sandwiched between the hills. Tongues of flame spat at us out of the darkness above as the enemy poured fire down on us. Before our drivers could laboriously turn the buses around, the fire from above took a severe toll of our force. Within a short time, our signals vehicle was full of wounded.

In the end, we managed to extricate ourselves, but the price we paid was high. Worst of all, we had suffered casualties to no purpose; we had not attained our objective. Beit Mahsir remained in Arab hands. What should have been a simple and successful operation ended up as a serious setback. Crestfallen, we got back to Abu Ghosh, where Yitzhak had set up advanced brigade headquarters. When I told him what had occurred, he shook his head and said: "I was afraid something like this would happen."

We talked over the whole situation, discussing what was to be done now. There was no question of giving up: unless we took Beit Mahsir, the road would remain closed, and no supplies could be got through to Jerusalem. Although the enemy would now be on guard against any future attack, I still adhered to the view that it wouldn't be hard to take the village if we made a determined effort. I proposed an additional attack, and Yitzhak agreed.

The plan for the second attack depended mainly on surprise, and the use of heavy covering fire from a Davidka mortar. I felt that under such conditions the village could be taken by a relatively small body of disciplined men sticking strictly to the assault plan. Some of the other officers, however, were dubious about the feasibility of crossing such difficult terrain, at night, with the heavy Davidka. They were sure that the Davidka's crew would be detected and ambushed on the way. To meet these objections, I consulted Amos Horev.

Amos Horev had a deceptively cherubic appearance. He was young and small and slow-moving, with blue eyes and curly hair —and behind that façade lurked a man of relentless energy, in war a fearless and intelligent soldier, very receptive to new ideas and tactics. I always found it a pleasure to work with Amos, and, as usual, on this occasion he did not disappoint me. After making a reconnaissance of the area, he reported back that it would be possible to bring a heavy mortar close to the walls of Beit Mahsir, under cover of darkness. If he were given twenty men to carry a Davidka and its bombs, he would undertake to get them to that position, where they would provide the necessary close-range supporting fire. With that, he overcame most of the objections to the plan, although Yosefele and Itty were still noticeably lacking in enthusiasm for the operation. Because of the manner in which the first attack had miscarried, their objections did not carry much weight.

This time, everything went off precisely according to plan. Amos slipped through the hills with twenty men and the Davidka, and had it in position on time. Before first light, the Davidka opened up on the village, making the usual ear-splitting bang, and the assault force went in. The Davidka had done its morale-shattering work well; our troops met practically no opposition. Thanks to Amos Horev's boldness and initiative, the attack was an unqualified success.

Shortly afterwards, Menahem's battalion, which was protecting the flanks of Amos's assault force, found itself heavily engaged by a large Arab force counter-attacking with close-artillery support. Some of our men were driven from their positions, but they counter-attacked in their turn, and drove the Arab reinforcements back.

With the repulse of that counter-attack, Beit Mahsir was firmly in our hands, which meant that we now had complete control over the road from Jerusalem as far as Bab-el-Wad. Although it had been blocked with heavy rocks and boulders, and even dug up in a number of places, it did not take us long to repair the road and render it fit for service once more.

We had cleared the road from Jerusalem to Bab-el-Wad, which was the aim of our operation; but the route from Tel Aviv was still blocked. A short way to the west of Bab-el-Wad the Arab Legion occupied the fortress of Latrun, and thus controlled another vital section of the road. It was a curious reversal: previously, we had been able to get through the coastal plain, while the hilly portion of the road was barred to our convoys. Now, the hilly section was secure, but the stretch at the edge of the coastal plain was under enemy control.

We were convinced that the continuation of the route to Tel Aviv—from Bab-el-Wad westwards—would be cleared by other forces, opening the way for supply convoys from the coast. We were encouraged in this belief when some members of the Givati Brigade (some of my Canadian volunteers among them) slipped through from the west on foot carrying supplies. They told us that their brigade was, indeed, trying to fight its way eastward to us, but was being held up, with heavy losses, at Latrun. Despite repeated attempts to take it, the fortress continued in the hands of the Legion, effectively blocking the road.

Time was passing. Night after night I waited, nerves jangling, at the appointed crossroads for a sign of the Givati men from the west. Nobody appeared. Our patrols towards the west failed to link up with the Givati forces. As for a convoy, not a sign! Meanwhile, in Jerusalem, the situation was worsening. Now that the British had left, the other Arab nations had formally joined the group pressing in on us. The enemy attacks were growing stronger, while our men lacked the arms and ammunition to hold out much longer. We had to find a way of getting the supplies through. There was no prospect of a quick conquest of Latrun by the Givati Brigade. We had no news from army headquarters; despite nightly struggles with the signals set, Yitzhak couldn't establish radio contact with Tel Aviv.

In these desperate circumstances, I proposed a new approach: we should try to open up a new road cross-country, by-passing Latrun. I pressed Yitzhak to authorize a reconnaissance probe to the west to seek out such a route. At first, the idea was regarded dubiously; but as the Jerusalem situation grew graver and no other solution appeared to be in sight, I was granted permission to plan the operation.

Clearly, the smaller the patrol, the better its chances of success. I asked for Amos Horev to be put in command of the party. I would go along, with two or three others: that was the entire "force". We would drive in an armoured car, followed by a light four-wheel-drive truck, to give us a "lifeboat" if we ran into trouble; since we would be driving through enemy territory, our chances of running into trouble seemed pretty high. When, or perhaps if, we got through to Tel Aviv, the reconnaissance route would be improved, and made ready for heavily laden vehicles.

At the last moment, our patrol was joined by Yosefele. That was typical; he had opposed this whole operation from the start, but he was such a brave and daring soldier that when he heard of the reconnaissance — a risky undertaking, as he knew — he absolutely insisted on taking part. We were also joined by another well-known figure, Benny Mahrshak. Benny officially served as the Palmach's "education officer", but his function was nearer to that of a Red Army political commissar. I couldn't have asked for a better group of companions in an expedition where our lives would be on the line; every man in the armoured car would be a ranking Palmach officer of proven valour and wide combat experience.

With the operation approved and planned, we began last-minute preparations. We spent hours digesting every detail of the latest reports from Harel patrols which went out every night to reconnoitre the area west of Bab-el-Wad. They reported that to the northwest, in and around Latrun, there were enemy forces, but that the area to the southwest seemed to be clear.

On the afternoon of May 19, Amos gave us our final briefing. He warned us of the dangers of getting across the open plain. If the vehicles were knocked out, each of us would be on his own, and have to make his own way back to our lines. None of us had to be told what our chances were; that sombre knowledge added to the general feeling of tension and anticipation.

As evening grew near, the Palmach soldiers came to sit around us. The mood of these boys and girls, who were usually so high-spirited, was uncharacteristically subdued. They knew about our mission, and they had a pretty good idea of its chance of success. Sitting there on the cool grass, they began to sing, not the usual throaty, vigorous songs of the Israeli pioneer, but lingering melodies, slow and touching, with thrilling harmonies. For all their frank and direct manner, these youngsters were very shy about their emotions, and they rarely displayed their feelings. Listening to those melodious voices float out into the gathering dusk, I knew that this was their way of wishing us godspeed and good luck.

We waited for darkness to fall. It seemed like an eternity before Amos called us together and gave his final instructions. We got into the armoured car, each one taking up position. I opened up my firing slit, and gripped my rifle; I had managed to acquire a Lee-Enfield rifle, which had been my favourite type of weapon in the Canadian Army. I liked the feel of its walnut stock — somehow, it gave me confidence.

It is the nature of war that petty matters sometimes overshadow major concerns. Here I was, setting out on a perilous mission, knowing that it would be a miracle if I were still alive and in one piece this time tomorrow, and uppermost in my mind was my annoyance over a trifling incident. I had a small knapsack, containing all my personal belongings and treasures, which I wanted to put beside me in the armoured car. However, Amos insisted that all baggage go in the truck. He was quite right, of course: in an emergency, any superfluous piece of equipment inside the car could be dangerous. But I was disappointed in an almost superstitious way, and was glad to have the counter force of my trusty Lee-Enfield.

The armoured car moved off down the darkened road, towards the Bab-el-Wad crossroads. I peered out through my firing slit, but the wooded hills along the road were already in complete darkness, and there was nothing to see. Anyway, this was still our territory, and there was little likelihood of encountering hostile forces.

Very soon, we reached the junction. Here we met the light truck, and held a last-minute conference. Then the car turned off the road to the left, driving cross-country. We were now in enemy territory. Our foot patrols were out, trying to help us on our way, and every now and then we would encounter one in the dark. Amos would stop and would receive a whispered report on what lay ahead.

After a while, there were no more patrols. Now we were deep into no-man's-land, and completely on our own. As we bumped along in the dark, with our lights out, we peered into the hostile darkness, alert for the slightest suspicious movement. Every now and then, Amos would stop the car. We sat, trying not to breathe, straining our ears for any sound of enemy activity. After a few moments, when we were sure all was clear, Amos would give the signal and the driver would quietly engage the clutch and drive on, praying that the blackness ahead didn't contain a gully.

The strain was terrific. At any moment we could be challenged, and when our identity was discovered we would find ourselves the target for a hail of bullets. I thumbed the safety catch of my Lee-Enfield, confident that if that happened we would give a good account of ourselves, but less confident that, once discovered, we would ever escape. And we knew that if we were captured our deaths would be slow and painful.

I don't suppose anyone knows the precise route we followed. Amos was heading west towards Hulda and Tel Aviv, but there were no landmarks to speak of in that undulating plain.

We drove on and on. Finally, after what seemed like an eternity (but was, in fact, no more than a few hours), we were challenged — in Hebrew!

We were overjoyed. When we identified ourselves and told the guard where we were coming from, he listened with a broad grin which said very clearly: who d'you think you're kidding? He was sure we were spoofing, and absolutely refused to believe that we had just driven right through enemy-held territory from Jerusalem. Still sceptical, he checked with his headquarters and then waved us through — to the main Tel Aviv road.

Our mood was strange. We were too numbed by our sense of relief to be able to rejoice. None of us had any illusions about the odds against our mission, and when it went off smoothly, the anti-climax was as overpowering as the hours of tension which preceded it. Later, however, Amos gave me a memento of that night drive: a map with our route roughly pencilled in, and his signature at the bottom.

As soon as we got through, work went ahead on improving the route, following more or less the same path. Amos returned two weeks later, with a convoy of jeeps carrying the weapons, ammunition, and reinforcements we had promised to send to Jerusalem. Later still, that rough track was secretly improved— an incredible task, incredibly successful—and made passable for heavy trucks. After that, regular convoys moved along it, by-passing the Legion garrison at Latrun with their precious supplies. The route became known as the "Burma Road", and its creation ended the blockade. Without it, Jerusalem's situation would have been hopeless.

The war ended with Latrun still occupied by the Legion, and the rough route we had reconnoitred was paved and renamed "The Road of Valour". For the next nineteen years, up to the 1967 war and the Israeli occupation of Latrun, it remained the only road connecting Jerusalem to Tel Aviv and the rest of Israel.

CHAPTER TWENTY-TWO

Mortars and Red Tape

It was still dark on the morning of May 20 when we entered the outskirts of Tel Aviv. We drove on into the city, until the pleasant tang of sea air indicated that we were near the beach. There was no sign of life at that early morning hour; the silence of the city was a strange contrast to its usual hustle and bustle. The armoured car rumbled through the empty streets, till Amos dropped me off at the Pension Brandshtetter. It was here that I had stayed when I arrived in Tel Aviv two months — only two months — earlier, and naturally enough I came to seek shelter here on my return.

Amos and the others bade me farewell and went on their way. As the lights of the armoured car receded, I turned and staggered into the hallway of the pension. I was in a state of complete exhaustion, and was thinking delighted thoughts about the warm bed with clean sheets that awaited me. My blissful plans were interrupted when I found the inner door locked. There was no one about, and I didn't want to wake Mrs. Brandshtetter, so there was nothing for it but to hold out till the morning. I lay down on the floor and slept as well as I could till dawn.

When it was fully light, I went over to the door and knocked till it was opened by the proprietor. Macbeth seeing Banquo's ghost couldn't have reacted with greater surprise than Mrs. Brandshtetter; she nearly fainted when she set eyes on me. I was a grotesque sight: I hadn't shaved, or even washed properly, for weeks. I was wearing my paratrooper's jacket, its original camouflaging reinforced by filth and grime accumulated in the hills of Jerusalem. I was red-eyed and emaciated, and almost certainly stank, and Mrs. Brandshtetter was understandably astonished to find such an object at her door in the early morning.

After she got over her surprise, she took me in hand. When an infantryman is in the field, there are some things he envisions, like dreams of paradise: a good hot bath, a shave, a clean towel, white sheets, and a soft, comfortable bed. Mrs. Brandshtetter wasted no time making these dreams come true. In true motherly fashion, she heated up some water for a hot bath, and while I was wallowing luxuriously in the tub, she prepared a lavish breakfast. I ate my fill and then went to my room, to collapse into bed for a few hours' blissful sleep. When I awoke — clean, well-fed, and rested — it was like being reborn.

My hostess told me that Colonel "Mickey" Marcus was staying near by, and I immediately went over to renew our acquaintance. I first met Mickey when he came to Toronto accompanied by Shlomo Shamir to bring me instructions about recruiting Canadian volunteers for Hagana. We took an immediate liking to one another, and our friendship grew fast, to the point where he was determined to exchange rings — my Queen's Own ring for his prestigious West Point ring. After about twenty-four hours, when I realized how important my Queen's Own ring was to me, I had some difficulty talking Mickey into calling off the deal.

When the fighting began in Palestine, Mickey had volunteered his service, and at that unforeseen meeting in Tel Aviv he and I had a lot to talk about. He related his impressions from a recent visit to the southern front, where Israeli forces were fighting the Egyptians, who were advancing in a giant, well-armed column. I told him about Jerusalem, and about the "Burma Road" by-pass route we had just established. (This information was to be of use to him sooner than either of us expected, for Mickey was appointed commander of the troops fighting in the Jerusalem corridor, where he met his death by tragic accident.)

In the course of our conversation, Mickey told me of the formation of a "new brigade" (this cryptic name — a security cover for the 7th Brigade—often creeps into historical accounts, with confusing results). The brigade's first assignment would be the capture of Latrun. The brigade's commander was to be Shlomo Shamir, and Mickey invited me to join it as co-chief-of-staff, sharing the post with Vivian (Chaim) Herzog. I rejected the proposal, for a variety of reasons. I didn't like the idea of divided function, with neither Herzog nor myself gaining clear authority. As for serving under Shamir, since his combat experience fell far short of mine, I immodestly felt that he should serve under me!

So I rejected the offer of a post with this mysterious new brigade without a second thought. There were other, more important things to occupy my mind. I had to report to Ben-Gurion, organize supplies for Jerusalem, and check on how "my" Canadian volunteers were getting along. (It was hard to believe that just a few weeks had passed since I volunteered to visit the Harel Brigade, to pass the time until the Canadian volunteers began to arrive!) These matters had first priority with me, and I could undertake nothing else.

The first task was a visit to Ben-Gurion. He was very pleased to see me, and appeared excited and gratified over our success in reconnoitring an alternate route to Jerusalem. I described the situation in Jerusalem, where the Israeli forces were unable to reply to the Legion's incessant shelling. I told him that among the vital supplies I hoped to take back to Jerusalem over our cross-country route was a large quantity of four-inch mortars. I recalled that these mortars had been in an advanced stage of preparation before I left Tel Aviv, and casually asked if they were now ready for action. He told me that they were not yet ready, and that he could not understand why; he asked me to look into the situation and report back to him.

My inquiries into the mortars amazed me. Before I left for Jerusalem, Hagana workshops had already produced a number of four-inch mortars as well as bombs for them. Artillery command had recruited a battalion which was to train with the mortars and take them into combat. Since one month ago, mortars, bombs, and mortar crews were all in Tel Aviv, it seemed reasonable to expect to find the mortars and their crews now tested and trained and ready for action. I was quickly disillusioned. The mortar battalion was sitting idle: neither mortars nor bombs had been delivered. If it hadn't been so tragic, it would have sounded like a joke: the mortar crews were in one place, the mortars in another, and the bombs elsewhere again. . . .

Further inquiries revealed that there was a reason, of sorts, for this: the Ordnance Corps inspectors would not certify the mortars or their bombs, both of which they considered unfit for use; without their approval, weapons could not be delivered to the battalion.

I went off to inspect the mortars and their bombs with Dr. Neir, a Weizmann Institute scientist and former mortar sergeant who was now involved in production of the weapons. At first sight, I must confess I felt some understanding for the reluctance of the Ordnance Corps inspectors to accept responsibility for such crude products. The "mortars" were no more than sewer pipes with steel wire bound about them. As for the bombs, they also looked too primitive to inspire much confidence. They were roughly cast, and almost every one showed cracks or imperfections. It was hardly surprising that the Ordnance Corps regarded these contraptions as a greater menace to our own men than to the enemy!

After a detailed explanation from Neir, however, I became

convinced that appearances were deceptive, and that the mortars were, in fact, quite safe to use. For all their home-made appearance, the reinforced sewer pipes were strong enough to withstand the detonation of the ignition cartridges; furthermore, the tests we conducted showed them to be surprisingly accurate. As for the bombs, it was Neir's opinion that the cracks did not constitute any danger. The explosive filling the bombs was very stable, and it could only be set off by the detonator, which was only armed when the bomb was in flight, and could therefore not be ignited before impact with its target.

All this showed that there were no grounds to fear for the safety of the mortar crews. After giving thorough consideration to all the possible snags, I saw no reason why the mortars and their bombs could not be delivered to the army for immediate use.

I reported my findings to Ben-Gurion, who as Defence Minister (in addition to his post as Premier) had taken complete control of the military machine. He was taken aback when I described the situation in detail, and was appalled to hear that even the mortar battalion was not yet trained, since its officers lacked the necessary know-how. When he asked me if I could take the necessary steps to get the mortars into action as quickly as possible, I agreed—but only on condition that I was given full and complete authority over all phases of the operation: production, distribution, and training of the crews. I could do it only if I were authorized to issue orders and make sure they were obeyed by all concerned.

Not surprisingly, Ben-Gurion was astounded at my conditions. "No head of state has ever signed a letter giving such wide authority!" he snapped indignantly. Clearly, he was upset—not with me, but at the principle involved in my demand. But I remained unrelenting, and in the end he realized that these weren't normal times, and extraordinary measures were needed to deal with extraordinary problems. Grudgingly, he gave in, asking me to go outside and dictate the letter to his secretary. Within a few moments, I was back in his office with the letter. Still angry over my insistence, he picked up his pen and, with evident displeasure, scrawled his signature at the bottom of the page. Then he shoved the letter across the desk and dismissed me with a curt "Get to work!" I did not need to be told twice.

I promptly went to the hard-working commander of the Ordnance Corps, Ben-Artzi, who insisted on my written acceptance of responsibility, but saw that the mortars were promptly delivered to the mortar battalion, which had been awaiting them eagerly. Within two weeks of receiving their new weapons and bombs, the first crews were trained and ready to go into action.

In the course of my work on the mortars, I had an opportunity to meet the dedicated civilian workers employed in their production. After beleaguered Jerusalem, Tel Aviv and its surroundings appeared quite peaceful, and the war seemed a long way away. But the people there were as closely involved in the war effort as their cousins in Jerusalem. I learned this during a night visit to a foundry near Tel Aviv, in the company of Mr. Villinchuk, a leading industrialist who was then civilian head of production. The whole area was blacked out, of course, but the foundry was brightly lit by the blast furnaces, making it clearly visible for miles around from the air. In the course of our visit, Egyptian planes appeared overhead and began to drop bombs. Since there were no anti-aircraft defences or Israeli planes to bother them, the Egyptian pilots were free to take their time and aim their bombs at leisure. As the bombs crashed all around, seemingly closer and closer to the foundry, some of the workers hesitated; then, laying down their tools, they began to head for the shelter. Mr. Villinchuk, a man in his sixties, quietly called on them to carry on with their work, and they obeyed, ignoring the bombs. This incident is typical of the spirit of the Israeli civilian population, which made such a decisive contribution to their country's victory.

In addition to supervising the production and delivery of the mortars, I was also commander of the mortar brigade, with Neir as my second-in-command. When I visited the battalion in training, I was very encouraged to learn from the men of this unit that many of them had Second World War combat experience: some as partisans, and others as members of regular military formations. They were a tough bunch, anxious to go into action and very glad to get hold of the weapons they were going to use. Their commander, Shmuelik Gorodetsky, had a similar record: he was a young Polish Jew, and was reported to have commanded an artillery brigade in the Red Army. With that experience, he seemed ideally suited to his present command.

I had come to arrange for the mortar crews to adopt a standard firing drill, but soon found myself running into unexpected opposition. Gorodetsky was reluctant to follow my instructions, and insisted on introducing his own methods, which, he claimed, were far superior to mine. Neither of us would give way, and we argued quite heatedly, and publicly. The situation became uncomfortable. The officers and men of the battalion knew Gorodetsky and had considerable respect for him, whereas I was an unknown newcomer, "outside top brass". Clearly, they were solidly behind their own commander, and resented my interference and my new-fangled ideas. As commander of the mortar brigade, I had the authority to impose my viewpoint, but I felt that, since the men of the battalion obviously backed Gorodetsky, this would hardly be the ideal way of resolving our differences and gaining the confidence of all concerned.

Accordingly, I made Gorodetsky a "sporting offer": I proposed that we take two mortars out on a firing range, and try out our respective methods to see which was better. He cheerfully agreed.

A large audience flocked to watch our "duel". Almost all the senior artillery officers came along, many of them, I'm sure, looking forward to my forthcoming defeat at the hands of "their" man. As we prepared, the atmosphere was tense. Gorodetsky, who was to fire first, carefully set up his mortar, aimed it, and announced that he was ready to fire. I walked up to his mortar, and checked his aim. Not believing my eyes, I asked Neir to doublecheck my observation. Then I straightened up and informed Gorodetsky—very loudly—that if he were to fire with the mortar at its present inclination, not only would the bomb fall far from the target, it would land on a nearby Jewish village! My words produced considerable consternation. The assembled artillery officers took a close look and discovered, to their horror, that I was quite right. Thereupon, I set up my mortar, aimed it, and (sometimes life is sweet) dropped my bombs right on target. With that, the issue was settled; thereafter, the battalion followed my drills and orders without question.

I was naturally very concerned about what was happening with the Canadian volunteers I had helped recruit. Before leaving for Jerusalem, I thought I had made arrangements for their reception and training. On my return to Tel Aviv, I was very upset to find that these arrangements had been discarded, and that on arrival the Canadians had been dispersed among various units. I was not the only one who resented this dispersal of the Canadian volunteers. Many of the men themselves complained bitterly of the breach of confidence, since I had given them to understand that they would be serving in a Canadian unit, under my command. This wasn't a matter of "Canadian patriotism" on their part: most of these men had extensive combat experience, and they resented having to serve under officers who, in many cases, had no idea of what to do.

While I was touring the various units, trying to locate the Canadians, they told me of a peculiar custom very characteristic of the Israeli Army in those chaotic times. Since the general army adjutant's office dealing with manpower was just being formed and was still ineffective, each unit ran its own recruiting campaign, exercising a great deal of initiative and ingenuity in trying to attract newcomers. Their "recruiters" were particularly keen on enlisting the Canadians, whose combat experience was a most valuable asset at a time when commanders were at their wits' ends to find trained personnel. Some of the Canadians told of being approached by representatives of many different units, each using every method imaginable — even offering financial incentives — to persuade the newcomers to join his outfit.

Before finally relinquishing the idea of a separate Canadian unit, I went to visit the only group that had managed to stay together, by joining the Givati Brigade fighting at Latrun. When I put the question to them, I found them of two minds. On the one hand, they were still attracted by the idea of the Canadians getting together. But at the same time, they had already seen a fair amount of action with Givati, they felt well integrated, and they had grown quite attached to the brigade and its officers, who, for their part, were obviously reluctant to lose such a fine group of soldiers. That being the situation, I hesitated to cause any upheavals.

By this time, I was having second thoughts myself. I felt responsible towards the men I had recruited in Canada, and to the promises I had given them. In addition, I was sincerely convinced that a separate Canadian unit would have been a hell of a big asset to the Israeli Army, and I regret, to this day, that I wasn't given the opportunity to prove it. But now, with the men I had recruited scattered all over Israel, the idea was clearly no longer feasible, and I ceased to pursue the matter. But wherever I was posted, groups of Canadians followed me, and I helped anyone who wished to do so with all the influence at my command.

By early in June, after I had put them through a fast but thorough training course, the first mortar battery was ready for action — in Jerusalem. I understood from Ben-Gurion that I would personally command it, taking it back to Jerusalem and leading it into action. My memories of crouching helplessly in Jerusalem, unable to hit back at the Arabs who were dropping shells all around us, were so vivid that I couldn't wait to get back with our mortars. I was also excited by the prospect of taking part in the first convoy back along the "Burma Road", in which I took a proprietorial pride. I knew that Amos Horev was organizing the first convoy and that part of our mortar brigade and its weapons were to be on it. It seemed fitting that I should be part of it.

Ben-Gurion thought otherwise. He decided that it was more important to stay in Tel Aviv with the brigade and continue its training, since Neir was fully competent to lead the battery to Jerusalem. Despite my regret, I had to agree with him on both counts. The battery was loaded on jeeps and sent to report to Amos Horev.

Shortly after that first battery left for Jerusalem, the first truce went into effect on June 11. But there was near certainty that the truce would not outlive its four-week term; more mortars and men had to be tested and trained in anticipation of the renewal of fighting. We pushed on with the training, frantically trying to get as many mortar men as possible ready for the next round.

CHAPTER TWENTY-THREE

Dissension

It is probably appropriate to draw back for a moment from my jeep's-eye view of the war to summarize briefly what was happening in the broader picture. On May 14, 1948, while we were clearing the road down to Bab-el-Wad, the British mandate over Palestine came to an end; on that day the British troops, who for the previous week or so had been gradually withdrawing towards the ports, left Palestine for good. Their departure was accompanied by two important events, which occurred within hours of one another: to wild celebration, the State of Israel was proclaimed in Tel Aviv by Ben-Gurion, head of the provisional government; and the armies of Egypt, Transjordan, Syria, and Iraq openly launched a full-scale war against the new state. Advance units and "volunteers" from these countries had been involved in helping the Palestinian Arabs fighting against us much earlier; but now, the full weight of their armed forces was committed to the campaign. It seemed like a hopelessly one-sided battle. The Arab armies were organized formations, well supplied with the most modern equipment and arms. They were professionals who had long been trained as regular armies; their officers had attended staff colleges in France and Britain. Where there was a lack of local officers, as in Transjordan, the Arab Legion was commanded by British officers seconded to their posts by their government.

The Jewish forces, on the other hand, consisted of a rag-tag, ill-clad assortment of groups which had operated hitherto in a clandestine or semi-clandestine manner, never enjoying the equipment, the training, or the organization of large regular formations. While the Arabs had armour, artillery, and air support, the Jewish forces had almost none, their arms consisting almost entirely of light weapons which had been procured illegally or produced in underground workshops. There was a great shortage of everything — vehicles, uniforms, the most elementary military equipment, guns, and, above all, ammunition. It was, in fact, a home-made army, an army where the only medium artillery were mortars made of drain pipes, and armoured cars were ordinary cars with iron-plate sheeting fixed around them.

Outsiders looking at the two sides gave the heavily outnumbered and outgunned Jews little chance. Yet they overlooked two factors. First, thousands of Israelis had seen combat with various armies during the Second World War, and while Israeli officers had not studied at staff colleges, that was not always a disadvantage: they displayed an unorthodox approach which enabled them to improvise and overcome what conventional military thinking would have regarded as insurmountable odds. The second factor was even more important and should not be forgotten, even today. The Jewish forces were fighting in their own country, on familiar terrain, and with the knowledge that this was a battle for survival; thousands of years of history were behind them, urging them on as they fought for their homeland. For example, the Palmach took the fortress of Nebi Yusha through the incredible heroism of volunteers who acted as human torpedoes; they blew up the defensive walls with sticks of dynamite wrapped around their waists. Courage like that evens up almost any odds.

At first, the tide of war seemed to be running in the Arabs' favour. The Arab Legion increased its pressure on Jerusalem.

The Iraqis and Syrians advanced on the north and east, taking over large sections of the country and isolating many Jewish settlements. But the principal threat came from the south, where the Egyptian Army, the largest Arab force, advanced up the coastal plain in a great column, its infantry backed by air and armoured support. After overwhelming the Jewish border settlements, the Egyptians thrust northwards, and military experts prophesied that it would not be long before they reached Tel Aviv.

Grim as the situation seemed, the Arabs did not have things all their own way. Small kibbutzim like Yad Mordechai and Negba, held by a few dozen lightly armed settlers, managed to delay or even halt the advance of large Arab units lavishly backed by air and armoured attacks. At the same time, the newly proclaimed Israeli Army — spearheaded by the units of the Palmach — immediately went on the offensive, launching lightning raids to wrest back from the Arabs several important strongpoints handed to them by the departing British. And all the while, the army was getting better organized, Jews were flooding into the country from the refugee camps at Cyprus and Europe to be recruited and trained, and weapons were being acquired and brought in. With Czechoslovakia as an intermediary, the Soviet Union began to send in large quantities of Second World War arms, commencing with captured German MG 42 machine guns and service rifles, and going on to slightly antiquated but still very serviceable Spitfires and Messerschmidt fighter planes.

As the Israeli Army gained strength, the Arab armies began to lose ground. Far from the battlefronts, however, the Arab political leaders still boasted of their imminent victory. On May 24 (the day after Ben-Gurion gave me complete control of mortar production and training, and nine days after the Arab armies officially entered the fray), the United Nations Security Council called for a cease-fire, warning that it would apply sanctions against any state whose army disregarded the call. Since their armies seemed to have victory within their grasp, the Arab leaders ignored the resolution, predicting quite accurately that no sanctions would be applied. On June 2, there was another cease-fire resolution; this time there was talk of sending an international force to back it up. But the Arabs again rejected the truce — and no international force materialized. Under the command of the British general Glubb Pasha, the Arab Legion pressed home its attacks on Jerusalem. The Egyptian Army continued its onslaught on the southern front, as it tried to break through to Tel Aviv, which its planes continued to bomb regularly.

But an Israeli counter-offensive was also in progress. Our troops were threatening Latrun, while Jaffa, Haifa, Acre, and Safed were now securely in Israeli hands. As it acquired new men, arms, and equipment, and learned to operate in regular units, the Israeli Army was rapidly becoming a formidable fighting force.

The morale and fighting spirit of the Arab armies declined as they saw that victory would not come as easily as their leaders had promised. At the same time, these leaders were sobered by the bad news from the battlefront, and began to have second thoughts about a truce. They now declared themselves ready to halt the fighting, hoping that a breathing-space would give them time to reorganize their armies and deliver the decisive attack. On June 11, 1948, the long-heralded truce finally went into effect. The Security Council sent the Swedish Count Bernadotte to the Middle East at the head of a team of observers to supervise the truce and act as mediator between Israel and the Arabs.

But from the very first, the truce was tentative and insubstantial. Only the wildest optimists believed that the war was over. Everyone knew that it was only a matter of time before the Arab armies mounted a new offensive on the new state.

The first truce was a period of great activity in the Israeli Army. The respite in the fighting gave time to reorganize the hastily formed units, to train new recruits. New service departments were established: intelligence, planning, signals, manpower, supply services, air force, and navy. Ben-Gurion, in his capacity as minister of war, set up a highly centralized system with power emanating from his office, although the country continued to be divided up into regional commands: north, central, Tel Aviv, Jerusalem, and south.

But the country was also divided in another sense, a far less healthy one. Political disputes and dissension raged at all levels of Israeli society, including the cabinet and the army command. Ben-Gurion headed the cabinet as the leader of the left-of-centre Mapai Party, the largest political group in the country. He was acutely aware that many of the senior commanders of the Palmach, and of other units, belonged to the leftist Mapam Party.

I learned at first hand about the problems that this produced when Ben-Gurion and I discussed the introduction of conventional military organization, including a code of military law, both of which I advocated strongly. Ben-Gurion tended to favour these innovations and he was also impressed when I told him of how Harel had introduced badges of rank and some measure of military discipline. He referred me to Israel Galili to discuss the matter further.

Galili was and still is a legendary figure; for many years he was the head of the Jewish Defence Council ever since his introduction to military affairs in 1920 as a ten-year-old runner. At this time he was, in effect, Ben-Gurion's chief adviser on military policy — and a member of the left-wing socialist Mapam Party. His horrified reaction to my suggestion that markings of rank be introduced was predictable and our discussion turned into a fierce argument. My attempts to talk him round by giving examples of what we'd done in Harel proved literally worse than useless; he remained unconvinced, and I am sure that it was no coincidence that Harel was shortly afterwards ordered to remove all badges of rank.

Apart from that incident, I was not directly involved in political struggles. I felt that if Israel was to be a democracy the army should be a modern disciplined force, with politics totally eliminated. My proposals about discipline, military law, and rank insignia were aimed only at improving the army's efficiency; I regretted that they were regarded as sensitive political issues.

Ben-Gurion's tussle with the left wing was largely conducted behind the scenes, but a far more serious crisis was brewing up on the right, and the conflict soon came out into the open. The Irgun Tzvai Leumi (Etzel) was founded during the British mandate as a breakaway organization which opposed Jewish Agency policy and refused to accept Hagana control. It conducted its own violent campaign against the British government, which brought it frequently into sharp conflict with the official Jewish leadership. As the British mandate came to an end, the Etzel emerged from underground and joined in the fighting against the Arabs. With the proclamation of the state, and the establishment of the official Israeli Army, the new government reached an agreement with the Etzel leaders whereby they would dissolve their separate units and integrate them with the regular army formations. Unfortunately, this merger could not come about overnight, and the Etzel was still partly autonomous when the cease-fire was proclaimed on June 11.

All might have been well but for the fact that the Etzel leaders were dissatisfied with the truce, whose terms included a ban on the introduction of weapons and fighting men into Palestine. While the truce was still in effect, the Etzel ship *Altalena* arrived from Europe, carrying a cargo of military equipment and hundreds of volunteers. The government, regarding the arrival of this ship in Tel Aviv as a challenge to its authority, as well as an embarrassingly flagrant violation of the truce terms it had just accepted, ordered regular army units to stop it from discharging its passengers or cargo. The Etzel command ordered the landings to proceed. It was time for a showdown.

I was in Tel Aviv at the time of the *Altalena* confrontation; from my hotel window I watched the clash develop. I saw the regular army units open fire from the shore. Their shells were horrifyingly effective, causing casualties and finally setting the ship on fire, which triggered off further roaring explosions as the ammunition on board blew up. For those tense hours, as the battle of the *Altalena* raged, and later as I watched the ship burn, the newly founded state seemed to be on the brink of civil war. But while Ben-Gurion and the cabinet stood firm, the Etzel leaders backed down, and the crisis subsided. The incident is a source of controversy to this day, with the Etzel leaders bitterly critical of Ben-Gurion for preventing the *Altalena* from landing its badly needed munitions and personnel. But it was not the ship, or its cargo, which was at issue: the question was whether the elected majority would stand for private armies — and the answer was a clear and unequivocal No!

Early in July I received perhaps the greatest honour of my life: Ben-Gurion gave me command of the 7th Brigade. This promotion came through at a time when the truce was nearing its end, and when the crisis within the Israeli command was reaching its height. While the army was making frantic efforts to prepare for the seemingly inevitable renewal of fighting, some senior officers resigned in protest at Ben-Gurion's introduction of formal discipline and organization, and his moves to reduce the influence of rival political groupings in the senior command. In this confused situation, Ben-Gurion appointed me to head the brigade in the same way that he had given me unlimited authority to get the mortar battalion organized: he simply made the appointment.

At that time, the Hagana chief of staff, Brigadier Ya'akov Dori, was more or less incapacitated. He had just been hospitalized with a bad attack of ulcers. I went to see him at once to discuss my new command, but although he received me most cordially, he was clearly in such great pain that I hesitated to discuss serious matters with him. When I mentioned the confusion I was encountering when I tried to find out about the 7th Brigade, he grimaced with pain and grasped his stomach with both hands, saying, "Exactly what I expected!"

Dori, an active and experienced field commander, enjoyed great respect, and his absence at that critical time was a serious handicap. If he had been at his post, he would doubtless have taken matters in hand, and provided the leadership that was so sorely lacking. Yigal Yadin, his operations officer, was too self-effacing to step in to fill the void left by Dori's absence; at this time, leadership and control seemed to be entirely in the hands of Ben-Gurion.

Although Yadin was officially chief of operations, when I visited him he seemed unable to give me clear-cut instructions about my duties or the tasks of the brigade. It may be that Yadin's vagueness was an expression of his resentment of Ben-Gurion, who had appointed me without consulting army command. Certainly, all I got out of him was the rather vague information that the brigade was in a bad state after suffering heavy casualties in the Latrun fighting — and a promise of two weeks to reorganize before we were called upon to undertake active operations.

I continued my rounds, seeking advice and instructions on my new field of operations in the north from anyone in a position to help me. Professor Rattner, a former commander of the Hagana, now head of planning at army headquarters, proved to be of great assistance to me in explaining the strategical problems I would be facing in Galilee. Above all, I have very vivid memories of him pointing to a map of Galilee, and singling out the crossroads at Sasa. "If you control these crossroads," he said to me very emphatically, "you control the whole of Galilee!" A sound observation, and one that I was to remember in the months ahead.

Years later, I was to remember another incident from those days: a member of Rattner's staff, a man named Yisrael Ber, was especially courteous and helpful; after serving as Ben-Gurion's security adviser, he was ultimately tried and convicted of espionage for the Soviet Union!

On July 5,[1] when I went to Ein Shemer, the base in central Israel, to take over the brigade, my reception was a sobering experience, confirming the reports about the poor condition of the unit. Military etiquette requires that the outgoing commander formally greet the incoming officer and hand over the command to him. Shlomo Shamir, the previous commander, was not at brigade headquarters. Nor were his senior officers, with the exception of Baruch Amir (Kertzman), the brigade quartermaster, who proved to be the senior officer present, and accordingly turned the brigade over to me.

It was not an auspicious beginning, but worse was to follow. In an attempt to obtain some kind of picture of the brigade's condition, I asked the quartermaster for a complete inventory of the brigade's equipment. His reply was startling: things were so chaotic that he couldn't fulfil my request! Instead, he signed a document absolving me of any responsibility for the equipment until a proper inventory could be made. An encouraging start.

Next, I tried to find the numbers of troops and their condition. The armoured battalion, the 79th, was up to strength and fairly well equipped, but the ranks of the two infantry battalions were sadly depleted. 72nd Battalion was almost non-existent, with a temporary commander. Not surprisingly, morale was at rock bottom in the entire brigade. Under the circumstances, it was difficult, but vitally important, for me to find out exactly what happened at Latrun.

The 7th Brigade (the "new brigade" that Mickey Marcus had mentioned to me) was largely manned by newly arrived immigrants who were rushed from the ships to the battlefield with

[1]See Appendix.

little chance for the brigade to organize or train them. Their supporting weapons were nearly non-existent; Chaim Laskov's armoured 79th Battalion was the exception, and it consisted almost exclusively of home-made armoured cars and a company of infantry mounted on half-tracks. As luck would have it, this hastily organized force, under its fairly inexperienced commander, was given as its first task an assault on Latrun. Latrun, of course, was held by Jordan's regular forces and was a tough nut for any unit to crack, even a battle-hardened and experienced one.

The operation was not a success. It would be unfair to call it a total disaster, since the brigade did succeed in capturing two key Arab towns — Beit Jiz and Beit Susin. Even the assault on the main objective, the Latrun police fortress, was not a disgrace. The 79th Battalion succeeded in breaking through, and had actually captured and occupied the fortress when, under heavy counter-attack, Chaim Laskov received permission to withdraw his battalion. The supporting infantry from another brigade had failed to show up, making his position untenable.

But over all, the operation was a failure, and the entire brigade suffered enormous casualties. It was a bitter baptism of fire for our troops, most of them hastily trained immigrants who were so badly equipped that they did not even have any headgear to protect them from the merciless semi-tropical sun.

A first taste of action can be decisive in establishing the morale of any unit; after the attack on Latrun the morale of the 7th Brigade was at rock bottom. Everyone was blaming everyone else, including Shamir, the brigade commander, who significantly was not there to tell me his side of the story. I'm sure that my reports on the sorry state of the 7th Brigade did nothing to forward Shamir's career, although, in some mysterious manner, these reports disappeared — to my knowledge they never reached Ben-Gurion, and I could not locate them in my files at brigade headquarters — and Shamir went on from one high command to another.

I was just settling in at Ein Shemer trying to absorb all of the information I had just gathered about my new unit when a visitor presented himself. If it had been General Eisenhower or King Farouk, I could not have been more astounded. It was the jack-in-the-box of my life, Leo Heaps, the incredible Canadian who had popped up beside the Rhine in 1945 in a paratrooper's uniform to greet my Queen's Own company and was now standing as large as life in front of me at 7th Brigade headquarters in the middle of Israel four years later.

If I was astonished to see him, I was even more astonished by the message he bore. He announced that he had been sent by Yigal Yadin to take over command of one of the brigade's battalions, in place of Chaim Laskov, who he understood had been promoted to command of the brigade! I lost no time in correcting the error: I was the commander of the brigade, and Chaim Laskov remained in command of his battalion, the 79th, which was serving under me!

There was no room at the inn for poor Leo, who was obviously an unwitting pawn in Yigal Yadin's continuing game of challenging my appointment by Ben-Gurion. At the first opportunity, I confronted Yadin over his behaviour. When he made no attempt to deny or excuse his actions, a hot and unpleasant exchange ensued.

But for now I had to put Leo and Yadin and everything else out of my mind, and get down to work. My introduction to the 7th Brigade had shown clearly what a poor state it was in and made me very pleased to have a two-week breathing space to get it into shape. I began to lay out a training program, but as I was doing so, orders arrived from the army command to leave our base in central Israel and move north. There was to be no training; our positions were to be in the front lines. Furthermore, we had to move immediately, to be in position by July 7, the day before the truce was due to expire. I sent a message to headquarters protesting the order. I had taken over command on the express understanding that we would have two weeks to reorganize, and I didn't feel that the brigade was yet prepared and fit to play an active role. My protests weren't heeded, and the order remained in force. We had to go. Ordering Chaim Laskov to supervise the brigade's transfer to the north, I set out for an air reconnaissance of my new sphere of operations.

CHAPTER TWENTY-FOUR

The Seventh Brigade in Action

I have never been a white-knuckle flier, but as our tiny Auster bobbed and weaved its way over the Arab positions, the hot July sun made the cabin into a Turkish bath, until I became almost nostalgic for the D-day landing craft I had known and hated. My discomfort was not helped by the fact that the pilot, a man with an uncertain sense of humour, had taken my instructions about flying low to get a good view rather literally, and was making uneasy jokes about my overweight making it difficult for him to make the plane climb, whenever that became necessary. In the hilly country of Galilee, it was necessary fairly frequently.

A shimmering, silvery haze blanketed some of the high hills as we struggled to gain altitude in the hot, rarified atmosphere. We crisscrossed all of Galilee, catching clear views of snow-capped Mount Hermon, beyond the Syrian border, and of the lush greenery around the Hula swamps and the Sea of Galilee. Between the Jordan Valley and the coastal plain lie the hills of Galilee — mostly barren, and inhospitable, with little vegetation to cover the bare, eroded slopes. The hills were rocky and steep, getting higher the further north we flew. The narrow valleys were filled with the silver-green foliage of olive trees. There were few roads; the ones I saw ran along the valleys, and were dominated by the mountains on both sides, as were the rough dirt tracks linking the hilltop villages. The area was not densely populated, and there was little trace of Galilee's ten thousand villages and two million inhabitants, which Josephus described at the time of the Roman conquest.

Seen from the air, the strategic situation in western Galilee was easy to grasp: the Jews controlled the narrow and densely populated coastal plain, from Haifa Bay up to the Lebanese border, while the Arabs occupied the hills and mountains inland. Topography clearly favoured the Arabs. The hill areas seemed almost impregnable to attack, while from their positions on the heights overlooking the coastal plain, Fawzi el-Kaukji's Arab "Army of Liberation", consisting of Palestinians, Iraqis, Syrians, and an assortment of other volunteers, threatened the port of Acre and the Haifa-Acre road, the main Israeli communication route.

On top of that, the Arabs also held one salient feature on the coastal plain itself: about four thousand yards east of the road, Kaukji's men occupied a mound named Tel Kissan—the site of many ancient settlements. Those prehistoric settlers chose a good spot: the mound dominated an important section of the plain, as well as sitting astride an important route into the hills. In Kaukji's hands, Tel Kissan was a menace to our positions, while simultaneously serving as an outpost which protected the main Arab concentrations. As we flew over, I took a long and careful look at the mound's defences — First World War-type Turkish zigzag trenches. I was interested and pleased to note that these had only been dug on the western side, which faced our lines, while the eastern, or rear, section showed no traces of defence positions. I concluded that Tel Kissan must be taken, and that, moreover, it might be taken fairly easily if approached from the rear under cover of darkness.

Yehuda Werber objected most strongly to my order. When the brigade arrived in the north, his 71st Infantry Battalion was scheduled to move into Acre to defend the town against an Arab attack which intelligence reports had warned us to expect as soon as the truce ended. Now I was telling him to take his men out of their defensive positions and launch an attack on Tel Kissan! He reminded me that when I took over the brigade, before its move northwards, he had told me in no uncertain terms that his battalion was completely inoperative, and could not be relied upon to fight without reinforcements and time to reorganize. In the meantime, he had received neither; his whole "battalion" numbered one rifle company instead of three or four.

I understood Yehuda's feelings very well. I knew that he was still badly shaken by his experiences in Latrun, and his pessimistic statements were all the more effective, coming as they did from such an impressive figure of a man. Yehuda was a Sabra, but his two-hundred-pound frame, his red hair, and his blue eyes made him look more like a hulking Viking warrior. As I looked at him standing morosely in front of me, I remembered how I myself had felt when ordered to lead a thirty-five-man "company" into the Hochwald. But I knew that he and his men would never regain their composure and confidence if they were left to sit around demoralized on defensive duty. So I insisted that he carry out the attack, expressing my confidence that the operation would go through without casualties. "If you come in from the rear, under cover of darkness, you'll be able to take the place with a single platoon — and the Arabs will run for their lives!" Yehuda had served as an officer in the Jewish Brigade (he was a lawyer in civilian life) and my explanations must have reassured him; after his initial opposition, he became convinced that the attack would be feasible, and agreed to lead the assault in person.

After he led his men off in the dark, I spent several sleepless hours waiting for his report. Success was vital to the morale of the whole brigade. Failure was likely to be the prelude to a whole string of failures as the men became fatalists. Then the word came through. The operation was a complete success! Under cover of night, Yehuda had led his men on a long and difficult march behind enemy lines. They had approached the mound from the rear, taking the defenders by surprise, and the position was seized with next to no resistance. Carried out so daringly and competently, the victory had an amazing and electrifying effect on the brigade's morale, instantly restoring the men's self-confidence. From then on, nothing seemed to hold us.

With the conquest of Tel Kissan, we now had complete control of the coastal plain, and the way was opened up for an attack on Arab positions in the hills. Now that the brigade had demonstrated its assault potential, I felt that we should exploit our initial success and carry the fight to the enemy as soon as possible. We had been given a defensive role, but I wanted to take the initiative from the enemy and keep him off-balance.

Morale was now flying high and the men were eager for action. I saw that they got it. Tel Kissan was captured before dawn on the day the truce ended; the following day, Yehuda's battalion went on to capture the Arab villages of Ar Ruweis and Ad Damun, on the foothills at the edge of the plain. At the same time, Arele Yariv's (Rabinovitch) 21st Battalion, temporarily attached to the brigade, captured two other small villages further to the north, straightening out our lines and, for the first time, giving us a firm foothold in the hills, all along our front. These operations cut road links to ten other Arab villages, lengthening and sapping enemy lines of communication throughout the whole of western Galilee. Our advance also meant that we were within striking distance of the Arab towns of Shafa Amr, Tarshiha and Tarbiha, and Magdalkrum, while at the same time the Arab threat to Acre was removed; with the loss of their foothills positions and the road connecting them, Kaukji's forces would find it extremely difficult to launch an attack on the town.

Ours were not the only Israeli successes to occur immediately after the over-confident Arabs had rejected an extension of the truce. A combined task force was led by Moshe Dayan in an attack that captured Lydda Airport, Egyptian attacks from the south were thrown back, and Israeli forces widened the Jerusalem corridor by taking several Arab villages. Pride in our successes combined with the good news from other fronts to brighten the mood in the brigade even further and there was a noticeable atmosphere of expectancy and optimism.

The success of the brigade's first operations had earned us a much-needed breathing space. Yehuda Werber's gallant but under-strength 71st Battalion withdrew to base after handing over its positions to local militia forces, which were called out for full-time service. The rest of our line, to the north, was held by the 21st Battalion, which had suffered a bad mauling in an abortive action near Jenin, and was under-strength. But it was well led by Arele Yariv, one of Israel's ablest officers, now a cabinet minister, while one of its company commanders, Dov Yarmonovitch, was an exceptionally fine soldier, a brave and inspired leader who headed most of the battalion's assaults. The men, Sabras for the most part, showed great resilience in over-coming their previous setbacks.

Having gained a breathing space the hard way, we now began an intensive period of training and reorganization. I moved from battalion to battalion inspecting, helping, encouraging. One battalion seemed likely at one time to pose an especial problem; the 72nd Battalion had been nearly annihilated in the earliest battles of the brigade, and was non-operative when I took over. The 72nd soon came under the command of Jackie Nursella, a sallow, deceptively mild-mannered American who had been living in Palestine for many years. Jackie had not been in the previous battles of the brigade, but had served with the Palestinians in the Jewish Brigade of the British Army, gaining valuable experience that he soon put to damned good use. The battalion was placed in reserve in a former British Army camp north of Acre, where we initiated an intensive training program, augmented by occasional combat patrols, to harass the enemy.

Very quickly, the 72nd Battalion seemed to be infected with a renewed feeling of confidence.

The brigade's third combat formation was the 79th Armoured Battalion (subsequently known as the 73rd) commanded by Chaim Laskov, which was in relatively good shape when I took over the brigade.

The 79th had given a good account of itself at Latrun, capturing the fortress before being forced to relinquish their conquest. During those first few days after Latrun, the men of the 79th were sullen and bitter. But, despite this, the 79th impressed me as a well-led and well-trained body of men and I looked forward to working with its commander, Chaim Laskov, and his second-in-command, Baruch Erez, a former South African.

Several days after moving from Ein Shemer to our northern positions, I was advised that Chaim Laskov was to be transferred from his command of the 79th Battalion to a rather vaguely defined position supernumerary to establishment, as military governor of the western Galilee, putting the troops under my command under his jurisdiction. The motive behind this appointment is not clear to me to this day; but it did not affect me, since I continued to take all my orders directly from Moshe Carmel, the commander of the Northern District (in which Laskov's sub-district was located, which put him under Carmel's jurisdiction as well). The 7th Brigade continued to be under my direct command.

At the same time Joe Weiner (a former permanent force sergeant-major in the Canadian artillery who had been with me in the mortars) was appointed to command the 79th Battalion in Chaim Laskov's place. To all intents and purposes, however, the battalion continued to function under the effective command of Baruch Erez, who had been with the battalion since its inception.

During our short breathing space, while the combat units were undergoing training I organized advanced courses for the brigade's officers and NCOs to improve their professional skills and widen their knowledge. Aside from their obvious direct benefit to the brigade, these courses also helped us to deal with a military problem of a rather unusual nature. At this time the war in Israel was becoming a romantic war, a place for well-intentioned young men to play heroic roles in their own real-life war movie. This attraction meant that we were afflicted with what might be called "the plague of the phoney officer".

The stream of volunteers pouring in to Israel from all over the world included a number of impostors pretending to have been experienced officers in their countries of origin. It was often difficult to check the validity of such claims, and many of these men were duly sent on to my brigade, which was faced with the task of discovering whether or not they were genuine. I developed a very fast — but totally reliable — test to find out whether they were, indeed, officers. Our officers' advanced training course included lessons in unarmed combat from a competent instructor, a former officer in the American Marines. I would pit the new arrivals against the instructor, and he lost no time in discovering whether his opponent was an infantry officer. The reasoning behind the test was simple: to be an infantry officer, a man has to be tough. If someone failed to put up any kind of show in unarmed combat, it was doubtful if he had ever served as an officer in an infantry outfit. This test eliminated ninety per cent of the phoneys. The rest were weeded out by a former regimental sergeant-major in the Black Watch, a leather-lunged disciplinarian, who would put the officer through his paces on the parade ground. Anyone who stumbled under his orders was instantly under suspicion. A man who doesn't know how to drill or can't grasp new drill procedures fairly readily is unlikely to have been an officer in a regular army unit.

These tests were both effective and necessary, as the following story will show.

One day, a man came to the brigade, introducing himself as a colonel in a South American army, and announcing that he had

46, 47. A jeep-borne (46) and infantry assault on two Arab villages in the Galilee.

48. A view of the brigade headquarters at Sasa during Operation Hiram.

49. The Israeli flag flies over a captured strongpoint in Sasa.

50. A distorting lens does strange things to this view of the distinguished Dunkelman wedding party.

51. B.D. and Yael celebrate their wedding at the reception.

52. 1976. B.D. pictured on the Golan Heights with the current commander of the 7th Brigade beside the brigade's memorial. Across the border in Lebanon, Mount Hermon looms in the distance.

53. Prime Minister Rabin greets visitors from Toronto, Mr. and Mrs. Ben Dunkelman.

what brought her to my headquarters as a "messenger". Before we parted, I had an opportunity for a good long look at her. My impression from the previous day was confirmed: she was very beautiful.

I spent the morning at headquarters in consultations and conferences. When I finally finished all my business, I invited Yael to come and have lunch with us. Yehuda came along, as did my second-in-command, Yosef Eitan (Eisen), and Yael's boss, Motke. We all went to Victor's, a nearby restaurant famous for its Arab dishes.

It was a memorable meal. By the time it was over, I was charmed and infatuated. During the next few days, I was extremely busy with preparations for the first attempt to mount what came to be known as Operation Hiram, which meant that I saw little of Yael, but she was rarely out of my mind. I suppose I must have shown something of my feelings — or perhaps Yehuda or Yossi "informed" on me; in any case, the men of the brigade seemed to guess the reason for their commander's preoccupation, and they exhibited great interest in the budding romance.

The behaviour of two of my closest assistants was especially noteworthy. One was my personal adjutant, Max Chiniz. Max was a strongly built man who had served with the Hagana in the north for many years, making a name for himself with his daring and courage. The other was Yossi, my driver. He was a tiny man, yet was wiry, tough, and strong as an ox; he was afraid of nothing and no one, and ready to fight at the drop of a hat. Very few people could get along with him, since he was notorious for his sharp tongue and his short temper. These idiosyncrasies may be explained by his past: he had been a partisan in Europe, fighting first with the Polish Army and then in the ranks of the Red Army. Later, he rejoined the Poles; when the Polish Division was transferred from Russia to Palestine, he deserted and remained in the country as an "illegal immigrant". Now, in addition to serving as my driver, Yossi acted as my personal bodyguard and nursemaid. When he was around, anyone looking at me the wrong way was risking his life.

Even though they were very different personalities, Max and Yossi made a great team, and with them beside me, I had a great feeling of personal security. They watched over me like a pair of mother hens, and their concern extended to my personal life. Hitherto, if I stopped to speak to a girl, which was hardly unnatural behaviour for a thirty-five-year-old bachelor, they would do their best—in every possible way, including some very unfair ones—to discourage me from showing too deep an interest. But with Yael, their behaviour was totally different; they saw what was afoot, and, like a mother with grandchildren in mind, did everything to encourage me, missing no opportunity to tell me what a wonderful girl she was. Their view gained strong confirmation from another quarter: when Chaim Laskov came to visit me, I wanted to introduce him to Yael. He surprised me by announcing that they were already more than acquainted: he was a close friend of the Lifshitz family, and regarded Yael as a younger sister. He told me wonderful things about her and her family. This warm recommendation meant a lot to me, coming as it did from the man who was my best friend at that time.

Chaim, and other friends acquainted with the Lifshitzes, told me many details about Yael's background. Her father, David Lifshitz—known to one and all as "Abba" (Hebrew for "Father") —was a well-known figure in the Yishuv. Born in Russia, he originally came to Palestine as a boy, in 1912, to study at the Gymnasia Herzlia in Tel Aviv, where he attended school with such famous classmates as Moshe Sharett, later to become Israel's first foreign minister and second premier. On graduating, he returned to Russia to study engineering, only to be swept up by the Russian Revolution of 1917. He was captured by the Whites and sentenced to death; while awaiting execution in prison, he was unexpectedly reprieved on the whim of a White general, who had him released. He later became a district commissar for education under the first Bolshevik government, but he had no interest in remaining in Russia. With his wife and year-old son, Avigdor, he escaped across the border to Turkey, and then set out for Palestine. Here, his engineering knowledge was soon put to good use, and he became one of the founders of the Palestine Electric Corporation. When I met him, he was manager of the Haifa branch of the Palestine Cold Storage Company, and, in addition, was working in a senior Defence Ministry post, engaged in procuring supplies for the army. Yael, the Lifshitzes' second child, was born in Palestine.

Like any other infatuated man, I was desperately anxious to be with the girl who had smitten me. I knew that I would soon be up to my neck in feverish activity when the truce expired; since my arrival in Palestine six months earlier, I hadn't had a leave, and I felt that I both needed and deserved a rest. Turning the brigade over to my second-in-command, Yosef Eitan, I went on leave, looking forward to a few days with Yael. It was a wonderful leave, but it didn't work out precisely as I had planned.

On arrival in Haifa, I found a message from Meir Weisgall, who had just arrived from Canada, and was bringing messages from my father and mother. When I contacted him, he insisted that I join him for dinner that evening. I pleaded a previous engagement with Yael, but he was not to be put off. "Bring her along!" he commanded, and I had no choice but to bow my head and accept the invitation.

Meir Weisgall had come a long way since 1928 when, as a gifted young journalist, he had been hired by my mother to edit the Toronto *Jewish Standard*. In the intervening years he had gained a prominent position in Zionist affairs, rising to become the confidant and assistant of Chaim Weizmann, the president of the World Zionist Organization, and, later, first president of Israel. Meir was, and is, a colourful character, a man well known for his rough-and-ready wit. Weizmann, by contrast, was a dignified and somewhat aloof man, and Meir was the only person who dared to use earthy and even obscene language in the great man's presence. But Weisgall was very close to Weizmann, supporting him in his many struggles with rival Jewish groups and leaders, and on Weizmann's death, Meir succeeded him as chancellor of the Weizmann Institute of Science at Rehovot. In all his activities, whenever he encountered hesitation or opposition, Meir was aided by his exceptionally forceful character.

Of course, I was looking forward to meeting him and hearing news of my parents. But there was nothing further from my mind than accepting his dinner invitation. I had another — and far more important — plan for the evening: this was to be the day when I'd propose to Yael!

My agreement to join Meir for dinner had left me in an awkward situation. What was I to do? Finally, I hit upon a solution: I'd propose to Yael first, and then we'd go on to Meir's hotel.

I went to collect Yael in my staff car. As she got in beside me, I was all determination, but during the drive I found myself tongue-tied and embarrassed. I tried to broach the subject in all kinds of roundabout ways: I asked her where she would prefer to live, in Rehovot or on Mount Carmel? Would she like to visit my family in Canada? So it went on: I was beating about the bush, without the nerve to pop the ultimate question. Ben Dunkelman, who had always prided himself on his frank and direct manner, was stumbling over his tongue, incapable of bringing out what he had to say!

The drive was too short for me to overcome my hesitation and before I could get to the point, we reached the hotel. I climbed out of the car, cursing myself for my cowardice.

It was already evening when we arrived at the blacked-out hotel. Meir was waiting outside to greet us, and I introduced Yael. On meeting her, Meir's reaction was typical: since it was dark where we were standing, he took her by the hand and led her into the hotel, where he placed her under a lamp and subjected her to a careful scrutiny. Then his face broke into a broad grin, and he pronounced: "Well, she certainly looks all right to me. Is it okay if I phone your mother and break the good news to her?"

I squirmed. At that moment, there was nothing to report to my mother or to anyone else, for that matter. I had yet to ask Yael to marry me, and I could only guess what her answer would be when I did get around to asking. So far, my broad hints and indirect queries had evoked no response.

Disregarding my embarrassment, Meir kept up the pressure throughout dinner, riding roughshod over our sensibilities and conventional good manners. "Vos wartst de?" he reverted to Yiddish, "What are you waiting for? Where are you going to live?" As time went by, he became more and more convinced that we were meant for one another, and he made no secret of his convictions. He kept asking me: "What's the matter, don't you love the girl?" Then without waiting for my answer, he would turn to Yael and put her through a parallel interrogation. "What's the matter, can't you make up your mind?" he would scold her. (Fortunately, this wasn't Yael's first encounter with Meir, and she was not totally unprepared for his manner.) There was little subtlety to this barrage of well-meaning prods and my confusion and discomfort grew by the minute. I felt, probably with some reason, that the whole dining room was following the conversation with fascination, for Meir is not given to whispering. . . .

Finally, I could stand the pressure no more. When Meir's attention was elsewhere for a moment, I desperately hissed at Yael, in an aside: "Is it all right with you?" On her wordless nod of acceptance, I proudly made my announcement: Yael and I were going to get married! It was about one month since Yael had come to my headquarters with her message and encountered such a rude reception.

Meir, of course, was overjoyed. Shouting "I must tell Rosie!" he rushed out to wire my mother. He returned in high spirits, still belligerently inquisitive. Why hadn't we told him immediately? he wanted to know. He wouldn't believe my story about wanting to keep it a secret. I'm sure he would have believed it even less if I'd told him that the question had just been popped, right there at his dinner table, while he asked the waiter about dessert. Ever since that dinner party at Hotel Lev Harcarmel, Meir has always insisted that he proposed for me. Although that is something of a Weisgallian exaggeration, he can justifiably claim that the timing owed a great deal to his pressure.

That evening I had some slight revenge on Meir for his storm tactics. As I had no money with me, he had to lend me the cash to buy the wedding rings. That loan was somewhat unique: I am a member of the Weizmann Institute's board of governors, a body charged with raising funds for the Institute. I believe that I'm the only governor who ever reversed the normal procedure by borrowing money from the board. . . .

Meir's urging had created a fairly unconventional situation: here I was announcing that we were to get married, and I hadn't even met Yael's parents, let alone asked them for their consent. This oversight was put right the next day, when I went to their beautiful home on the top of Mount Carmel. There I found that my worries about leaving them in ignorance were groundless: Israel is a small country, and "Abba" Lifshitz had been receiving full and up-to-date reports of our romance.

In the meantime, Yael and I had decided to get married right away, inviting only immediate family and a few friends. But when they heard of this, the Lifshitzes asked us to postpone the ceremony, for what to us seemed like an intolerably long time, pleading for ten days' grace so that they could invite "a few" friends, as they put it, and hold a proper wedding. To us, it seemed like an eternity, but we allowed ourselves to be persuaded.

For a short while, our forthcoming wedding was the most

important subject in the world, and we permitted ourselves to forget the war. But reality broke rudely into our idyll; on September 10 the air-raid sirens sounded, and an enemy plane roared overhead, dropping its bombs on the city. One of these hit a children's home, killing forty children.

A short time later, when the raid had ended and we were at dinner, the war intruded once more. The phone rang: it was Motke Makleff, asking me to report immediately to his home on the Carmel, for urgent orders. As I put down the receiver, I noticed a whimsical smile on the face of my future father-in-law. I suspect he was thinking that the argument about the wedding date had been clinched: whatever Yael and I wanted, the next few days would keep us busy with other preoccupations, and there would be no time for frivolities like wedding ceremonies.

CHAPTER TWENTY-SEVEN

Operation Hiram

Yael's father drove me to Motke's home, where I found Moshe Carmel, head of Northern Command. He and Motke briefed me on the gravity of the situation. Under cover of the truce, Kaukji's forces had reorganized and regained their aggressiveness. Their forays in western Galilee had encountered a vigorous response from the 7th Brigade, and our sector of the front was now relatively quiet. But in northern Galilee, the Arabs were conducting an active campaign. They had laid siege to the mountain settlement of Manara; when the Carmeli Brigade tried to send in reinforcements, Kaukji's troops ambushed the relief column, inflicting heavy casualties. The Arabs remained in control of the heights around Manara, from which they dominated the north-south road linking the Metulla area with the rest of Israel. Despite the loss of Nazareth, and the beating they had taken from the 7th Brigade, Kaukji's forces were now strongly entrenched in central Galilee, and their attacks in the north were taking on menacing proportions.

It goes without saying that Kaukji's actions were flagrant violations of the truce agreement, and Israel had demanded United Nations intervention. There had been five days of continual negotiations, through the mediation of United Nations observers, but the Arab commanders had cockily rejected Israeli demands for preservation of the cease-fire. This intractable attitude on the part of the Arabs pleased me; it clearly saddled them with the blame for breaking the truce, thus removing the last political obstacles to a full-scale operation against Kaukji for which I had been pressing. When Moshe Carmel advised me that I'd command the operation to be mounted against Kaukji forces, I had no hesitation in announcing my readiness to take on the task. My assault plan had long been ready, planned to the last detail. In fact, the operation had actually been launched a month earlier, and all the preparatory phases had been successfully completed when, at the last moment, the assault was called off.

The essence of the plan was simple. Kaukji controlled most of the Galilee hills, while our forces were in the plains and foothills to the east, south, and west. Since access to the hills was easiest from the west and south, it was on those sides that the Arabs expected us to attack. Kaukji had concentrated most of his forces to the west, because continual pressure from the 7th Brigade convinced him that any threat would emanate from that side. None of his forces were in the east, for what seemed like very good reasons. The terrain on that side was very rugged; and the single road, from Safed to Meron, was blocked. This road was difficult at the best of times; it began three thousand feet up, at Safed, and then snaked down to the valley bottom where it crossed five large culverts designed to carry off the winter rain-water. Our scouts reported that all of these had been blown up and surrounded with anti-tank mines and booby-traps. With the road seemingly impassable, and in the absence of sizable Israeli forces in the Safed area, Kaukji obviously felt secure from attack on that side, which was why I planned to mount the attack from the east.

I felt that we could mount a successful attack from Safed, if two essential preconditions could be met: the assault force had to be concentrated at Safed, and the road had to be made usable—and both operations had to be carried out in complete secrecy to ensure that Kaukji did not reinforce his exposed eastern flank.

These conditions seemed impossible; but having already gone through all the preparatory stages, I was able to explain convincingly to Moshe and Motke what had to be done, and how it could be done.

Over a month previously, on September 16, my entire brigade had clambered onto trucks at their bases in and around the coastal plain. Then, as darkness fell, the long column set out. Making an enormous detour, so as to ensure that it traversed only Jewish-populated areas, the column headed south, then turned east by way of Afula and Tiberias, and then made its way up the steep and winding road to Rosh Pina and Safed. That night drive was a major feat. Strictly forbidden to turn on their lights, the drivers strained their eyes to follow the twisting roads. As the column followed its long and arduous roller-coaster route in the pitch darkness, it seemed that only a miracle could get us through without some of the vehicles taking a wrong turning, or running into each other, or just plunging off the narrow roads. But the brigade's provost company performed that miracle; before first light, the whole brigade was safely in Safed, without any mishap. On arrival, the units were swiftly dispersed to take up places of concealment, where they were to hide until zero hour for the assault, that evening.

While the brigade was engaged in that nerve-wracking night trek, one small unit of skilled and devoted men was engaged in an even more perilous undertaking. Under cover of darkness, the brigade's engineering company crept along the blocked Safed-Meron road, and stealthily began to remove the obstacles and mines. Everyone knows that this is a most dangerous and delicate operation at the best of times. Now, it was doubly difficult. Working close to an Arab village, the engineers had to do their delicate and dangerous job while groping in total darkness, desperately trying not to make a sound which might be heard by some alert look-out. Since the task of clearing all five culvert areas could not be completed in one night, the engineers began their work one night before the assault, which made it all the more important for them to remain undetected. If the Arabs realized what we were up to, the following day would give Kaukji sufficient time to deploy some of his forces in positions overlooking the road, making it impossible for the following night's assault to go forward as planned.

Somehow, the engineers performed the impossible. Under the command of A. Nissan (Nissenbaum), a most diligent and efficient officer who had received his engineering training in the British Army, they had accomplished a large portion of their task before the approach of dawn forced them to withdraw.

On the morning of September 17, we had gone a long way towards fulfilling the preconditions for the operation: the brigade had arrived safely in Safed, and many of the obstacles on the road had been removed. That night, the engineers would set out as darkness fell, and complete their task. At the same time infantry would be slogging their way up the hill towards Meron. As soon as the road was fit for use once more, the assault units would move in to the attack.

Everything was ready. As the daylight hours dragged slowly by, tension rose in anticipation of the impending assault. All day from my observation post I anxiously scanned the hills through my binoculars, searching for any signs of unusual Arab activity that would indicate that they sensed something afoot. To my relief, everything was peaceful and quiet; they seemed to have no inkling of our preparations. If so, we would achieve total tactical surprise, and the operation was ensured of success.

Evening was drawing near, and it would soon be time for the troops to move off. Then, as tension was nearing its peak, high command ordered the attack postponed!

The explanation wasn't hard to find. That day Count Bernadotte, the United Nations mediator, was murdered in Jerusalem. Feeling in the United Nations was running strongly against Israel, which was held responsible for the crime, which I, like many Israelis, believe was committed by an *agent pro-vocateur*. Although Kaukji's provocations gave us every justification for attacking, our operation was, nevertheless, a technical violation of the cease-fire—and, as such, it might be seized upon by hostile powers as an excuse to intervene directly against us.

At first, the attack was only postponed. Then came a second postponement, then a third. Finally, the whole operation was called off. On September 27, I ordered the brigade to move back to western Galilee. Once again, we travelled in silence by night, taking great care to conceal our movements from the enemy. I didn't want Kaukji to know that an entire brigade had massed in Safed without his knowledge — it would give him a fair idea of what we were trying to do. For the time being, I was obliged to relinquish the plan, but I had a feeling that a day would come when it would be implemented. For the same reason, I ordered Nissan to replace most of the mines and booby-traps, and to remove all signs of repair work on the culverts, so that the enemy would have no idea the obstacles had been altered in any way. Our precautions were highly effective. Though thousands of men knew of the preparations for the attack, the Arabs had not the faintest idea of our activities. It was an impressive display of field security.

Now, a month later, seated in Motke's home in Haifa, I re-minded Moshe and Motke of the attack which had been called off. Now that we had the green light for a full-scale operation against Kaukji, my proposal was simple: we go ahead with the attack, as planned.

I was in for an unwelcome surprise. Motke did not agree to my suggestion. Instead, he proposed that we launch an attack from our present positions, in the west, and drive into the hills along the Nahariya-Tarshiha road! He considered that my plan for an attack from the east was impractical, stressing the difficulties of moving thousands of men secretly, at night, over rough roads, and the enormity of the task facing the engineers in making the Safed-Meron road usable. Why not take the direct approach?

I considered his whole idea incomprehensible, and said so. Most of Kaukji's combat units were now strongly entrenched in defensive positions in the west, covering the approach roads. I had encouraged this by keeping up constant pressure from the west. As a result, helped by their topographical advantages, the enemy defences were now strong enough to hold up a force far larger than ours. I agreed with Motke that the main objective of any operation must be the capture of the Sasa road junction. While planning the operation, I constantly remembered Professor Rattner's advice that whoever controlled that junction controlled Galilee. There are few roads in the region, and the main routes converge at Sasa in the north; one glance at the map sufficed to prove that it was the key to Galilee. But I saw no possible hope of getting through to Sasa if we attacked from the west, as Motke proposed. It would be just plain stupid to launch a frontal attack at the precise point where the enemy is strongest— and expects us, into the bargain!

Regarding the objections to my plan—I had no hesitation in dismissing them. Nissan's engineers remained confident of their ability to clear the road within the time allotted. As for moving the brigade to Safed—we had already done that once; when repeated, it would be the most carefully rehearsed operation I had ever taken part in. In addition to that full-scale dress rehearsal, I had carefully prepared all my officers in staff exercises, using an enormous relief map of Galilee to go over every detail. Admittedly, it was a complicated operation, but I had full confidence in the staff of 7th Brigade. My previous chief of staff had been replaced by my old friend Yosef Eitan, who also did excellent work as my second-in-command. He was assisted by a very able intelligence officer, David Garfinkel. Yosef Mann, our signals officer, left little to be desired in the brigade's communications. The quartermaster, Baruch Amir, lacked formal military training but he was doing a fine job in supervising our supplies. He was greatly assisted by Isa Yuval (Salzman), our reliable and industrious adjutant, who had served with the British Royal Army Service Corps, and was now in charge of administration. Hoter Ishai, our DAQMG, served as general troubleshooter, tidying up any loose ends and helping wherever needed. Given such a first-rate staff—and, above all, given the officers and soldiers of the combat units, a fine body of brave and devoted men — I had no doubt that we'd overcome all obstacles in carrying out the plan.

Motke, possibly playing devil's advocate to draw me out, continued to press for an attack from the west. As before, in the heated discussions over the plans for the Nazareth attack, I made it quite clear that I would resign my command rather than adopt a plan which I considered to be impractical and certain to result in heavy losses to our forces. I insisted on the advantages of my plan, and finally, after much discussion, I was greatly relieved when Moshe Carmel came round to my view. He agreed to proceed with the attack — from the east!

I was convinced that the decision was a correct one, and my certainty even affected my personal plans: my future father-in-law had been invited to take part in our meeting. Having heard of the plans for the forthcoming operation, he again suggested postponing the wedding, but I confidently insisted on sticking to the original date, ten days ahead. I was sure the campaign would be successfully completed by then.

I now hurried to my headquarters to put Operation Hiram into action. The preliminary phases went like clockwork. On the evening of October 27, the engineers slipped out to the Safed-Meron road, and began their now-familiar task of clearing the road. At the same time, the rest of the brigade moved off from its bases in western Galilee. Once again, the provost company did fine work in directing the column, but this time our blacked-out drive over the mountain roads was not quite flawless: missing a turning in the darkness, one of the trucks plunged over a cliff. Fortunately, its occupants escaped with their lives, although they suffered a bad shaking up. But the rest of the vehicles got through without mishap, and by dawn, men and vehicles were concealed in the hills around Safed, ready to attack that evening. It was October 28, 1948.

We were facing a formidable enemy. Kaukji's forces consisted of three brigades of his Arab Army of Liberation, a brigade of local irregulars, and several battalions of Syrian regulars. His troops also had a number of artillery pieces on loan from the Syrians, and several squadrons of armoured cars manned by Iraqis, Germans, and other volunteers. As we had discovered during our attack on Nazareth, he was backed by some Spitfires (at that time, they did no more than buzz ineffectually overhead, but they were a potential threat, and in the hands of skilled and aggressive pilots could do terrible damage to our forces). Our intelligence reports told us that Kaukji's forces were rapidly building up their strength: there was a constant flow of reinforcements, and the training of his troops was also improving. But most of the Arab forces were concentrated in the Tarshiha area, facing west, with some units laying siege to Manara. Their mobile reserves were stationed in central Galilee, near the villages of Maghar and Ar Rama, where they were strategically placed to move in any direction they were needed. These reserve forces caused me my greatest concern: if they were moved north, they could disrupt our advance.

To overcome this powerful adversary, the 7th Brigade had received some significant reinforcements. These included some local militia units, recruited from among the tough frontier kibbutzniks of eastern Galilee; a company of Circassians (Moslems of Russian origin); and another company of Druze, now an integral unit of the Israeli Army. These auxiliary troops were placed under the command of Yehuda Werber. Yehuda's own

71st Battalion was attached to the brigade's other infantry battalion, the 72nd, both under Jackie Nursella. Our side had not been idle during the truce either, which meant that the two infantry battalions now each had a support company equipped with three-inch infantry mortars and light machine guns. The brigade's armoured battalion, the 79th, was now commanded by Baruch Erez, the well-qualified South African who had previously been its second-in-command.

The brigade's support weapons, too, were far more impressive than anything we had ever possessed before. In addition to two heavy mortars and some antiquated artillery pieces, the initial stages of the attack would be covered by three medium bombers now attached to Northern Command. Heavy support, indeed. But in practice, these powerful weapons brought us no benefit, and even caused some trouble. The "artillery" consisted of two antiquated French 75s, whose trajectory was too flat for them to be of much use in the hills. We had no direct contact with the bombers, and no way of controlling them; the result was a tactical error which might have proved very serious. As for the medium mortars, their officer refused to obey my orders during the operation, claiming that he was "in support" and not "under command" — shades of the tank commander in the Hochwald! All in all, I had little joy from my support units. . . .

When we moved out of western Galilee, our positions were taken over by local militia, while the Oded Brigade was ordered to launch heavy diversionary attacks towards Tarshiha, to deceive the Arabs into thinking that our main attack was coming from the west. To help in the deception, I detached a troop of the 79th Battalion's armoured cars to assist Oded; the cars kept constantly on the move, maintaining a very heavy fire, and successfully convincing the Arabs that they were a much larger force.

While the main Arab forces were tied down in the west, we would move into a three-phase attack, aimed at the Sasa road junction, whose capture would lead to the destruction of Kauk-ji's forces and the capture of central Galilee. The first phase of the attack consisted of an attack on Meron, where our forces would blow up the bridge, making it impossible for Kaukji's reserves in Maghar and Ar Rama to reach the battlefield; at the same time, the engineers would be clearing the Safed-Meron road. In the second phase, we planned to take Kaukji's head-quarters at Jish, which dominated the Sasa road junction. Jish was not heavily defended, and its capture would make it a base for the third phase: the capture of Sasa, which was undefended.

After completing the three-phase plan with the capture of Sasa, we intended to move on to Tarshiha and Tarbiha, taking the forces there in the rear, and then to advance northeast and retake Malkiya.

Quite aside from the military importance of these villages, some of them had great historical significance for Jewish sol-diers. For example, Jish (known in Hebrew as Gush Halav) was the last village in Galilee to hold out against the Roman legions, its defenders fighting on for two years after the rest of the province was overrun. Even then, they were not defeated in battle, but starved out. Weakened by hunger, they had to ac-knowledge defeat; but they fell on their own swords rather than surrender. Now, two thousand years later, Jewish soldiers were again going into battle in these same hills.

Brigade headquarters was at Safed, a quaint little town where Jewish rabbis and sages have maintained their schools for many centuries. Perched high on the hills overlooking precipitous cliffs and valleys, Safed is a mecca for painters who try to capture the brilliant colours of its magnificent views: the snow-capped mountains of Syria, the blue Mediterranean to the west, the Sea of Galilee to the east, and the purple hills all around. With less artistic purposes in mind, I carefully studied this wild mountain-ous terrain, both by means of aerial reconnaissance and from a

vantage point in Safed. After close observation of enemy dispositions in the area, I was satisfied that the Arabs were unaware of
our plan to attack them from Safed: there was no sign of defensive positions covering the Safed-Meron road.

On October 28, just before dusk, the units formed up in their
staging points. Then, as darkness was falling and the units were
getting ready to move off for the attack, we were appalled to
hear the roar of planes overhead. In amazement we watched
planes with Israeli markings approach from the south, and
proceed to bomb the main road between Meron and Jish! Here
we were, taking enormous pains to conceal our intention of
attacking in this area, and, without clearance from me, some air
force staff officer had decided to stage a raid! After the air strike
had ended, I wasn't surprised to observe the lights of three Arab
vehicles on the road; they were heading north, from their base at
Maghar towards Jish. But fortunately the enemy still seemed to
have no clear idea of what was happening.

Darkness fell. The entire brigade was now on the move. The
engineers were working full out to repair the road, with some
armoured cars from Baruch's 79th Battalion close behind, to
protect them in case of need. At the same time, several small
Arab villages to the north of the road were being taken by the
79th Battalion's infantry company, moving in armoured half-
tracks under the command of Moshe Engel.

To keep our movements secret, I had insisted on complete
radio silence. As a result, I could not know what was happening,
and I now transferred to a mobile advance headquarters, with
my staff. Previous experience had taught me that advance headquarters ought to move as a combat unit. Accordingly, we were
accompanied by two troops of jeeps mounted with machine
guns, and one armoured car serving primarily for signals
equipment and personnel. As we moved off, I rode in the armoured car. This proved to be an unfortunate choice; the car's
regular driver fell sick shortly after we started off, and his

inexperienced substitute missed a turn in the road. Normally that would have been only a minor mishap; on this occasion, his oversight was more serious, since when the car ground to a halt, we found ourselves hanging precariously over a cliff which plunged a thousand feet into a deep valley. The moonlit view was spectacular but unattractive. While the car teetered there, its front wheels dangling in space, we swiftly but carefully clambered out of the back. Somehow, despite the vehicle's precarious position, we managed to salvage it. But I'd had enough — I got into one of the jeeps.

Despite that mishap, I was feeling fairly confident, although some misgivings still nagged at the back of my mind. We had taken on some incredibly difficult tasks: clearing the Safed-Meron road, capturing Meron, and blowing up the bridge there. Each one of these had to be completed by first light: failure in any one of them would allow the Arabs to move up their reserves, making our advance immeasurably harder and costlier. The planners at Northern Command doubted our ability to get everything done by morning; were they right?

By now, the engineers were hard at work, removing the remaining obstacles and repairing the culverts. They worked with daring and dispatch, clearing detours wherever the road was impassable. But such activity could not long remain undetected: the Arabs, alerted by the noise, opened fire on the engineers. The armoured cars now moved into action, opening up over the sappers' heads and pouring a heavy fusillade into the enemy positions. This took the pressure off the engineers, allowing them to get on with their labours. At 3.30 a.m., well before daylight, the engineers finished their task: the road was cleared!

Immediately, 79th Battalion moved ahead to the junction with the Meron-Jish road. According to plan, one troop of armoured cars now turned left and headed south, to help 72nd Battalion in taking Meron. At the same time, two companies of the 79th — armoured cars and infantry in half-tracks — raced for Jish.

Jish is on a high hill, some four thousand yards from the crucial Sasa road junction. Kaukji had made it his main headquarters and base, but, believing it to be impregnable, he had left it only lightly defended.

As the Romans had learned two thousand years previously, those hilltop fortresses, defended by men of determination, are almost impossible to take by frontal assault. Our only advantages were speed and surprise, and we used them to the utmost.

Under the command of Amos Benin, the armoured cars roared along the road, closely followed by Engel and his company of half-tracks. It was an awe-inspiring sight to see them hurtling recklessly up the hill towards the enemy with all their guns blazing into the night, while the other units poured effective supporting fire into Jish and the neighbouring village of Safsaf. The assault was spectacular and daring. The armoured cars rushed the defence positions, overwhelming the Arabs before they had time to get organized. Within a short time, the 79th Battalion was in possession of the whole area. Baruch ordered his men to spread out and cover the flanks, so as to consolidate the newly captured positions and make them a firm base for the attack on Sasa which was to go ahead as soon as it could get organized.

Sasa was to be attacked by Jackie's 72nd Battalion. By early morning, the men of his battalion had completed the occupation of Meron and blown up the bridge to the south. After being relieved by 71st Battalion who took over the defensive positions around Meron, the 72nd Battalion made its way towards Jish, with the company of former Etzel soldiers in the vanguard.

It was a complicated plan, for it required one group to leapfrog over another, leaving small bodies of men in the rear and on our flanks to defend our line of advance. But it worked. The captured positions were consolidated and defended by the 71st Battalion, and by the auxiliary companies commanded by Yehuda Werber, while the 79th were freed to join Jackie's men on the short sharp attack on Sasa.

Dawn was breaking. We were in firm control of Jish, and the

area around the village, but there was no time to rest on our laurels. Our unexpected attack had taken Kaukji by surprise, but he would soon get over the shock. Sure enough, a force of his infantry moved down from the north, supported by armoured cars, to launch a powerful counter-attack on our positions around Jish. They advanced with great determination from Sasa crossroads, but by now we had the crossroads under the fire of our guns, and 79th Battalion's armoured cars and half-tracks were also in position to engage the enemy armoured cars in a running battle. At the same time, a group of our infantry moved fast along the base of Mount Atzmon, to attack the Arabs from their southern flank. The brigade headquarters troop went into action here with their light machine guns and were an important factor in stopping the counter-attack. It was a short but fierce engagement; finally, our forces pushed back the enemy, taking control of the Sasa junction as they did so.

It was still the morning of October 29, the first day of our offensive, and we had taken all our immediate objectives. By noon, all organized Arab resistance was at an end, and our brigade headquarters was established at Sasa.[1]

We now sent out detachments to seal off the roads in all directions, trapping the remnants of Kaukji's forces which were retreating north in a steady stream up the road to Malkiya. We sent armoured cars towards Malkiya, while another force headed for Tarshiha, where the Oded Brigade's diversionary attack from the east had tied down most of Kaukji's forces. Our surprise attack took them from the rear, and they quickly ceased all resistance. When evening fell, all our objectives had been taken.

I was too tired to feel any real elation. This was my fourth consecutive night without sleep: on the night preceding the operation, I had been fully occupied with planning and preparations. Then followed the night of the move to Safed, and the night of the assault itself. Now, as we stood in the darkness under

[1]Appendix, paragraph III.

the olive trees of Sasa considering how to exploit our success by eliminating all remnants of Arab resistance, I, like the rest of my officers, was in a bad way; we could scarcely keep our eyes open. In fact, we decided to hold our consultation standing up, because we dozed off as soon as we sat down. Some of our men were detailed to keep prodding us awake as our red-rimmed eyes scanned the maps.

At dawn the next morning, our forces reported the recapture of Malkiya. This meant that thirty-six hours after setting out from Safed, we were in effective possession of the whole of Galilee. Operation Hiram had succeeded brilliantly, almost beyond our expectations. With the roads in our hands, the remnants of Kaukji's thoroughly beaten forces were creeping north into Lebanon, using watercourses and rough shepherd tracks through the hills. Although some four hundred of his men were killed, the main body got away across the border. As they ran away with our units close at their heels, Kaukji's men shed their weapons, their packs, and even their shoes. They had taken a humiliating thrashing. In addition to their casualties, we gathered some rich booty: fifteen hundred rifles, three cannons, two armoured vehicles, twenty cars, four machine guns, and three anti-tank rifles. All this was a very useful addition to our armament and was very graciously received.

More surprisingly, our booty also included large numbers of cattle, abandoned by their fleeing owners. At a loss what to do with them, I turned the beasts over to the local kibbutzim, for which I later received a stern reprimand from Ben-Gurion. He told me I should have held on to them until they could be turned over to the "appropriate authorities"; all my explanations that I was commanding soldiers, not cowboys, failed to appease his indignation. He might have been even more indignant if he had been able to attend our wedding reception, where hundreds of men of the brigade appeared, carrying trays of meat. . . .

After inspecting our positions at Malkiya, I ordered patrols out. One of these was headed by Lieutenant Aya Feldman, the fine young officer who had led that famous bayonet charge in western Galilee. While his patrol advanced along the Lebanese frontier, Aya was killed by a sniper firing from a hilltop inside Lebanon. Aya's death naturally came as a shock to all of us, because he was very popular in the brigade; but it was doubly shocking because it occurred at a time when the fighting seemed to be over. In the whole operation, the forces under my command suffered three dead; considering the size of the tasks we had tackled, it's amazing that we got off so lightly. It was a repetition of my proud record in the Canadian Army, where — with the exception of the Mooshof attack — units I led suffered relatively few casualties.

Our low casualties were no accident, however. The whole attack was planned in such a way that we conducted a minimum of frontal assaults. For the most part, the operation had consisted of carefully planned troop movements, which were unopposed because they crossed difficult terrain where there were next to no enemy forces. When we attacked enemy positions, we came by surprise, from the rear. As a result, we had gained a brilliant victory at an unusually low cost to our men.

Aya's patrol wasn't the only one to come under fire from across the Lebanese border. Other units were also subjected to sporadic sniping from the adjacent hills, so I asked Northern Command for permission to occupy the strategically located border villages, explaining that representatives of these villages had approached us with the request that we occupy their communities and defend them against Kaukji's troops who were seeking asylum there. The request was not as strange as it may seem; these villagers were mostly Christians, who had endured centuries of Moslem persecution, and they were always friendly towards the Jews.

At that time, straight after Operation Hiram, it would have been easy to advance into Lebanon. Even if we had driven as far as their capital, Beirut, I am certain that there would have been no resistance from the Lebanese, who were welcoming our forward patrols with flowers, like an army of liberation. These forward patrols went well beyond the frontier; some of my men actually reached the banks of the Litani, where millions of litres of fine, fresh water — enough to irrigate enormous areas in Israel as well as the Arab countries — pour to waste in the Mediterranean. That flowing river was a tempting sight, and we thought longingly of what Israel would be able to do with it if we could retain control. But high command sent firm orders: we were forbidden to occupy any Lebanese town or village — and our troops were to withdraw from the Litani!

Although the sniping from beyond the Lebanese border was relatively minor, it was an irritant. As I was considering the problem, I was approached by my old acquaintance Shmuelik ("One Shot") Gorodetsky. Once again, Operation Hiram had left Shmuelik a sadly frustrated man. The ancient artillery pieces he commanded were of little or no use in those mountains, which called for high trajectory weapons. As a result, he had dutifully trailed along behind our advancing troops, hauling his guns without ever getting the satisfaction of firing them.

Now, eager as always for a chance to make a bang, he came up to me and proposed that he fire a few shells at the snipers across the border who were bothering us. For want of any other means of dealing with the problem, I told him to loose off a round or two, taking care not to hit any village. Delighted, he brought up his guns; the next time a shot was fired from the hillsides opposite, he sent a couple of shells in that direction.

The result was startling. Hitherto, no more than a few sporadic shots had been fired at us. Now, as the shells landed, a veritable fusillade rang out as dozens of concealed riflemen sprang up, enraged, to return our fire. Shmuelik's shells had stirred up a hornets' nest. I had no interest in provoking a battle across the border, and I considered it advisable to cease the exchange instantly, before the situation got out of control.

Once again, poor Shmuelik had the misfortune of receiving an order which owed little to conventional military protocol:

"Shmuelik — cease fire and get the hell out of here!"

CHAPTER TWENTY-EIGHT

Two Weddings

Operation Hiram was at a triumphant end. After four nights without sleep, I was utterly exhausted, and when I lay down on the cement floor of advanced headquarters at Malkiya I instantly fell asleep. I was sleeping the sleep of the dead when I was rudely disturbed. It was Yosef Eitan, accompanied by my adjutant, Max. When their shaking failed to make me open my eyes, they resorted to a judiciously applied bucket of cold water. I sat up, spluttering and indignant.

"Get up!" they shouted, "Yael is on her way here!" To my befuddled mind, this news was as welcome as an Arab counter-attack! But I scrambled to my feet, while Max explained that he'd had the greatest difficulty in dissuading her from coming all the way to Malkiya. After much cajoling, she had finally consented to wait for me at rear headquarters in Sasa. "But I don't think she'll wait long," he warned. "Unless you get there fast, she'll come up here to find you!" The threat had its effect: the road from Sasa to Malkiya winds through ten miles of wooded hills adjacent to the Lebanese border. The area was still no-man's-land, infested with enemy stragglers and snipers. If she tried to get through, she might run into an ambush. I hurried back to Sasa to intercept her.

Only five days had passed since Motke Makleff's summons interrupted our tranquil discussion of wedding plans. But they had been long days—for Yael as much as for me. She spent the whole of the time at Northern Command headquarters, glued to the signals set, anxiously following the progress of our attack. But the information coming back was scanty and incomplete. She stayed there as long as she could stand the uncertainty, but in the end decided she had to find out for herself what was happening. Making the most of her connections at headquarters, she commandeered a jeep and set off to find me. Her search took her over lonely mountain roads which had yet to be cleared of mines and other dangers.

I must have looked a sorry sight when we met at Sasa. My few hours' sleep hadn't done much to make up for those five sleepless days. I was bleary-eyed and dazed. My uniform was filthy, and, needless to say, there had been no time to wash or shave. I probably looked more like a scarecrow than a victorious brigade commander!

Right from the start, my driver Yossi had appointed himself the watchdog of my romance with Yael, and he now did his best to make up for my bedraggled appearance by putting on a fitting reception for my bride-to-be. He disappeared somewhere, then reappeared occasionally, bustling about on some mysterious business of his own. Finally, bursting with pride, he returned to present the two of us with a magnificent dish of fried chicken which he had miraculously "requisitioned". Yossi's intentions were of the best, and I'm afraid I caused him considerable embarrassment and disappointment by asking him if there was enough chicken to go around for the rest of headquarters staff. Taken by surprise, he tried to bluster. "What d'you care? Go ahead—eat!" But I didn't relent, and he had to admit that there wasn't any more. He then looked completely bewildered when I told him that I couldn't touch his offering.

This wasn't the only incident of the kind. However long he was with me, Yossi could not grasp that I wouldn't accept preferential treatment, particularly not with regard to food. I adhered to the principle we followed in the Canadian Army: I would never eat until I was sure my men had been fed. This habit was respected by my subordinates, but poor Yossi never seemed to comprehend such inexplicable behaviour.

I was still in a sorry-looking state, and Yossi did what he could to help me clean up, rigging up a bucket of water as an improvised shower. When I had made myself look a little more presentable, he drove Yael and me back to Northern Command; still exhausted, I slept most of the way. When I reached headquarters, I arranged to get leave for the wedding.

The wedding ceremony was held at the beautiful Lifshitz home on Mount Carmel, and it was conducted by Rabbi Kniel, the chief rabbi of Haifa. We had planned a quiet wedding; but plans are one thing and their implementation is something entirely different.

It is the Israeli custom to announce forthcoming weddings with newspaper notices inviting all friends and acquaintances. Judging by the turnout, those notices must have been seen—and accepted — by nearly the entire Israeli Army, Navy, and Air Force! Needless to say, the 7th Brigade turned out en masse, bearing some very welcome trays of meat, a wedding present from Kaukji. The reception turned into a large-scale garden party as swarms of guests came to congratulate us. It was a very gay and lighthearted occasion, marred only by one thing. There were still no scheduled airlines serving the new state, connections were haphazard, and no members of my family could reach Israel in time for the ceremony. The Dunkelmans have never forgiven me for not giving them enough notice. Can I blame them?

Although I was granted leave to go on a honeymoon, it seemed that the army was following me everywhere. For one thing, Moshe Carmel strolled up to me during the party and casually asked me to report at Northern Command headquar-

ters the next morning. It seems he expected me to deliver a
lecture on the planning of Operation Hiram—on the first day of
my honeymoon! I never found out whether or not he was joking.
In any case, I chose to believe that he was, and failed to deliver
the lecture.

That lecture was comparatively easy to evade, which is more
than could be said for Yossi, my driver, who seemed determined
to accompany us on our honeymoon. Needless to say, I didn't
relish that idea, and I tried to get rid of him by insisting that he
go on leave. I underestimated his tenacity. Undeterred, he returned to our seaside hotel at Nathanya, and after no more than
a casual knock at the door, barged straight into our bedroom to
notify us that he was ready to drive us anywhere we wanted.

Our honeymoon lasted for ten glorious and peaceful days,
marked by only two noteworthy events. The first was a visit from
Ben-Gurion and his wife, Paula, who came to explain that a
cabinet session had kept him from attending our wedding. We
were greatly honoured by the visit—spent at the home of Yael's
parents—as well as by Ben-Gurion's present: a set of his works,
with his personal inscription, which we treasure to this day.

The second event began in a somewhat more ominous manner. I was approached by an emissary from Sheikh Marzouk,
who informed me that I had grievously offended the Druze: I
hadn't invited them to my wedding! This was a grave affront to
the feelings of my friends and comrades-in-arms from the villages of Yanuh, Jatt, and Yerka, as well as the Druze inhabitants
of Shafa Amr.

I was appalled by my thoughtlessness. I had been instrumental
in enlisting the aid of these brave people for Israel's war effort; I
had been in close and friendly contact with them ever since—
and then I went and forgot completely that they would not, of
course, read the Hebrew and English newspapers, and would
therefore not see our wedding notices! Highly embarrassed by
my oversight, I did my best to assure the emissary that it had

been completely unintentional. After offering my heartfelt apologies, I was relieved and pleased to receive a very tangible token of their forgiveness: we were invited to the Druze villages for a feast and a "fantasia" in honour of our marriage! It was a great honour and privilege, and we accepted the invitation with gratitude.

I had no doubt about the sincerity of the Druze and their feelings towards me, and had full and implicit faith in them and their hospitality. Nevertheless, as I thought about the forthcoming festivities, I had some misgivings about what might happen there. The Druze regard all their people as kinsmen; nevertheless, there is always a certain amount of feuding among the various clans and villages. The three villages that had invited us were involved in a particularly bitter and long-drawn-out vendetta, and there had been open hostility among them for years. In addition, there had recently been some regrettable incidents in that area, and several Israeli soldiers had been killed in the clashes. I was worried about what might happen when all these people got together for the first time in many years. From my youthful days with my Arab and Bedouin friends I was familiar with the "fantasia" and knew that the main feature of a "fantasia" is the shooting: it is the custom for every man who carries a gun to blaze away with it. Usually, the shots are directed at the sky — but sometimes a bullet can go astray. . . .

Bearing this in mind, I took certain precautions. Although I did not anticipate any premeditated disruptions, my preparations for the reception were made with the thoroughness of a military operation. Indeed, it resembled a military operation in other ways. My brigade's 79th Armoured Battalion provided an impressive escort: no less than an entire squadron of armoured cars, each with its complement of machine guns and heavier armament. It was an unusually formidable wedding procession.

On the morning of the appointed day, our column moved up the rough serpentine tracks which led into the hills. Yael was quite apprehensive, but I held her hand and tried to reassure her, while cautioning her to be ready for surprises. They weren't long in coming.

As we proceeded on our way, we were met by companies of fiercely moustached Druze, who lined up on both sides of the road with raised guns, which they fired off close above our heads. We drove along under a triangular wedding canopy of flying bullets. Impressive, but a little unnerving. Yael, who is rather timid by nature, flinched as the salvoes echoed all around us, but she gamely did her best to overcome her fears. After the first shock, she gradually regained her composure, and sat at my side as white as a ghost. Again, I cautioned her: "This is just the beginning. . . ." I knew what was to come.

We stopped at the first village. Yael and I were conducted to a central square; above us, the rooftops were jammed with people waiting to welcome us. As we stood there, a platoon of men came marching towards us, their white kaffia head-dresses fluttering in the breeze. They were led by a dapper officer, breeched and booted, and very handsome with his bristling moustaches. He brought his men to attention before us; then, turning, he marched smartly in our direction, with his pistol drawn. He halted in front of Yael, dropped on one knee, raised his pistol, and emptied it at the sky, just inches from her face. I stood close by her, watching her anxiously out of the corner of my eye: I was half afraid she might faint. But I had no cause for concern. Yael was still on her own two feet, and was now entirely her usual graceful self. She had passed the test of the "fantasia"!

The festivities were lavish and extravagant. A banquet had been prepared for us in each of the villages, and each mukhtar (mayor) in turn invited us to his feast. Each was conducted in the same manner: our hosts brought in and set down before us great circular pans of lamb stew, and trays piled high with meat. Sitting beside me in the place of honour, Yael was the only woman present: the Druze do not consider it becoming for their women to join in public revelries. As guests of honour, we were expected to initiate the proceedings by dipping our hands into the steaming plates. After we took our first mouthful, we were followed by the mukhtar, and then the other dignitaries, and finally all the other guests joined in lustily. Outside the banqueting hall, the men of the village were playing all kinds of games, accompanied by wild cheering and firing in our honour. Meanwhile, the women, though confined to their quarters, found their own way of joining in the festivities: their singing and chanting was clearly audible.

The same ceremony was repeated in each of the villages, and we were expected to partake heartily at each banquet. Even with my healthy appetite, trained from infancy at the groaning board in the "Kibbutz Dunkelman", I found this a formidable task. Yael, who eats little at the best of times, found herself in deep trouble: she couldn't, of course, refuse any food without insulting our charming hosts. Accordingly, she was obliged to go through the motions of eating, putting on a convincing show by chewing each tiny mouthful hundreds of times, with great relish.

The last banquet was held in Sheikh Marzouk's village, where we were led into a high-ceilinged, domed room and seated on a raised dais, above our hosts and fellow-guests. This banquet resembled the previous two, with the same ceremonies and rituals, but there was one important difference: the guests included mukhtars and dignitaries from the other villages, who had gathered under one roof for the first time in years. In our honour, they were setting aside ancient but continuing quarrels; today, they were joining together for a banquet and a "fantasia". This reconciliation was an unprecedented event. It was wonderful to feel that we were directly instrumental in ending the bitter hostilities which had set these men at each other's throats for so long.

The revelries were growing wilder and more unrestrained by the minute. In the streets all around the house, the tempo of firing was increasing with every passing minute until it sounded as if a full-scale war was going on outside—and even inside the building, some guest or other would frequently demonstrate his enthusiasm by blazing away at the ceiling. Judging by the wild shrieks coming from that direction, the excitement in the women's quarters was also reaching a peak. Sheikh Marzouk now extended an invitation from his wife, who asked Yael to join her in her quarters and accept a wedding gift. By this time, however, Yael was reluctant to move from my side, and she contrived—as gracefully as she could—to refuse the invitation. The sheikh did not press her. Instead, he himself went to the women's quarters and personally brought Yael the present. It was a magnificent, hand-wrought gold necklace, which his wife had taken off her own neck.

Touching as this gesture was, it was quite overshadowed by what was happening in the hall, where I saw men who had not spoken with each other for years shaking hands and patching up their differences. Slights were brushed away, feuds forgotten, and vendettas settled in a veritable frenzy of reconciliation. It was profoundly touching to see former enemies embrace, rejoicing in their renewed friendship—a kind of microcosm of universal peace and brotherhood. It was impossible to watch without being moved.

But this new-found harmony was still very fragile, as we soon discovered. Ironically, the disruption came from two of the Jewish guests. While the Druze were reviving old friendships, these two — our old friends Mordechai and Chaim — were continuing an old feud. Ironically, the seeds of their feud lay in the fact that they had supported different factions among the feuding Druze. Now, as the Druze were overcoming their own differences, several of them decided to sponsor a reconciliation between Chaim and Mordechai. The two men were coaxed — dragged almost — to the centre of the hall, and their Druze friends stood around, smiling encouragement as they waited for the pair to shake hands. But these expectations were premature: at loggerheads on everything else, the two foes were united in their mutual hatred. To everyone's consternation, neither of them would hold out the hand of friendship.

In the midst of that general festival of reconciliation, this unfriendly act was like a bombshell. The atmosphere of friendship which had filled the hall a brief moment ago was now rudely shattered, and the air suddenly filled with tension. There was a deathly silence. Then, worse than silence, the shuffle of feet as the Druze of the various villages began to line up alongside their respective Jewish "champions", who stood face to face, glowering at each other.

The situation was explosive, and a flare-up seemed inevitable. One false move could lead to bloodshed: every man there was armed. I was very worried about Yael, and concerned for her safety if a brawl should erupt. Fortunately, I had earlier taken the precaution of ordering the armoured cars drawn up around the building. Now, as I saw what was happening inside the building, I quickly decided to create a diversion: I ordered the squadron's crews to open up with all their automatic weapons.

Instantly, dozens of light and heavy machine guns let fly with a thunderous roar which reverberated from all sides. It was a most impressive display of fireworks, and the deafening din had its desired effect: without exception, all the guests froze in open-mouthed admiration of this massive fusillade, which far surpassed anything they'd ever experienced before. The Druze were delighted! With such a stupendous "fantasia" going on, the two opposing camps quickly abandoned their eyeball-to-eyeball confrontation to run outside and enjoy the fun. Ironically, those automatic weapons had restored the peace!

The danger was past. Nevertheless, I decided not to risk any further incidents. Seizing the opportunity, we quickly bid adieu to our hosts. I accompanied Yael to our car, and with the armoured car escort in our wake, we drove away. As we sped back down the hill, I breathed a heartfelt sigh of relief. It had been a joyful and unforgettable feast. I was glad that it had ended on a happy note.

CHAPTER TWENTY-NINE

From Soldier to Settler

On November 5 the ten glorious days of our honeymoon came to an end, and I went back to being a soldier. But it was a very different kind of soldiering now. To all intents and purposes, the War of Independence was at an end. The last battles of the war, fought shortly after my return to duty, resulted in the Egyptians' being driven back across the mandatory border of Palestine, until they retained only the narrow coastal strip around Gaza. Meanwhile, in the Jerusalem sector the Arab Legion had been contained, although the Israeli forces did not succeed in recapturing important objectives like the Jewish quarter of Jerusalem's Old City, Latrun, or the Etzion settlements, and the Arabs held the "Triangle", a strategic salient which nearly cut Israel in two between Haifa and Tel Aviv. (Shamir, now the commander of that area, refused my offer to bring the 7th Brigade in to straighten out the Triangle, for reasons best known to himself.) But new Jerusalem was firmly in Israeli hands, while the vital supply corridor to the city had been maintained and even extended. In the north, the success of Operation Hiram had given us control of the whole of Galilee, and there was little further fighting in our sector after the destruction of Kaukji's army. The Syrians maintained a small foothold around the captured Jewish settlement of Mishmar Hayarden, from where they threatened Rosh Pina; but after witnessing

Kaukji's fate, the Syrians were careful to refrain from provocations.

After months of danger and tension, the 7th Brigade had to get used to the humdrum task of manning the positions facing the Syrians. In good weather it might have been fairly pleasant, but winter was another matter. Just as foreigners find it hard to believe that summers in Canada are uncomfortably hot ("But wouldn't that melt all the snow?" is one famous response), so those who have never been to Israel find it hard to believe that the winters can be cold. A single night in our positions opposite the Syrians would have taught them otherwise. In the north, the winter nights are bitter and our inadequate uniforms afforded little protection against the chill winds that whistled from the snows of Mount Hermon.

In these conditions the men soon became bored and disgruntled. In fact, the men of 72nd Battalion's English-speaking company began to complain so bitterly that their complaints soon became a demand to be demobilized; whereupon their commander got them together for a pep-talk, in which he told them in no uncertain terms how privileged they were to be allowed to defend their own country again, after two thousand years of dispersion. That kind of rousing speech was not unusual; what made this one remarkable was the fact that, unlike most of his listeners, the officer was a Gentile! When he first joined the brigade, he made no secret of the fact that he was on leave from the British Army. In view of Britain's attitude at that time, this should have made him an object of suspicion, but I placed complete trust in him, which he fully justified. In time, he became the commander of Israel's first paratroop school.

Our tasks now consisted of uneventful patrols and guard duties, leaving us plenty of time and energy for more interesting occupations. In flagrant defiance of the law, we undertook many trips across the Lebanese border, where the villagers welcomed us in a most friendly fashion and fed us royally. Another piece of law-breaking was more personal: Yael moved to Safed to be with me. Hitherto, I had strictly forbidden men of the brigade to bring wives or girl-friends to our operations area. I tried to keep the rule myself, but Yael simply informed me that she was coming to Safed, and there seemed to be nothing much I could do about it. With military activity at a standstill, there was little I could do to impress my bride with my heroism. However, since an icy fog enveloped the hotel where we were staying, and since our room was unheated, it became my regular duty to enter the bed first, to warm the chilly sheets for my pampered young bride.

Now that we were free of active combat duty, I could devote more time to organizing the brigade and improving its training. There was also time to deal with something that had worried me for a long time, the fact that the Israeli Army lacked a proper code of military law. I'd had many opportunities to observe how badly such a code was needed. On one occasion during the Galilee campaign, I ordered a stand-to in one of the battalions (which means that everyone, without exception, must man his post). Yet when I went there to inspect the unit, I found that the battalion's commander was absent! This was such a shocking example to set his men that I decided to lay charges against him. But because there was no legal structure in the army, there was no point in laying formal charges — and when I informed my superiors about the incident, they "punished" the man by transferring him to another unit, where he continued to serve as an officer!

This absence of a legal structure was bad for military efficiency, and it was often bad for ordinary soldiers. I remember one particularly shocking example, which I witnessed during my service in Jerusalem. A Palmach officer paraded his whole battalion to denounce a young soldier, whom he accused of cowardice under fire. To my horror, the officer pulled the boy out of

line, slapping and punching him to "punish" him for his behaviour. Then, having been deliberately disgraced in front of his
comrades, who watched all this in tight-lipped silence, the boy
was shoved back into line to join them, crushed with shame.
Quite aside from the degradation, I was horrified by the idea of a
man being summarily punished because his nerve failed him, let
alone a seventeen-year-old who had been perhaps facing death
for the first time. I can't blame the officer concerned. Palmach
discipline relied heavily on social pressure engendered within
the tightly knit framework of a platoon or section where everyone knew everyone else; in a unit as large as a battalion, it
couldn't function. In the absence of conventional military law,
the commander was at a loss and simply made up his own rules
and punishments.

Now there was time to work on this pet project of mine, and I
also had the right man to do it. One of the officers in the brigade,
A. Hoter Ishai, was a lawyer who had served with the British
Army and had become an expert on the subject of military law. I
set him to work on drawing up an original code, largely based on
the British model. As a result, among its other "firsts", the 7th
Brigade was the first Israeli unit with a regular legal structure. A
copy was sent to high command, where it made such a deep
impression that Hoter Ishai was promptly transferred to army
headquarters to promulgate a general body of Israeli military
law.

As it turned out, my brigade was not called upon to conduct
active operations after the successful conclusion of Operation
Hiram. But at that time it still seemed quite likely that hostilities
would be resumed in the near future. In case that happened, I
prepared a plan for an offensive against the Syrians. After close
study of the terrain and of enemy dispositions, I became convinced that a reinforced 7th Brigade could encircle the Syrian
Army, capture Kuneitra, and drive on to Damascus! I presented
these plans to Moshe Carmel, at Northern Command, and to his

chief of staff, Motke Makleff. The plan sounded grandiose, but it was no more ambitious than the previous plans for the conquest of Nazareth and for Operation Hiram, both of which had been carried out with complete success.

I was summoned to meet with Ben-Gurion to discuss these plans for the Syrian front. After a useful discussion, we went on to discuss over-all questions of military organization, training, and tactics, which provoked him to ask me to present him with written memoranda. Towards the end of January 1949, I concluded many weeks of discussions and research by handing him two reports dealing with a number of vital topics: training, discipline, the selection of officers, mobilization of reserves, the tactical role of armour, and co-operation between armour and infantry.

Ben-Gurion greeted my report on military matters with enthusiasm, and it later was adopted by the Israeli Army and fully implemented. He expressed the hope that I would stay on in the army, and offered me command of the entire armoured corps! It was both an honour and a challenge to receive such an offer, which seemed to hold out hopes of going to the very top of the military hierarchy. With the command, I would attain the rank of "Aluf"—full colonel—which meant that I would be subordinate only to one man, the chief of staff. This would assure a secure and promising future for me in Israel.

At this point, the other half of my dual allegiance began to make its presence felt. Almost a year had passed since I had left Canada, and in the meantime I had acquired a wife whom my family had not yet met. The postal service to Israel during the war was less than perfect, but even the barriers it erected were not enough to stop volleys of letters from my parents getting through, all of them demanding that I show them their new daughter-in-law as soon as possible. Since the negotiations at Rhodes for an armistice with the Arab states seemed to be progressing well, I felt that I was safe in going to Canada for a few weeks, and applied for leave. In due course permission was granted. On February 7, 1949, Yael and I set off for Canada.

It was a memorable flight. At that time, only Sabena flew from Israel, and their planes followed no regular schedule. Yael was flying for the first time, and was more than a little apprehensive. Naturally, I exuded confidence, telling her how well maintained aircraft were nowadays and how rarely anything went wrong. And so on. My glib line of salesman's patter died away for a moment when I saw the antiquated DC-3 that was to carry us, and heard the blasphemous comments it provoked from some of our fellow-passengers, a group of volunteer pilots on the way home to the United States. Once we were in the air, my propaganda to Yael was further undermined as the pilots proceeded to loudly call the missing cylinders. They were right, too. We had to make two forced landings before the plane managed to struggle across the Alps. Yael's faith in aircraft and her husband took a severe beating; but in recompense we enjoyed an unscheduled stopover in Nice, while the plane was being repaired.

When we arrived in New York, my sisters, Zelda and Ronny, were there to greet us. They took one look at the little country girl I had brought with me, and then the two of them, lovely and sophisticated ladies of fashion, dragged her off for a shopping spree beyond Yael's wildest dreams. The next stop was Toronto where, amid scenes of great excitement, the family greeted Yael and welcomed me back after nearly a year of combat. It was good to be home.

But my mind was still back in Israel. In the course of our travels, the Arabs had decided that they had no hope of gaining a decisive victory over Israel. On the contrary — before the fighting was halted, their own armies were in imminent danger of destruction. They decided to call it a day. On February 24, 1949, an armistice was agreed between Egypt and Israel, followed in the coming months by similiar agreements with Transjordan, Lebanon, and Syria.

On April 1, 1949, Yael and I returned to Israel.

I had given Ben-Gurion's offer of command of the armoured corps a great deal of thought and had finally decided to turn it down, with regret. It was a dazzling prospect to be so close to the top, and the challenge and the responsibility, along with the honour and the glory, would have meant a great deal to me. Certainly, it would have changed my life. But in the end I turned it down for the same reason that I turned down the command of the 1st Battalion of the Queen's Own: I was not a soldier. When men were needed in time of war, I'd be there; but in peacetime I wanted to get out of uniform, back to normal civilian life.

Ben-Gurion accepted this explanation of my decision not to accept his promotion. He also accepted my suggestion that now my most important contribution might be in the civilian arena. But he did extract a commitment from me: "Whether as a soldier or as a civilian — promise me you will remain in Israel!" I promised.

I was not able to keep that promise, although I fully intended to do so. In our first few months back in Israel, Yael and I rented a little apartment in Haifa, on the Carmel. There we soon learned that our first child was on the way. My excitement was dampened by the news from Toronto that my mother's cardiac condition was causing the family a great deal of concern.

Meanwhile, I plunged into the business world in Israel with an enthusiasm and energy that surprises and pains me when I think of it now. The economy of the new state was in pitiful condition; unless we could get it going, bankruptcy might achieve what the Arabs had failed to do.

Immigration was a major cause of the economic problem. At the time of its proclamation on May 14, 1948, Israel had a Jewish population of just over six hundred thousand. In November 1949 it reached the one million mark, and continued to climb as immigrants poured into the country in a steady stream. Most of them were penniless. There was next to nothing to prepare for their reception—no jobs, no food, and no houses. Squalid transit camps of shacks and tents sprouted everywhere as the authorities desperately tried to cope.

In these circumstances, with Ben-Gurion's encouragement, I decided to enter the housing market. Making full use of my business contacts, I arranged for engineers from U.S. Steel to come in and put up a model Quonset hut—ugly as sin, but cheap and easy to erect, and the ideal solution to the desperate need for temporary housing. The entire Israeli cabinet came to inspect it and, satisfied with what they saw, gave me a written order for five thousand units. Encouraged by this, I made further arrangements with U.S. Steel to import a light mobile steel fabrication plant, which would be very useful for construction.

As if that wasn't enough to keep me busy I also acquired, with official approval, the franchise to bottle Coca-Cola in Israel. An unimportant product in itself, perhaps, but symbolically important, since its establishment in Israel was likely to encourage other American firms to expand into the country, which badly needed such investment.

For the same reason, I was horrified to discover that our valuable foreign currency was being spent on importing uniforms from Europe. I knew a little about setting up uniform plants as a result of my 1939 experience in Canada. I plunged into that project, too, renting a factory in Acre and lining up the necessary machinery in Canada, together with key personnel to come and get the operation going.

On all three business fronts, things seemed to be running smoothly and I was confident that the one hundred thousand dollars I had spent would be recovered when the projects got going. But there were one or two clouds on the horizon. One official regulating the construction field had looked at me pityingly and asked why I wanted to compete with Solel Boneh (Israel's largest contracting firm, owned by the Histadrut Labour Federation, and thus the possessor of much political influence). The Coca-Cola franchise idea was apparently unpopular among existing Israeli soft drink manufacturers. And, despite the help I received from Golda Meir, the Minister of Labour, the uniform factory was running into strong labour opposition (our friends in the Histadrut again), because it, like any other efficient clothing factory, was to be run on piece-work lines. And my applications for permission to import the necessary machinery for these various projects were still awaiting official clearance. No doubt it was just bureaucratic delay....

CHAPTER THIRTY

A Home in Toronto

While all three of my business ventures were at this critical stage, we received a telegram from Toronto: MOTHER CRITICALLY ILL. I dropped everything and we left for Canada at once, arriving on October 8.

On her deathbed, Mother extracted two promises from me. She wanted to be buried in Israel; and she asked me to promise that I wouldn't name our child after her but after my youngest sister Theo (Theodora), who had died tragically while very young. She would not relent until I gave her my promise.

Of the two vows, I kept one. Mother's final resting place is in Kibbutz Degania, near the Kinneret, as she wished.

As to my second vow: my grandmother, Dora Miller, the matriarch of the family, released me from it. My first daughter, born on Mother's birthday and two months after her death on October 20, is named after her grandmother: Rose.

I spent the two months between my mother's death and the birth of my daughter in a state of high tension. On top of the emotional upheaval was the knowledge that I had left Israel with all of my projects hanging in mid-air. I was eager to get back to get working on them again as soon as Yael was fit to travel.

Then the word came from Israel. Every time I opened a letter there was more bad news; one by one, like successive blows to my stomach, the projects were turned down by the government for various reasons. I bombarded the authorities with letters and telegrams, trying to get permission for my projects. Officials who had promised their help were suddenly very evasive and unable to give me any clear commitment. I felt as if my ribs had been kicked in; I knew now what it was to feel like an outsider.

In the meantime, while we were temporarily in Toronto, my wife and baby daughter and I had to eat. I was heavily in debt, with no reserves left. My father renewed his perennial pressure on me to rejoin Tip Top Tailors. As long as I was here in Toronto, why couldn't I give a hand?

I was very wary of getting entangled once again, so I cautiously agreed to a compromise. I would spend part of my time at Tip Top Tailors, while the rest of my time would be my own to devote to some private projects, which seemed likely to be interesting and profitable.

We bought a home in Toronto for the time being. There was no furniture, of course; all of my furniture was in Haifa, waiting to be uncrated. Sadly, I sent instructions to reload the crates on a ship and send them back to Canada. Yael, of course, found it hard to accept the idea of living in Canada, far from her family and friends, although she was given a warm welcome here and made to feel very much at home. The welcome came not only from my family and friends. In view of my wartime record, Parliament passed a special act, granting her immediate Canadian citizenship — a splendid gesture. Equally unusual (for a Sabra!) was the kind invitation she received to join the Queen's Own auxiliary chapter of the Independent Order of the Daughters of the British Empire. The IODE is usually regarded as an extremely aloof and snobbish WASP organization, but Yael was made to feel at home there.

Soon we began to put down other roots in Canada. In 1951 our second daughter was born. In honour of Lady Wingate, we named her Lorna.

But although I was predictably becoming more and more

involved in running the family business, Israel was never far from our minds. On one occasion, it took the form of a telegram signed jointly by Ben-Gurion and Golda Meir. The second Israel Bonds campaign in Canada was in difficulties. Would I take over as chairman of the Toronto campaign?

Since my return, I had been too busy — and too poor — to return to my former Zionist activities. But I could not remain indifferent to such a request, and I threw myself into the appeal. The campaign went very well, aided by a daring innovation: we made an appeal in the synagogues, during the High Holidays, when the Jewish community turned out en masse. At first, the idea ran into strenuous opposition, but I refused to give in. The appeals were made to packed synagogues, and results were so satisfactory that the idea has now caught on in almost all the Jewish communities in North America, and in other places, too.

Whenever we could, Yael and I undertook visits to Israel to visit kith and kin and see what was happening to the new state. I always loved those visits. Besides my over-all love for Israel, I am deeply attached to the small, everyday things: the food, the sun, the landscape. There was the pleasure of seeing my many dear friends, while, needless to say, Yael has many more links to maintain.

Every time we went there, I secretly hoped that some opportunity would come up, some opening which would permit us to settle in Israel. But each visit showed us how hard it would be to move our growing family, and establish ourselves there.

There's a link between the size of our family, and our visits to Israel. Since Yael was always eager to go to Israel, we had a semi-humorous agreement: the "contract" said that after every journey, we'd have another child. We didn't keep the deal a secret, and our friends knew what to expect after each of our Israel trips.

In 1953 our third daughter was born: Deenah.

On every visit to Israel, I would spend as long as I could —

hours and sometimes days — with Ben-Gurion. Even when he was unwell and was officially seeing no one, he was a wonderful host to me — courteous and friendly. We had long talks on general Israeli affairs; as usual, I found him bright and incisive, and he listened carefully to all I said. But he was obviously upset that we were living in Canada. "How can you live anywhere else but Israel?" he would ask me. I tried to explain about the difficulties which had foiled my attempts to settle in Israel, but he brushed them off as secondary. "You come and live here!" he said. "You'll see — the problems will work themselves out."

He didn't remind me of it then, but both of us remembered that I had given him my word of honour that I'd live in Israel. That unfulfilled commitment preyed on my conscience, even though I felt that it was no fault of mine I hadn't kept it.

In January 1957 Yael and I visited Israel. It was shortly after the 1956 Sinai campaign, and the Israeli Army was occupying the Sinai Peninsula. Ben-Gurion asked me to go down and take a look around. When I came back, I told him my impressions of all I'd seen. Stressing the importance of Sharm a Sheikh, which controls the Tiran Straits, I urged Ben-Gurion not to relinquish this strategic position. He became indignant at the very idea, and assured me that he had no intention of withdrawing. A few days later, I heard the announcement on Israel radio: in response to United States pressures, Israel was withdrawing from the whole of the Sinai Peninsula, including Sharm a Sheikh. Clearly, President Eisenhower's men had exerted enormous pressure.

In 1957 our fourth daughter: Daphna.

With the passing of the years, it became clear that my dreams of settling in Israel would have to be postponed. I was now firmly established in business in Toronto, running an airport hotel and creating a large shopping centre, apart from my role in the family business. At the request of the Jewish community I had become involved, as chairman, in the creation of the Island Yacht Club — now one of Canada's largest. My ties and responsibilities were not the type that could be sloughed off with ease. Our children were all born in Canada; this is where they had their schools and their friends, this is their natural environment, and where they feel at home. Rose, our eldest, was twelve: it would be hard for her to adjust to a new life in a new country.

My father kept trying to bring me back into the management of Tip Top Tailors, but I refused to commit myself. In the end, Dad forced the issue in a characteristically direct and simple manner. One day, he called me to him and once more asked me to take over the company. Yet again, I refused. Whereupon he said: "I'm going to Florida."

I was caught by surprise. "What about the business?" I asked.

He shrugged his shoulders. "Let it go bankrupt!"

I was left with no choice. I took over what I knew would be an enormous workload. As I told myself, it would be for a short time only. . . .

In 1963 our twin sons, David and Jonathan, were born. We now had six children, and decided to abandon our arrangement about trips to Israel.

Over twenty-five years have passed since my "temporary" return to Canada; all that time my life has been divided. My everyday activities, my work, my family, and my friends — all these have focussed my attention on the immediate Canadian environment. But at the back of my mind and never far from the surface of my consciousness, there was the constant tug of Israel, and the hazy hope that, somehow or other, I'd be able to realize my dreams and make my home there. It may sound pretentious, but my situation is not unlike that of the mediaeval Jewish poet Yehuda Halevi, who lived in Spain but dreamed of the Holy Land: "I am in the west, but my heart is far away, in the east." My links, my concerns, my worries, and my preoccupations were largely bound up with Israel, with its development and its problems, with its failures and its triumphs. Like Yehuda Halevi, my heart was there, in the sun-drenched landscape I got to know so well, as a farmer and as a soldier; it was there with the people, alongside whom I had worked and fought and suffered and wept and rejoiced.

My heart's links were more than a jaded figure of speech. In the nerve-wracking weeks which preceded the Six Day War, in late May and early June 1967, when the Arab armies were massing on Israel's borders and the United Nations forces had been ordered out, I felt strongly that the state was in danger of imminent destruction. The only path open to Israel, I thought, was to launch a pre-emptive strike, before it was too late. I sent off telegrams, urging the Israeli leaders to strike fast — but before I found out that they were doing that precise thing, my worry and concern exacted their price from my body. On June 5, while Israel was battling for its life, I was battling for mine, following a near-fatal cardiac seizure. After forty-eight hours in an oxygen tent, I was through the worst of the crisis, and my complete recovery was hastened by the news of Israel's victory over three powerful Arab armies, in the course of six days. After that, I may be forgiven for claiming that, for better or worse, my heart is in Israel!

After the near-fatal heart attack, my life underwent great changes. I sold the business, which was now flourishing, and received a substantial price for it. Yael and I followed one of our dreams by opening an art gallery, which, with simple modesty, we named The Dunkelman Gallery. We were particularly privileged to be chosen by Kahnweiler to be Picasso's exclusive representative in Canada. This involvement with art and artists has given both of us a great deal of pleasure.

In addition, I was able to indulge many of my old hobbies and sports, especially those connected with the outdoors. I went on treks in Alaska and the Yukon, and on photographic safaris in Africa. I did a lot of sailing and boating. Clearly, my heart was stronger than ever before, despite that attack.

Early in 1973 I visited Israel for the 7th Brigade's twenty-fifth anniversary. It was a great occasion: along with the other former commanders of the brigade, I had the honour of being presented with a ceremonial trophy. It was wonderful to see all my old companions and comrades-in-arms again, and to be reminded of the almost legendary position the brigade holds in the hearts and minds of the people of Israel.

During this visit, I went on a tour of Israeli positions in Sinai and found many things which disturbed me. Taking full advantage of my role as elder statesman, I pointed out the deficiencies I'd noticed. My comments were listened to politely enough, but there was a great atmosphere of absolute self-confidence and assurance, and I knew that my comments were falling on stony ground. In a way, I was pleased to find the Israeli commanders so full of self-assurance, since this is such a valuable attitude for an officer to have; but I couldn't help harbouring a sneaking suspicion that it may be overdone (the Maginot Line is a case in point) and perhaps verged on an unwarranted arrogance.

A few months later, on October 6, 1973, when the Yom Kippur War broke out, it became regrettably clear that my premonitions were not misplaced: there were serious deficiencies in the Israeli chain of command. But Israel's forces recovered from their surprise so quickly that once again the United Nations had to intervene to protect the endangered Arab armies. During the fighting, my old brigade, the 7th, covered itself in glory once more. I was proud to hear of that; but I was saddened to hear of the heavy price it had to pay.

On the face of it, my life has been incomplete. I have achieved some success in my undertakings, whether as businessman, or soldier, or in the other roles I have played. But I haven't always achieved what I desired. I've had a lot of fun in the outdoors world that I love—but most of my life has been spent in cities. I have built a home—but not necessarily where I wanted it to be.

As a loyal citizen of Canada, I've worked and fought for this country, and I feel deep bonds with Canadians of all ethnic origins. But I am not a citizen of that other country I have cherished and defended.

And yet, with all my dissatisfaction that things haven't worked out precisely as I wanted or expected, I feel now as I did when I came back to prosperous, secure Canada from my second trip to Palestine in 1936, leaving behind me the Jewish settlers, struggling with their enormous difficulties — arduous living conditions, constant dangers, and back-breaking toil. At that time, as I looked around at the people enjoying the luxuries and comforts of this rich land, I remember saying to myself: "My life has been fuller than any ten of theirs put together. I'm in my early twenties, yet if I were to die tomorrow, I would die a happy man, because I have lived such a full life, in such a short period of time."

My life has been passed shuttling to and fro, from Canada to Israel and back again. (Even now, as I write, work is going forward on a villa that Yael and I are having built in Israel, just outside Nathanya. When it is completed, who knows what we will do.)

This shuttling to and fro, physically and in spirit, has given my life an additional dimension. My dual allegiance has given me the pleasures of two lives. When I think of the good men of two armies who fought and died alongside me, I realize that I have been lucky to live so much, and see so much, and feel so much.

I have been very privileged.

APPENDIX

Inaccurate Historical Accounts

Many of the events depicted in this narrative have been described in other books, which purport to be accurate and objective historical accounts. Regrettably, many of these display an astounding degree of inaccuracy, especially with regard to military operations. I believe that at least some of these inaccuracies stem from incorrect reports given to the historians by various officers and commanders whose involvement and personal interests may have induced them to tamper with the facts.

The following are a few random examples of this phenomenon; I have picked those having some bearing on the contents of this book:

I. "Haim Laskov": an unpublished account, describing his service with the 7th Brigade. (Mimeographed. Hebrew. Unsigned, and bearing no name of publisher. Received early in 1955.) In this account, which is on file in the Archives of the Israeli Army, Laskov describes himself (pp. 80-81) as taking command of the 7th Brigade on July 5, 1948, at a meeting in Ein Shemer. Further, he recounts handing over command to me on July 22, 1948. (NB These dates include the period of the Shafa-Amr–Nazareth operation.)

This version is incorrect. At no time did Chaim Laskov command the 7th Brigade. I took command of the brigade on or about July 5, 1948, before the brigade moved to the north,

327

and remained its commander until my release from the army in 1949. (For an account of my taking command of the brigade, see Chapter Twenty-two.)

II. Netanel Lorch, *The Edge of the Sword* (New York: G. P. Putnam's Sons, 1961). On p. 118, he describes the British as fulfilling their promise to keep the Sheikh Jerrah quarter neutral until their final withdrawal. If so, why was the Mount Scopus garrison cut off during this time, and why did the Palmach reinforcements have to sneak through at night to relieve it (see Chapter Nineteen)?

III. Lieutenant-Colonel G. Luria: *Ma'arachot* (Israeli Army official publication), January 1963. A description of Operation Hiram, which seems to be coloured by somewhat inflated accounts of the contribution of the Oded Brigade. For example, he criticizes the 7th Brigade for the tardiness of its advance (!) on Sasa. For a more correct description of the operation — including its lightning timetable — see Chapter Twenty-seven of this book. Oded's role in the operation was principally diversionary, and it was not charged with taking any of the main objectives.

The above are a few examples of the errors I have discovered in accounts of the 1948 war; they refer only to events of which I have direct personal knowledge. The presence of such errors casts some doubt on the reliability of the facts conveyed in these accounts. While the historians share some of the responsibility, it seems that the officers who reported these "facts" are principally to blame for the inaccuracies.

The above is not my view alone. In describing the Nazareth campaign, Jon and David Kimche (*A Clash of Destinies*, footnote p. 226) complain:

"Here we came up against an apparent contradiction of evidence which we could not resolve. This account of the war in the north is largely based on the contemporary eye-witness evidence of one of the authors. But it is not borne out by the reports and documents in the Israel Army Archives. . . . After consulting with some of the officers in charge of the Nazareth offensive, we have concluded that there remains an irreconcilable difference of emphasis between the participating eye-witness and the General Staff documentation."

I hope that the book I have written will be helpful in clarifying the events of the Israeli War of Independence. Historians seeking further details and a full bibliography are referred to the Dunkelman Collection in the Public Archives of Canada (MG 31 — G10) in Ottawa.

INDEX

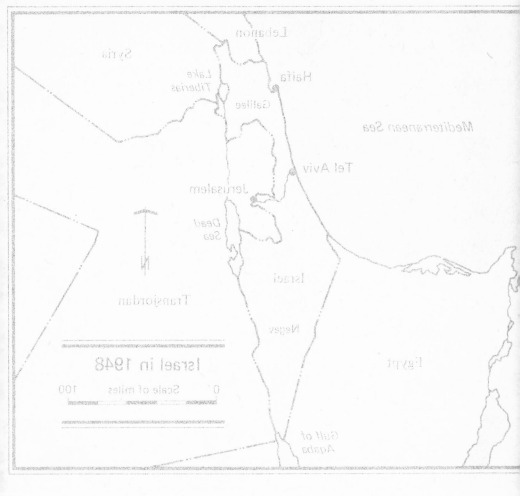

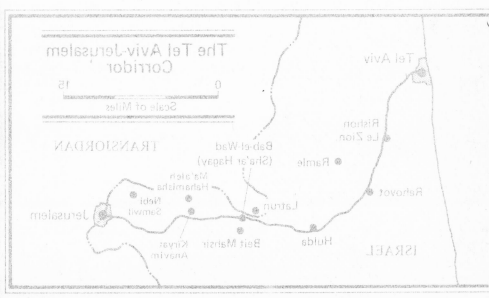

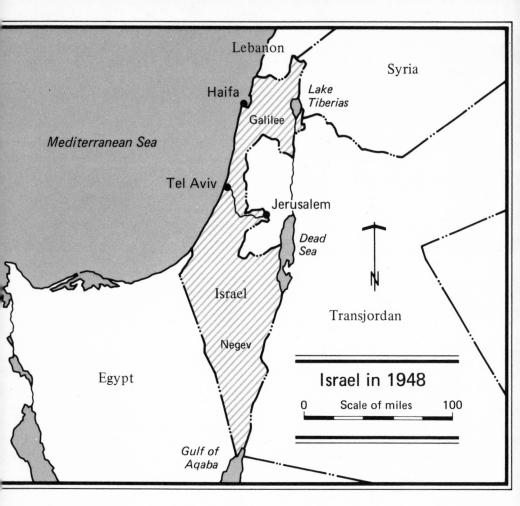

Mediterranean Sea

Lebanon

Haifa

Galilee

Syria

Lake
Tiberias

Tel Aviv

Jerusalem

Dead
Sea

Israel

N

Transjordan

Negev

Israel in 1948

Egypt

0   Scale of miles   100

Gulf of
Aqaba

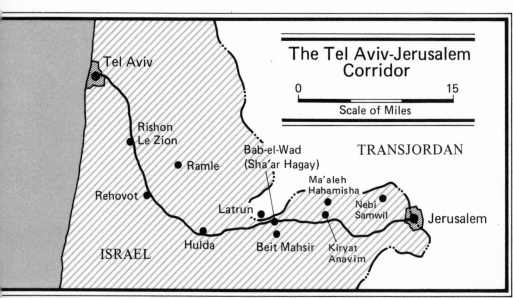

Tel Aviv

The Tel Aviv-Jerusalem
Corridor

0   15

Scale of Miles

Rishon
Le Zion

Bab-el-Wad
(Sha'ar Hagay)

TRANSJORDAN

Ramle

Ma'aleh
Hahamisha

Rehovot

Latrun

Nebi
Samwil

Jerusalem

ISRAEL

Hulda

Beit Mahsir

Kiryat
Anavim